D0171723

tuk tuk to the road

tuk tuk to the road

two girls, three wheels, 12 500 miles

Antonia Bolingbroke-Kent and Jo Huxster

First published in Great Britain in 2007 by Friday Books
An imprint of The Friday Project Limited
83 Victoria Street, London SW1H OHW

www.thefridayproject.co.uk
www.fridaybooks.co.uk

Text © 2007 Antonia Bolingbroke-Kent and Jo Huxster

ISBN - 13   978-1-905548-65-1

British Library Cataloguing in Publication Data

A catalogue record for this book is available from the British Library

Internal and cover design by Snowbooks Design

Map illustrations by Lorna Brown
www.lornaart.com

Typeset and printed by Omnipress Ltd

The Publisher's policy is to use paper manufactured from sustainable sources

In memory of Rose and Livs, our guardian angels

contents

a note from the authors

All blog posts written by Ants are indicated by .

All blog posts written by Jo are indicated by .

introduction

People often ask us where the inspiration to drive a tuk tuk from Bangkok to Brighton came from. The answer is simple – five years ago Jo went to Bangkok, fell in love with tuk tuks and decided that one day she would drive one back to England. Four years later we turned Ting Tong out of the gates of the British embassy in Bangkok and headed for home. Two continents, 12 countries, 14 weeks and the odd snapped accelerator cable later, we made it to our final destination – Brighton, England.

Anyone who has spent even five minutes in a tuk tuk might question why on earth we would consider undertaking such a gruelling journey in one of these noisy three-wheelers. Why not a nice comfortable Land Rover? Well, quite frankly, that would have been dull. The primary motivation for this trip was to take part in a challenging and novel experience, to explore the world in a vehicle that most people would consider travelling in for only a few miles. Plus, as we were going to be doing the trip in aid of the mental health charity Mind, then what better way to attract attention and sponsorship than a bright-pink tuk tuk?

Having ideas is one thing, but making them happen quite another. Turning our dream into the reality of a 12500-mile tukking extravaganza took determination, tears, stress, excitement and an unwavering desire to succeed. Last January we dived head-first into the unknown, spending the next four months working full time to organise everything: technology, insurance, medical training, finding sponsors, raising money for Mind, learning Russian and much more. It was often difficult to comprehend the enormity of what we were actually doing; instead of feeling scared, we felt like we were planning the trip for someone else. At other times, it felt like galloping flat out towards a vast brick wall with no idea what was on the other side.

But all the hard work paid off in the end, as the trip was a unique and amazing experience. After being back for six months, we are still digesting and reliving those 14 weeks on the road. It was the best thing we have ever done and, although it may sound like a horrible cliché, this past year has taught us that if you are determined enough, anything is possible.

Jo, Ants and Ting Tong
March 2007

prologue

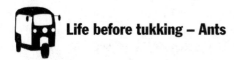 **Life before tukking – Ants**

It was a typical May day in Bangkok. The streets were the usual gridlock of tuk tuks, taxis and kamikaze bikers, the air stiflingly hot. In the Khao San Road dreadlocked travellers rubbed shoulders with immaculately dressed ladyboys and women hawked their wares to passers-by. There was nothing to suggest that today was anything but ordinary. But for Jo and I this was D-Day, the day when we would embark on a dream born years before. In the cloying, pre-monsoon heat we loaded up our tuk tuk for the first time and wove through the traffic towards the British embassy. Neither of us could get our heads round the enormity of the task that lay ahead – that finally, after months of planning and preparation, we were about to take the first tuk on the long road home. Was a tuk tuk really going to be able to make it all the way to Brighton? It was too late now for such questions. It was time for Lift Off.

Our journey had really begun 15 years earlier when Jo and I found ourselves in the same classroom in the autumn of 1991. Despite our different upbringings – Jo's in Surrey's leafy commuter belt, mine in the North Norfolk countryside – we were soon inseparable, our friendship forged on a love of sport, animals and subverting discipline. Winter weekends would be spent careering around the lacrosse pitch, thrashing other schools and gorging ourselves on match teas. In summer we would while away the evenings with long competitive hours on the tennis court, evenly matched and determined to beat each other. The holidays would see us frequenting the National Express between Norwich and London to stay at each other's houses. It's easy to look back on the past through a rose-tinted prism, but these early teenage years were a lot of fun, both in and out of school.

I often wonder whether the signs were there during those carefree years. At what point did the cracks begin to show? Jo was always extreme, non-conformist, a rebel – you could say anti-establishment. At an age when peer pressure was at its most potent, she was someone who dared to be different. It wasn't that she was an attention-seeker; it was just that she seemed to lack the self-consciousness that so commonly afflicts teenagers. While we thought we were at the cutting edge of fashion with our latest purchases from Kensington Market, Jo would go one step further, appearing at school in massive army boots, tie-dye, eye-poppingly short skirts and an undercut, a hairstyle synonymous with dog-on-string ketamine-heads, not public school girls. This, combined with her ridiculous sense of humour, was perhaps what I loved most about her. But was this necessarily an indication of what would happen a few years later? Did fate already have Jo in its clutch?

At the end of GCSEs, Jo left our school to do her A-Levels at Lancing College. It was then that things started to go wrong. She was miserable at Lancing from the outset, and my diary entries from her first term there speak of her unhappiness and desire to leave. On my part, I missed her terribly. But it wasn't until the following summer that I realised quite how unhappy she was. We were walking along the street in Thames Ditton one afternoon when I noticed some marks on her arms. I had never seen self-harm before, never heard of it even, but I knew those marks were self-inflicted. Nowadays self-harm is a recognised condition and rivals anorexia for newspaper column inches. A 2006 survey shockingly revealed that 25 000 teenagers are treated in British hospitals every year for self-inflicted wounds, but ten years ago it wasn't something you ever heard about. 'What are those marks on your arm, Ferret?' I ventured. She looked sheepish and smiled that nervous smile you do when you know you have done something wrong. Then she admitted she had done them to herself. They were tiny scars at that point – barely visible – and she assured me that she wouldn't do it again.

These assurances were soon forgotten. My diary from October 1996 records: 'I went to stay with Jo last weekend... I don't know what to do about her at the moment... she's cutting herself regularly... who the hell do I turn to for advice?' I felt helpless, out of my depth. We met up a few times during that term to go clubbing in London, and Jo covered up her arms with bandages and lied to anyone who asked. In November we celebrated our eighteenth birthdays dancing the night away at the SW1 club in Victoria with a load of friends, going home long after the sun had come up. In spite of the cutting, she was still the old Jo, full of laughter, energy and mischief. I could never have foreseen what lurked in the shadows of the immediate future.

A week later she was taken to a psychiatric hospital near Tunbridge Wells.

And that's when we lost Jo.

It all happened so quickly. One minute she was there – unhappy yes, but still Jo, still able to come out and have a laugh and celebrate turning 18. The next minute she'd gone, enveloped by the dark cloak of depression. Four weeks after she had been admitted, I went to visit her in hospital with her father and brother. The first shock was the hospital itself. Just before we arrived, one of Jo's fellow patients had cut themselves in the bathroom and there was blood everywhere. Someone else had kicked a door in. The whole place reeked of unhappiness and disquiet. Then there was the shock of seeing my friend. The Jo I knew and loved was vibrant, hyperactive and quick to laugh. The Jo I saw that day in hospital was a mere shell, hardly able to speak, her limbs a morass of self-inflicted wounds. She was also under constant one-on-one supervision in case she tried to harm herself. How on earth had it come to this?

Jo spent the next four years in and out of various psychiatric institutions in the south of England. She should have been doing her A-levels and then a degree, out there having fun. Instead she was on a cocktail of antidepressants and locked into a spiralling addiction to self-harm. As the months and years ticked by, I began to lose hope of Jo ever being able to escape from the abyss into which she had fallen. She took overdoses and cut herself so badly that she frequently had to be stitched up – with 128 stitches on one occasion. At one stage, voices in her head urged her to cut herself and to kill herself and others; thank goodness she had the strength to resist. It was heartbreaking to see her so unhappy and to see such a beautiful girl destroying her body like she was, knowing she would be scarred for life. I can't begin to imagine how her family must have felt.

While Jo was battling depression, I was leading a very different existence as a student at Edinburgh University. It was extraordinary to think how much our lives had diverged in such a short space of time. We had gone from seeing and speaking to each other daily to barely having any contact at all. My letters went unanswered, my calls were unreturned and when I did make the journey south to see her she was usually uncommunicative and numbed by drugs. Because I had never experienced depression and couldn't relate to her condition, I became frustrated with what I saw as an increasingly one-sided friendship; Jo didn't seem to care at all. It was naive of me to think that the normal rules of friendship still applied, to expect anything from someone who was so ill, but I didn't understand that when you feel like Jo did you become socially disabled and unable to communicate even with those closest to you. It was only when my own life crumbled during my second year of university, in 1998, that I understood what this felt like.

In a single week, my father lost his business, we lost our family home and my parents split up after 26 years of marriage. It was a massive shock and before long I was experiencing severe panic attacks, which lasted for the next three years. I now knew what it was like to not want to speak to people, to feel like you have fallen down a black hole from which there is no perceivable escape. Depression can make you very selfish; you're so caught up in your own problems and paranoia that you become disconnected from the world outside your own head. Jo had always been a compassionate, thoughtful, loving person, but she was so ill at times during these four years that it was as if she was locked in a glass prison, able to see and exist within the outside world but unable to communicate with it.

Looking back on it now, I see the fact that Jo recovered as little short of miraculous. She plumbed the very depths of depression and yet made it out the other side. Pinpointing the reasons why someone suddenly overcomes such an affliction is almost as hard as comprehending why and how they succumbed to it originally. In Jo's case it was a combination of factors, namely the right medication and the love and support of her family, friends and... ferrets. Above all, though, I put it down to her extraordinary strength of character. Many people who suffer from depression give up hope of ever seeing light at the end of the tunnel. The darkness is so consuming that they can't believe it isn't terminal. But even at her lowest points, Jo held on to that vital shred of hope that she wouldn't feel like that for ever. Her recovery should be an inspiration to all.

In the summer of 2002 Jo went to Thailand with her friends Hannah and Niki. It was a seminal moment. When she went on that holiday I knew she'd made it, that we'd got Jo back again. Little did I know that a small incident on that holiday would have such major ramifications, for it was here that she first encountered a tuk tuk, the ubiquitous three-wheelers that crowd the streets of South East Asia. It was love at first rev, and at that moment Jo dreamt up the notion of one day driving a tuk tuk from Bangkok back to England. Since Jo has never been the most conventional person, it was with only a slightly raised eyebrow that I greeted the news of her plan upon her return, although I'm not sure I ever truly believed the scheme would come to fruition. My doubts were coloured by my own experiences of hair-raising tuk tuk rides in Bangkok, which had always left me slightly deafened and vowing to take a taxi next time. Plus, I doubted one would make it as far as the city's airport, let alone England.

I should have known better. Jo is the most determined person I know, and this little plan of hers was here to stay. For the next four years, while Jo did a psychology degree in Brighton and I clambered up the ladder in the world of television production in London, the dream simmered. She would occasionally mention it in passing, but I didn't really think she meant business. Meanwhile, Jo was quietly gathering information and maps and beginning to show a very unladylike interest in mechanics. In September 2005, Jo and two of our other great friends from school, Anna and Lisa, came to stay with me for the weekend in Norfolk. At supper one night in the local pub, Jo piped up, 'Right, guys, I need your advice. I've got a year off before I start medical school next autumn, and I'm wondering whether to take the plunge and do this tuk tuk trip. Either that or I go and do a master's degree.' Fuelled by wine and lots of laughter, our vote was unanimous: the tuk tuk it was. None of us gave a moment's consideration to how she would do it or who she would go with, but we all thought it was a wonderful idea and celebrated with several more glasses of wine.

The following week Jo called me: 'Ferret, will you do the tuk tuk trip with me?' she asked, her voice filled with excitement. My immediate reaction was to say yes – how could I resist the temptation of such an adventure? This was the chance to go travelling together, the chance for which we had been waiting since a hilarious caravanning holiday nine years earlier. I put down the phone with a smile and went to bed that night dreaming of the open road and exotic places with unpronounceable names. Over the next few weeks, however, I was gripped by uncertainty and nagging doubts about the wisdom of my decision. If I gave up my job at ITV to go gallivanting around the world on three wheels, where would it leave me? Would I be throwing away all that I had achieved on a flighty whim? Was I striving for excitement when really I should just be sensible and get a bit of stability in my life? Put simply, I was afraid – afraid of stepping outside the box and doing something a bit different and afraid of losing my place on that overcrowded TV ladder. After weeks of sleepless nights and dreams of never being able to find a job again, I rang Jo in late October and told her that I had changed my mind, apologising profusely and feeling incredibly guilty about letting her down. She was far too magnanimous to point out that by pulling out I was probably putting an end to her dream, but I knew that was the case. It was far too big and dangerous an undertaking for Jo to do solo.

A few weeks after that, on 16 November, I was filming at the Eden Project in Cornwall when my mobile rang. It was my friend Rose's brother, Humphrey. 'She's done it,' he said. 'Rose killed herself yesterday morning.' My beautiful, sweet, vivacious friend Rose. Gone. Just like that. I knew she had been extremely depressed and when we had gone to the cinema a few weeks earlier she had confided in me that she had contemplated suicide. But there is a vast gulf between contemplation and action, and the fact that she had actually done it left me numb with incomprehension. That night I went for a moonlit walk and thought about Rose, the fragility of life and how you never know what's round the next corner. Her sudden death made me realise more than ever that you only live once and that opportunities like this trip should be grasped with both hands, not recoiled from. A few days later I called Jo and told her I had changed my mind – I wanted to do the trip with her after all. And this time I was sure.

So at the beginning of January, having waved goodbye to ITV, Jo and I found ourselves sitting at her parents' house in Surrey, crisp new notebooks in hand, wondering where on earth to begin. Since Jo was due to start medical school in September, we had only eight months to organise and complete the journey. It was going to be a huge challenge. Neither of us had ever driven a tuk tuk before, knew where to get one, or had any idea about how to plan such a massive project. We'd both done a lot of independent travel, but organising a backpacking trip round India and planning a 12 500-mile, two-continent tukathon are quite different matters. If we were going to be back by September and avoid the Asian monsoons, we would have to leave in April, May at the latest, which gave us four months to do everything. Not that we had any idea what 'everything' entailed at that point.

With four months until Lift Off, the only things we were sure of were our intended route and the fact that we were going to do the journey in aid of Mind, the mental health charity. Jo's four years of studying maps and trawling the Internet had made her determined to tackle 'the northern route' via China, Central Asia and Russia. Not only was this 'the road less travelled' but also it meant that we would be overland all the way, our wheels leaving terra firma only to hop across the Channel on the Eurotunnel. The alternative was to take the old hippy trail through India, Iran, Pakistan and Turkey, but the major drawback here was having to ship our vehicle across the Indian Ocean from Singapore to India. Not only would this dilute the overland experience but also, in the current political climate, the idea of travelling through Iran wasn't overly appealing. Labelled as 'the axis of evil' by George W. Bush in 2002, Iran's leaders' nuclear ambitions and threats against Israel had led to further threats of ballistic missile attacks from the Pentagon if Tehran didn't toe the line. Dodging US missiles was something we would rather avoid.

Our first major obstacle was China, country number three on our intended route. While flicking through the Rough Guide in January, Jo was horrified to read that it is illegal for foreigners to drive in China. If this was the case, then we would be forced to divert to the southern route, or take option number three – ship the tuk tuk to Japan and from there to Vladivostok on Russia's far eastern seaboard. It would be a toss-up between facing the dangers of Iran or taking on roads that had nearly spelt the end of Ewan McGregor and Charley Boorman's *The Long Way Round* expedition two years previously. Fortunately, neither situation ever arose, as, after extensive research, Jo discovered that it wasn't in fact illegal, just extremely complicated and expensive to arrange. First we would have to find a specialist Chinese travel agent to arrange our passage through the Dragon's Den. This agent would have to obtain special permission from the army, the police and the government, and we would have to follow a set itinerary and be chaperoned at all times by a Chinese guide. Plus we would have to get special Chinese driving licences, and our tuk tuk would have to be fitted with Chinese plates at the border. All this for the bargain price of £6530. It was going to be a huge chunk out of our budget, but Jo was determined. China it was, then.

With the Chinese issue under control, it was down to the organisational nitty-gritty. How and where were we going to find a tuk tuk? What visas and documentation did we need? What equipment should we take? How were we going to find financial sponsors for the trip? Which roads were too dangerous or too mountainous to tuk? Then in early February Jo dropped a bombshell: since a tuk tuk classifies as a motorbike on the International Driving Permit (IDP), we were going to have to get full motorbike licences. Quickly. The Chinese agent needed our IDPs within a month in order to process all our permits in time, so there was no room for error.

I'd barely even sat on a motorbike before, let alone attempted hill starts, U-turns or straddling a throbbing 500-cc bike dressed in full leathers. And Norfolk in February was not the ideal place to start. The next month saw me glued, freezing, to the back of a bike, exhaustively practising all the manoeuvres in the back streets of Norwich. My instructor, Paul, a grizzled 40-something with a broad Norfolk accent, encouragingly told me one day that I wasn't 'the most natural biker'. On more than one occasion, having broken yet another indicator and failed another U-turn, I wondered whether we'd ever make it out of the country, let alone back here. Test day came on 9 March and, quaking with fear despite having downed a bottle of Rescue Remedy, I mounted the bike. By some amazing stroke of luck, I passed, with only three minor faults. Much to her chagrin, Jo passed second time around, a week later.

With China and our motorbike tests under our belts, our mission was now in full swing. It was now that the countdown really begun.

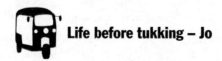 **Life before tukking – Jo**

It is very difficult to put into words what it feels like to suffer from depression. I think that to truly understand you have to have suffered it yourself, and I wouldn't wish that experience on anyone. I think an apt description would be cancer of the soul or malignant sadness. When you are depressed, the world is a very dark place, totally devoid of anything positive. Sometimes when I was really down, I would just hide in bed and cry and feel absolutely terrified. Other times I couldn't cry and just felt like a corpse with a pulse. I remember feeling really scared because I knew that I loved my family and friends, but I couldn't feel love for them. I felt imprisoned in my own mind and I had no idea how to escape.

I don't know what caused me to become mentally ill. My upbringing was loving and secure, and there seemed to be no trigger for my depression. A possible contribution might have been genetic: I am adopted, and my natural mother suffered many mental health problems throughout her adult life, eventually succumbing to her demons and committing suicide.

Ants and I first met when we were 12 at Wycombe Abbey. We quickly became best friends. We had a close-knit group of friends at school and, whether we were playing sport, rolling down hills or going for sneaky cigarettes in the woods, it was a good experience. At Wycombe we may have been thought of as a bit rebellious, but the worst we ever did was smoke and occasionally sneak into High Wycombe to go shopping – hardly deviant behaviour. In such an academic pressure cooker, it was important to conform and it was sometimes fun to act the clown and do the opposite of what was expected. I recall a £3 dare to wear my nightie to classes on a Saturday morning. I probably could have passed it off as an ethnic trend, but unfortunately the nightie was totally see-through and Ants' housemistress posed the question 'Why is Jo Huxster wearing her nightie?' After my GCSEs I went to a new school, Lancing College. It was then that my problems began.

I vividly remember Mum and Dad dropping me off at Lancing on the first day of term. Instead of feeling excited, I felt a sense of dread and was really struggling to hold back the tears as I hugged them goodbye. However, I made friends quickly and spent more time socialising than concentrating on my studies. From the outside everything appeared to be going well, but inside I struggled to feel happy and I would frequently cry in my bedroom, although I had no idea what the problem was. Another student told me that I would feel better if I cut myself, and so I did, carving the name of an ex-boyfriend on my forearm.

Some people are horrified and scared of self-harm, and I can understand why. It seems like such a destructive and horrible thing to do to yourself. Self-harming made me feel better because it distracted me from feeling down. Seeing my own blood was such a release from the negative thoughts in my head. I continued to self-harm intermittently during my first term at Lancing, but then my mood improved and the next two terms were better.

Ants and I spoke regularly during my time at Lancing, and she was very supportive. Sometimes I would just be in tears on the phone and she always did her best to cheer me up. I really missed my friends at Wycombe and wondered whether leaving had been the right choice, but Ants assured me that I wasn't missing out on anything.

Things started to go really wrong during the first term of my second year at Lancing. The feelings of sadness that had plagued me the previous year returned with a vengeance. I couldn't concentrate on my work and life felt utterly pointless. I spent a lot of time crying and began to cut myself frequently. My housemistress became concerned about my behaviour, and I was sent to see the school's GP, who referred me to a psychiatrist.

I had no idea what depression was or why I felt miserable and cut myself. I didn't know anyone who had visited a psychiatrist and thought only seriously mentally ill people did this. I think my comment at the time was 'I'm not crazy'. I recall being told that I had a depressive illness, and

I asked what it was called. I knew nothing about mental illnesses and assumed that there were lots of different types of depressive illness, just like there are many viruses. Mental health was not in the news so much a decade ago – the recent increase in media coverage has raised awareness, which is surely a good thing.

At the end of the winter term I was really struggling to cope with my depression and was admitted to psychiatric hospital for the first time. I naively thought that I would be there for five days, take some pills and then be back to normal. Unfortunately, the pills I was taking didn't make me feel any better and three weeks later I still felt the same. I was discharged from hospital over Christmas, but then I returned in the new year. I think the five days of my second admission formed one of the lowest points of my whole life. For some reason I got it into my head that I couldn't wee, and so I stopped drinking properly. This made the problem worse because I became totally dehydrated. I remember lying on the floor feeling terrified that I was going to die.

Over the next four years, I was in and out of different psychiatric hospitals like a yo-yo, spending over two years as an inpatient. I tried every type of medication they gave me, various forms of talking therapy and even a course of ECT (electroconvulsive therapy, whereby the patient is given a short general anaesthetic and an electric current is passed through their brain). The ECT didn't work, but I enjoyed the general anaesthetic, because it meant a few moments of respite from the depression. Most of the time I felt like absolute shit, but a couple of things kept me going through these years: first, my ferrets, and, second, something that my first psychiatrist had said to me when I was 18: 'Jo, I promise you won't feel like this forever.' This comment may sound quite insignificant, but when you are in the depths of depression you cannot see a way out and without this small glimmer of hope I might not be here today.

I got my first ferret when I was 19. It was all Ants' fault. We had always called each other 'Ferret' at school, and Ants suggested I get a pet ferret to cheer me up. Little did she know that this was to be the start of a total obsession with the smelly little creatures. I named my first ferret Ants in her honour, which I'm not sure if she saw as much of a compliment, because Ants was a smelly little white thing with red eyes that bit anyone who wasn't me. They say that a pet is good therapy, and Ants certainly kept me company when I felt low. My second ferret was called Zed, an amazing animal who wouldn't leave me alone when I was really depressed. If I cried, Zed would lick away my tears; when I was too down to do anything other than lie on the sofa, Zed slept down my T-shirt. Mum and Dad would bring Zed to visit me in hospital and she pottered up and down the corridor on her lead, providing some light entertainment and face-washing for the other patients.

I wasn't severely depressed for the whole four years that I was in and out of hospital, but I always felt low. I used self-harm to distract me from my feelings and it became an addiction of sorts, although when I was challenged about this I denied it. Even though I hated the scars that I got from cutting myself, I also felt that I deserved them. I was so frustrated with myself for not getting better and feeling like such a useless person.

My admissions to hospital usually happened after my behaviour became unmanageable at home. One time I had gone for a late-night walk and decided to take an overdose of diazepam to try and get some sleep. The next night my parents locked me in the house to keep me safe. I had other ideas and tried to climb out of my bedroom window, still half drugged from all the diazepam I had taken the previous night. As I tried to lower myself from the first-floor window, I fell on to the concrete and was found wandering the streets half a mile away with a broken wrist. This time they wouldn't discharge me and I was taken to the local psychiatric hospital. I never tried to kill myself, despite the fact that my behaviour sometimes seemed to indicate otherwise. However, I did think about death frequently and would often wish that I could just fall asleep and never wake up. Even when I took overdoses, it was to get some uninterrupted sleep rather than to die.

I don't know how I survived those four years, but I am not sure I would have survived if my family and friends hadn't been so amazingly supportive. Friends would phone and visit me in hospital. My family almost had their lives taken over by my illness. They provided such unconditional love and support and frequently visited me in hospital. One thing that I will always feel guilty about is that the people I love had to deal with me when I was depressed. When you are depressed, you don't care about yourself, let alone anyone else. During my illness, I feel I was a crap daughter, sister and friend. I can't even begin to imagine what it was like for the people who loved me to see me ill. If I try and put myself in their shoes, then I think it must have been awful and they probably felt so helpless, because I didn't respond to any treatment. I think Ants sometimes got frustrated with me, because she always phoned me and I would rarely get in touch with her. I felt that I had absolutely nothing to say for myself and couldn't bring myself to pick up the phone.

However, I don't regret being depressed, because living with regrets is not the best way to live your life. It is important to try and learn from past events and then move on with the knowledge and wisdom that you have discovered. Furthermore, suffering from depression has helped to shape the person that I am today and provided me with opportunities to meet some truly inspirational people. Who knows how my life would have panned out if I had never suffered from depression?

I often wondered whether I would ever truly feel better, but after trying nearly every antidepressant available my doctor finally found one that worked. This was such a shock and relief, because although I always dreamt of feeling better I often wondered whether I was going to feel depressed for the rest of my life. The medication lifted the dark cloud sufficiently for me to feel more stable and human, and the need to self-harm disappeared. I had always thought that the opposite of depression was happiness, even though my mum insisted that people who aren't depressed do not feel happy all the time. As an adult, all I had experienced was feeling low and I had forgotten what 'normality' felt like. I discovered that Mum was right and that life is not a continuously joyous experience – merely the day-to-day living, punctuated by some very happy moments and times when you feel a bit down. Not feeling depressed was like having the shackles of mental torment removed properly for the first time in my adult life. At last, I now felt able to start planning for the future.

During the following five years, I threw myself into studying, first passing an A-level and then going on to study for a degree in psychology. After my first year at university I went to Thailand with two friends, Hannah and Niki. Thailand was a turning point for me in many ways. It was the first time I had done something that felt really independent of my parents, because when I was depressed I had been too scared to ever stray far from home. It was also a time that I began to get used to my self-harm scars and come to terms with showing them in general public. In England I always wore long-sleeved tops, even in the summer, because I felt paranoid about people looking at me. It was so hot and humid in Thailand that I couldn't bear long-sleeved tops and so I wore T-shirts. I realised that people didn't stare as much as I thought they would, and I became much less self-conscious.

It was on this trip to Thailand that I first encountered a tuk tuk. Tuk tuks are to Bangkok what black cabs are to London, and they are definitely the most exciting way to explore the city. We had hired a tuk tuk for the day and gone whizzing around the sites of central Bangkok. At the end of the day the driver let me sit in the front seat and pose for a photo with my friends in the back. It was as we walked down the Khao San Road later that evening that I decided I would one day drive a tuk tuk back to England. Simple as that.

During the next few years while I was at university, the tuk tuk idea never left my imagination. I purchased an old motorbike to try and learn some mechanics and printed out hundreds of pages of information off the Internet about the different countries through which I wanted to drive. It was a dream that I was determined to make a reality, but the problem was finding a large enough period of time in which to organise everything and actually do it.

I couldn't think of anyone I wanted to do the trip with other than Ants. We had always planned to go on a gap year together, but because of my problems it had not been possible. I was thrilled when she eventually agreed, because at last we would fulfil our dreams of travelling together.

In January 2006, Ants and I started planning for the trip full time. We were sitting in my parents' front room and just thought 'Where the hell do we start?' Although I had first thought of driving back to England in a tuk tuk nearly four years ago, the logistics of an adventure like this were mind-boggling. We had so much to organise, and it was hard to know where to begin. Although we were both seasoned independent travellers, we had absolutely no experience of planning a huge overland trip. The next few months turned out to be an incredibly steep learning curve.

We knew that we wanted to do the trip for charity and, after much discussion, we decided to support Mind, the leading mental health charity in England and Wales. It wasn't too difficult a choice as we both had obvious personal reasons for supporting it. During one of my hospital admissions a representative from Mind gave me a leaflet on depression, which really helped me. It was before the Internet was widely available, and I didn't know much about depression. Reading the leaflet gave me more of an understanding about my illness and provided me with hope and inspiration that one day I would get better.

Our first experience of driving a tuk tuk was on a freezing day in a field in North Norfolk. We had tracked down a company in Thailand called Expertise, which was prepared to build us a tuk tuk for our adventure. Expertise also had previous experience of producing tuk tuks that could survive long overland journeys. By a strange coincidence, the guy that imported tuk tuks from Expertise to the UK, Scott, lived just a few miles away from Ants in Norfolk. Scott very kindly let us do a photo shoot with his tuk tuk and take it for a spin. Although we were in a huge field, Ants nearly managed to drive the tuk tuk into a ditch at the edge of the field. We worried that if we couldn't drive a tuk tuk around a field safely, how on earth were we going to drive one back from Thailand?

 **Ting Tong**

In January 2006 Ting Tong wasn't even a glint in her daddy's eye, and yet only eight months later she had successfully traversed a small handful of continents and sped into the record books. In the 14 weeks it took to drive from Bangkok to Brighton, she overcame terrains that would make even the most hardened 4×4 turn a funny shade of green: man-sized potholes, quagmires, desert, steep mountains – you name it, she conquered it. She may be pink, she may be a girl, but don't be fooled – this is one tough tuk tuk.

Ting Tong was born at the Expertise factory in Bangboo, a small village 20 miles from the centre of Bangkok. It's here that her lord and creator Anuwat Yuteeraprapa, the scion of an eminent tukking dynasty, has been building tuk tuks for four years. Anuwat's family has been in the tukking business for the past 40 years, and today he is Bangkok's undisputed three-wheeler king. Anuwat's tuk tuks are no ordinary tuk tuks. Not for them the polluted streets of Bangkok and a lifetime ferrying tourists between the Grand Palace and the Khao San Road. Each model is lovingly hand-built and the majority are exported to discerning customers in America, Japan and Europe. These are the crème de la crème.

Jo made contact with Anuwat for the first time in January 2006. She'd heard of his mastery via the Internet and knew that he was the man for the job. Whether he would agree to get involved was another matter. First, we were total strangers calling from the other side of the word – were we timewasters or the real deal? Second, building a tuk tuk for such a long journey meant a lot more work for him and his mechanics. He should know: only the year before, Expertise had built a tuk tuk for a German couple, Daniel and Susi. They had driven their tuk tuk 23 000 miles back to Germany, via Japan, Mongolia and Libya. Even though Anuwat's tuk tuks were already a cut above the rest, the experience had taught him that for one to make it this far it had to be custom-built to supersonic perfection. It would need to have a stronger chassis, raised suspension, a special long-range fuel tank, roll-bars, extra lights and special wiring and fuses. He already had a full quota of orders for the year; saying yes to Jo would put a lot of pressure on his factory. But Anuwat is never one to turn down a challenge, and at the beginning of February work began on what would become the most perfect tuk tuk the world has ever seen.

Meanwhile we pondered over a name for our chariot. Barbarella was mooted, but rejected by Jo on the grounds that she had no idea who Barbarella was. Then, inspired by watching too many episodes of *Little Britain*, I hit upon Ting Tong, the Thai bride played by Matt Lucas. It was perfect. Not only did it have the right ethnic origins, but also Ting Tong and tuk tuk share the same initials. Ting Tong it was.

Over the next three and a half months, six experts would work on bringing Ting Tong to life – Anuwat, his wife Dow, and mechanics Thart, Thung, Doung and Karm. The fact that it would be two girls driving this tuk tuk back to England spurred them on to even greater perfection. The steel chassis was reinforced, a 550-cc Daihatsu engine flown in from Japan, the suspension raised by 15 cm to give it extra clearance and roll-bars added at the sides. As Ting Tong began to take shape, her creators turned their attention to the details. More lights were added for increased visibility, special seats were ordered and, most crucially, her body parts were painted a perfect shade of pink. There was no chance this tuk tuk was going to get lost in the crowd.

Ting Tong's creation went (almost) seamlessly, and on Thursday 25 May 2006 Jo tuk to the wheel and drove her out of the Expertise factory for the first time. The pinkest, sleekest, hottest three-wheeler in history was ready to be unveiled to the world.

Ting Tong's vital statistics

Engine: four-stroke, water-cooled 550-cc Daihatsu
Fuel: unleaded petrol
Fuel tank: 50-litre capacity
Gears: five forward, one reverse
Cylinders: three
Wheels: three, with 12-inch rubber tyres
Colour: pink
Top speed: 70 mph
Electrical system: 12 volts
Braking system: 11-inch front disc brake, rear drum brakes

planned route

Lift Off: 28 May 2006, Bangkok, Thailand
Touch Down: 3 September 2006, Brighton, England
Average daily distance: 150 miles
Cruising speed: 60 mph
Full throttle: 70 mph

 **1 Thailand**

Random country facts: the official name of Bangkok is Krungthep mahanakhon amonratanakosin mahintara ayuthaya mahadilok popnopparat ratchathani burirom udomratchaniwet mahasathan amonpiman avatansathit sakkathattiya witsanukamprasit. Thailand is home to the world's smallest mammal, the bumblebee bat.

The mission begins on 20 May 2006, when we fly out to Bangkok to be united for the first time with the last, but most definitely not least, member of the team, our Formula 1 tuk tuk, Ting Tong. With a week of acclimatising, mechanical training and last-minute panic and preparation under our belts, we'll crank up her engine and take the first tuk on the long road home. So begins the tukathon.

After our baptism of fire among the city's bronchitic mêlée of traffic, we will wend our way north towards Laos, about 645 miles away. Our first major port of call will be Ayutthaya, the old capital of the Thai kingdom, once so teeming with temples that sunlight reflecting off their gilt decoration was said to dazzle from nearly three miles away. Today it is a UNESCO World Heritage Site, in memory of this illustrious past. Here we will turn east, taking in the wonders of the Khao Yai National Park, one of the locations used in the filming of *The Beach*, before tukking north towards Vientiane. We'll add another national park, the Nam Nao, to our list, before we get to Phimai, a small town in the north east of the country, which hosts one of Thailand's most impressive Khmer temple complexes, redolent of Cambodia's Angkor Wat.

About 200 miles from here we'll cross the Friendship Bridge into Laos. With one country down, it's a mere 11 850 miles to Blighty.

 **2 Laos**

Random country facts: Laos has only about 50 written laws. Laos is the most bombed country in the history of modern warfare. DJs are officially outlawed in Vientiane.

First on our Laotian agenda will be Vientiane, Laos' capital city. By all accounts this is a delightful spot, fusing a cornucopia of styles and influences: Lao, Thai, Chinese, Vietnamese, French and even Russian. Built on the banks of the Mekong River, this ancient city abounds with temples and things to see. We should have time to have a brief explore before we hit the road again and tuk off to Vang Vieng, about 100 miles north. As we drive up Route 13, we'll be following the valley of the Nam Ngum, home of the Hmong and Yao hill peoples. The scenery here is said to be spectacular – limestone caves, waterfalls and dense jungle.

Another 150 miles up Route 13 and we'll come to Luang Prabang, the second UNESCO World Heritage Site on our Grand Tour. We won't have time to visit all 32 temples in this former royal capital, but it'll be a good pit-stop at which to soak up the laid-back Laotian atmosphere. If time allows we'll squeeze in an excursion to the nearby Pak Ou caves and Kwang Si falls.

Heading north west from Luang Prabang we'll pass through Udomxai, one of the biggest settlements in northern Laos, before tukking the last 80 miles through the Luang Nam Tha province to the Chinese border at Boten. This last stretch is the Nam Ha national protected area, home to clouded leopard, tiger, elephant and 288 bird species.

 **3 China**

Random country facts: ice-cream was invented in China around 2000 BC. China is the fourth largest country in the world.

On 10 June we'll tuk into China. Due to Chinese laws regarding foreign drivers, we will be accompanied for the next 4375 miles by a Chinese government guide. Considering our Chinese language skills end at '*nee hao*', this is probably a very good thing.

Our itinerary while we are in China is all prearranged by the China Sea International Travel Service (CSITS) in Beijing. The next 28 days will be spent travelling north via Kunming, Leshan, Chengdu and Lanzhou, before turning west along the fabled Silk Route towards the plains of Central Asia. Our route will take us via subterranean caverns, the world's largest carved Buddha, the dense forests of Emei Shan, temples, bustling modern cities and remote tribal villages.

At Lanzhou we'll turn north west for the final leg of our Chinese journey. Lanzhou, once a vital stronghold on the Silk Route, will mark the beginning of our drive through the Hexi Corridor, a narrow strip of land sandwiched between the Tibetan Plateau and the Gobi Desert. This road takes us through Jiayuguan, the last fortress of the Great Wall, an isolated place with the same connotations in Chinese myth and legend as Siberia for Stalinist Russia. Tukking due west, our route then takes us through Xinjiang, China's remotest province, home of the Uighur people and gateway to the Islamic world. Hami and Urumqui will be our last pit-stops in China, before we enter Kazakhstan at the Khorgos border crossing. All going well, this will be on 7 July.

 **4 Kazakhstan**

Random country facts: Kazakhstan sells 400 000 barrels of oil a day. *Kokpar*, goat polo, is a popular sport here. The word 'Kazakh' means 'free' or 'adventurer'.

The name 'Kazakhstan' instantly conjures images of endless steppes, exotic bazaars, nomadic ger villages... and Borat. At the beginning of July our three-wheeled posse will be crossing the border and heading for Almaty. Our biker contacts in Almaty assure us that the roads in this area are good, so the 200 miles from here to the old capital should be easy-going. The Singing Dunes and Charyn Canyon are apparently not to be missed, so we'll be stopping for a cold beer or maybe a refreshing bowl of *kumys* (fermented mare's milk, a Kazakh speciality) before hitting the cosmopolitan hub Almaty.

Almaty is the commercial heart of Central Asia's richest country and will be a welcome respite after several weeks in China's western wilderness. While TT has a service, we'll get some R&R and perhaps even don our glad rags and sample the local nightlife: *The Long Way Round* team have told us that the Lord Nelson club is not to be missed.

From Almaty we'll head north up the M36 to the capital, Astana (meaning 'capital' in Kazakh). Our original plan was to travel through western Kazakhstan via the Aral Sea, but sadly the roads (if you can call them that) are too bad and we would probably have had to resort to hitching a lift on a camel or a Kamaz truck. This route via Astana shouldn't disappoint though.

A few hundred miles north west of Almaty we'll come to the southern end of Lake Balkash, Central Asia's fourth largest lake, which, according to a recent United Nations report, is sadly echoing the demise of the Aral Sea. Next it's Karaghanda, famous for coal and gulags, and then Astana, its glass skyscrapers rising incongruously out of the treeless steppes.

In Astana we will have to make a decision: either go due north to Russia via Petropavlosk, or tuk north west via Kostanai. Apparently the roads aren't great on either route so we're hoping some good local knowledge will be able to point us in the right direction. Then it's goodbye Kazakhstan and *zdrastvuyte* Russia.

 **5 Russia**

Random country facts: around six billion bottles of vodka are drunk in Russia annually, at a rate of 40 per person. Russia spans 11 time zones. According to the *CIA World Fact Book*, the population of Russia is 143 420 309.

At the border we'll turn west, open the throttle and head for Europe across the West Siberian Plain, one of the world's largest regions of continuous flatland, bounded by the Urals in the west and the Yenisey River in the east. Although we'll be a mere 1000 miles south of the Arctic Circle, the summer temperature here should be a balmy 20 °C.

First on our Russian agenda will be the city of Chelyabinsk, a key centre of military production during the Soviet era and scene of the world's worst nuclear accident before Chernobyl. The city is also the last metropolis on the eastern side of the fabled Urals, the geographical divide between Europe and Asia. As far as mountains go, however, they are little more than a wrinkle on the earth's surface, and our three-wheeled friend should tuk over them without any problems.

On our western descent of the Urals we'll go through Ufa, birthplace of Rudolf Nureyev and capital of the self-consciously autonomous Bashkortostan Republic, before tukking through the southern tip of Tatarstan and into the Volga region. This is the heartland of Russia. 'Mother Volga' is one of the nation's most enduring symbols as well as Europe's longest river, at 2303 miles. We'll be travelling through the area at the best time of year, when the river's banks become a haven for swimmers, sun worshippers and sybarites. As we tuk down the Volga we'll take in the cities of Samara and Saratov. The latter was home to Yuri Gagarin, the first man in space.

Next stop is Volgograd, a day's tukking down the Volga from Saratov. Better known by its former name, Stalingrad, the city was the scene of the Second World War's bloodiest battle. At least 600 000 German troops died here, and a further 180 000 were captured by the Soviets. The total number of Russian dead is unknown, but again the figure is probably around 600 000.

This will be an opportune spot for Team Ting Tong to relax, refuel and prepare for the final leg of the odyssey. We might even indulge in the odd vodka, knowing the legendary Russian propensity for the drink.

From Volgograd it's almost a straight line due west to England, via Lviv, Krakow, Prague, Cologne, Brussels and the Channel Tunnel.

6 Ukraine

Random country facts: the name 'Ukraine' translates as 'borderland' or 'on the edge'. Ukraine is one of the world's main centres of sugar production.

Ukraine gained its independence from Russia in August 1991 and is so far unblighted by mass tourism. Oxen still plough the fields in many parts and rural areas are yet to be tainted by the encroaches of the modern world.

Our first major pit-stop will be Kharkiv, 250 miles north west of the Russian border on the M03 via the towns of Krasny Luch and Slovyansk. Eastern Ukraine is an area little visited by tourists. During the Soviet era this was a military industrial centre; today it is the business (and mafia) end of the country.

At Kharkiv, Ukraine's second largest city, we'll take the M03 west for a further two days to the capital Kiev, the apotheosis of the nation's new-found wealth. Here, old women selling corncobs rub shoulders with Prada-clad urbanites, and blacked out SUVs and Mercedes are the norm. If time allows, we'll park up, kick back and check out some of the sights – mummified monks at the Caves Monastery, Independence Square and the Chernobyl Museum (the destroyed reactor is a mere 60 miles north of the capital), to name a few. But we'll have little time to loiter. Next stop is Lviv, 400 miles west on the M06.

Commonly billed as 'the Florence of the East' and 'the new Prague', Lviv is a city full of beauty and historical interest – and the obligatory Soviet-era tower blocks. Lonely Planet describes it as 'a true gem that is only now starting to get the attention it deserves'. We'll stop here for a night before the final lap of our Ukrainian tukathon. From here it's less than 50 miles west to the Polish border at Shehyni.

 **7 Poland**

Random country facts: Poland shares its borders with seven countries. Chopin and Copernicus both hailed from Poland.

By the time we reach Poland, the trickiest parts of the trip should be behind us. We'll have put over 2000 miles between us and the Central Asian steppes, and Brighton will be well within our reach. We hope!

We'll spend less than a week skirting across the southern underbelly of Poland, going via Rzeszow, Krakow and Opole before entering the Czech Republic 60 miles east of Prague.

Krakow is Poland's most historic city and was the royal capital for more than 500 years. Amazingly it was almost unscathed by the Second World War, which ravaged Wroclaw and Warsaw. Today it is a World Heritage Site. No other city in Poland has so many historic buildings and monuments, and nowhere else will you encounter such vast collections of art. This is a city not to be missed and we'll take a day out of our home run to explore its treasures.

Krakow is also famous for its close proximity to Auschwitz, a name synonymous with Nazi brutality and the horrors of the Holocaust. The camp is just south of our route and will certainly be on our itinerary if time allows.

This area of Poland, Upper Silesia, is heavily developed and industrialised and home to ten per cent of the population. It doesn't promise to be the most scenic part of our adventure so we'll open up the throttle and push on to the Czech Republic via Opole in Lower Silesia.

 **8 Czech Republic**

Random country facts: Pilsner and Dvorak are two of the Czech Republic's most famous exports. The national sport is European handball.

The Czech Republic will be a short but sweet fragment of our tukathon. We'll cut 200 miles across the heart of the country in about five days. We could do it in less, but since this is one of Europe's most historic countries it would be foolish to do so.

Prague is the obvious highlight, but it might come as a shock after the tourist-free expanses of Russia and Eastern Europe we'll have experienced. If we can bear the hordes, we'll stop here for a night and do the tourist thing before pushing westward towards Germany. Our route will take us through the dark forests and fairytale castles of West Bohemia as well as the ancient spa town of Karlovy Vary. Since Emperor Charles IV allegedly discovered the hot springs here in 1358, luminaries such as Beethoven, Karl Marx, Chopin and Peter the Great have all made the journey here to drink the curative waters.

Last up in the Czech Republic will be Cheb, a medieval town built on the banks of the Ohre River.

 **9 Germany**

Random country facts: the *autobahns* were begun by Hitler in the 1930s as a work-relief programme for the unemployed. Germany is the second most populous country in Europe after Russia.

Once into Germany we are well and truly on the home stretch. We'll probably spend only a day here, speeding west on the *autobahn*. Cologne's famous cathedral could be on the agenda if time allows.

 **10 Belgium**

Random country facts: Belgium is officially trilingual. The Belgians are the world's greatest beer drinkers.

Belgium and France will pass by so quickly we'll hardly notice we're there. Having spent a month traversing China, it's likely we'll tick off Belgium, France and the UK in a single day. I'm sure we'll find time to sample some of those famous chocolates though.

11 France – the home stretch

Random country facts: France has the highest per-capita consumption of cheese in the world. Napoleon suffered from ailurophobia, fear of cats.

France will be notable only as the last foreign destination of Tuk to the Road. After 12 weeks – we hope – on the road, we'll drive Ting Tong on to the train at Calais and head for those white cliffs.

12 England – and Brighton

Random country facts: only the queen is allowed to eat swans. The International Festival of Worm Charming is held in Totnes, Devon, every May. It is illegal to enter the Houses of Parliament in a suit of armour.

From the Eurotunnel terminal it's 65 miles to Brighton. What an amazing moment that'll be... and time for some serious celebrations.

chapter 1
countdown

 Tuesday 14 March, Kelling, Norfolk, UK

 The countdown begins

When Jo returned from a holiday in Thailand a few years ago and announced that she was going to drive a tuk tuk back from Bangkok to the UK, I never thought for a second I'd be sitting here four years down the line studying maps and wondering which route we are going to take through Kazakhstan. And now here we are, with two months until Lift Off, frantically planning every aspect of our 12 500-mile odyssey. Within the space of a few months I feel as if I have been transformed from an assistant TV producer to a bona fide explorer.

Until you embark on setting up a mission like this, you have no idea of the massive amount of organisation involved. Everything from which roads we are going to brave to which tent is the best has to be planned carefully. Nothing can be left to chance. Last weekend we were at the Royal Geographical Society, home of cutting-edge scientific exploration, to do a wilderness medical training course. There were scientists who study snow leopards in Siberia, biologists off to Greenland, botanists heading for Borneo... and Jo and I, the Tukkers. I think the weirdest thing we learnt all weekend was that the American military suggests a 'rectal Mars Bar' in the case of an unconscious diabetic. And that 25 000 people die in India every year from rabies. Gripping stuff.

This weekend it's off to the wilds of Devon for more training, this time for survival skills courtesy of Intrepid Expeditions. I'm horrified to see that the kit list includes mess tins and sleeping mats. Camping was never my forte, but I had better get used to the idea if we're going to survive in the Central Asian steppes, where there won't be a power shower or a wi-fi connection for hundreds of miles. Let alone sushi or a black cab. Just us, a pink tuk tuk and the Great Outdoors.

People keep asking if we're nervous, but at the moment it just doesn't seem real. It feels as if we are planning the trip for someone else. I wonder when it will seem real? When we switch on the engine for the first time and the GPS says in that irritating voice 'Go to the end of the road and turn left'? Or when we find ourselves stranded in a Russian pothole?

 Monday 20 March, Kelling, Norfolk, UK

 A mild case of Stockholm syndrome

We're just thawing out from having spent this weekend on the aforementioned survival course in Devon, where we had to skin various animals, build our own shelter and generally behave like Neanderthals. Believe it or not, it was surprisingly fun, despite the sub-zero temperatures and disgusting army rations.

As I drove down on Friday I was overcome by a desire to spend the weekend in a swanky hotel – the type with voluminous fluffy towels and delicious cream teas – rather than a Devon wood. My initial impression of Nigel and Kim, our captors for the next few days, did nothing to alleviate my fears – hardcore ex-Marines in big boots and army gear. Neither did the prospect of our first task, building a 'hasty shelter' for the night using little more than tarpaulin and rope. But things are rarely as bad as they seem, and a few hours later we were all happily hunkering down around the campfire discovering the joys of life in the woods.

On Saturday we crammed in a multitude of tasks – skinning rabbits, plucking pigeons, night navigation, building a proper shelter, purifying water, learning 101 ways to light a fire. Jo also taught Nigel and Kim a few of her own special survival skills. I think I can safely say that these were things they hadn't come across before, and they probably won't introduce them into subsequent courses.

All in all it was a brilliant weekend and I feel sure that if we get stranded in the middle of steppe, mountain or desert we will have Nigel – aka Uncle Nobby – and Kim's wise words echoing in our ears. Failing that, we will certainly have their numbers on speed dial.

One final thing: Jo and I have both come back suffering from a mild case of Stockholm syndrome.

 Saturday 25 March, Kelling, Norfolk, UK

 China here we come

It hasn't been the most eventful week in Tukland: no more survival courses in the depths of Devon or learning how to splint fractures at the Royal Geographical Society. However, on the logistics front we have made some headway since the China Sea International Travel Service (CSITS) in Beijing has now confirmed that we can enter China on 10 June. Since it will take us about 12 days to drive north from Bangkok to China, this gives us a start date of 28 May, which means leaving England around 20 May for a final week of planning and preparation. That will give us enough time in Bangkok to become acquainted with

Ting Tong, our supersonic tuk tuk, get some mechanical training and generally prepare ourselves for the next 12500 miles.

Other main news this week is that we are getting our fundraising action plan in place and exploring security issues. As we are two girls going solo, security is something we have to consider carefully. What sort of back-up are we going to have? What methods of communication are we going to use? How do we cope if we break down in the middle of nowhere? This week I have been talking to International SOS and Control Risks Group, professional security organisations, to see what they can offer us and at what price. Option one, having a two-man back-up team with us 24/7, comes in at a hefty £600 a day – laughably beyond our budget. Option two, at around £3000 for three months, is to have a remote assistance team, whom we call every day and who will warn us of any potential security or medical risks. Option three is to go it alone and trust in the power of Ting Tong. At the moment Option three is favourite, unless some kind corporation decides to throw a wad of cash our way.

Jo's off to India next week to see her fiancé Raja. Does anyone want to look after her ferrets?

 Thursday 6 April, Kelling, Norfolk, UK

 Skype on board

Exciting news! Skype confirmed this week that they are going to sponsor us. We are thrilled to be in cahoots with such a well-known brand and are looking forward to calling everyone via Skype from the back of the tuk tuk. If you haven't already discovered Skype, get on to it. It's amazing. I've been having Russian lessons via Skype with my teacher Vanda, she in her house in Sweden, and I in my house in Norfolk. Technology, eh?

It sounds like Jo is having fun in India. Her last email recounted an ear-piercing festival she had been to.

My friends Bella and Ewan have just come back from three weeks in Thailand, Cambodia and Laos and said that not only was it unbearably hot but that one night it rained so much in Bangkok that the water was up to their knees. By May it'll be even hotter, and with the monsoon looming there are bound to be a few more of these flash floods. I've been caught in them before and the volume of water is astonishing, incomparable to anything you will ever experience in this country. Fingers crossed that we don't get caught in any such downpours: tuk tuks are tropical beasts and not famed for their prowess in deep water.

 Monday 10 April, Kelling, Norfolk, UK

 So you wanna be a record breaker?

I just had lunch with Hugh Sinclair, who in 1991 broke the world record for the fastest traverse of the Americas by motorbike. Having heard about our expedition on the traveller's grapevine, he very kindly contacted us to offer advice. What a fount of information: I've come away with my brain bulging and a list of tips as long as my arm. Hugh's story is a funny one: he and a friend decided that they wanted to break a world record; they didn't know how or where, but it had to be a record. They weren't bikers but when they found out that there was no confirmed record for the fastest crossing of the Americas by bike, they decided that was what they would do. So they got their tests and set off: 35 days' riding, 40 accidents and an airlift later they did it. And Hugh has barely ridden a bike since! Glad to see that we're not the only certifiable people out there.

We just got back the results of a geopolitical security assessment we had done for the journey, looking at the potential medical and security risks we could encounter in each country. It makes nerve-wracking reading. Here are some of the highlights. Of Laos it says: 'Overland travel in general is becoming increasingly hazardous in Laos and most authorities advise foreign travellers to consider air travel between urban centres.'

Of Kazakhstan: 'The police and the National Guard may themselves present a threat... it is worthwhile noting that visitors are advised not to drive but to hire a driver or to take a taxi between locations.' Of Russia: 'The police can be particularly difficult to deal with, and the concept of corruption is endemic to the population at large.' It's great to have an assessment like this done and to be aware of the risks – it would be irresponsible of us not to – but it doesn't exactly fill me with confidence. The fact is, though, that we can't afford an expensive back-up team and are just going to have faith in the power of Ting Tong and our guardian angels.

Jo's back from India now so we're getting together tomorrow to work out our final plan of action. Only five more weeks to go, but so much to think about still.

 Thursday 13 April, Kelling, Norfolk, UK

 Five weeks until Lift Off

Gee, where do I start? So much has happened in the past few days that it's hard to keep track of everything. Organising this venture is the ultimate emotional rollercoaster: some weeks you feel like you are trying to climb a never-ending mountain, other weeks everything goes right and you are bowled over by the kindness and generosity of people. This week has definitely fallen into the latter category.

On Tuesday Jo and I drove down to Winchester to see Brussels-based expedition guru Sam Rutherford and his wife Bea. Sam was one of a team who drove from London to Sydney in two pink Land Rovers in 1997 and since then he and Bea have set up their own company, www.prepare2go.com, organising rallies and advising people like me and Jo on how to travel the world and make it back in one piece.

Talking to people like Sam, you pick up tips that you would never discover in a month of research. Perhaps his best pieces of advice were to keep our sense of humour – particularly in China, which allegedly makes India seem like the proverbial stroll in the park – and to never lose sight of the fact that the main thing is to get home safe. He also allayed our fears that someone might steal Ting Tong: it seems that our decision to paint her pink is in fact a stroke of genius since it would be pretty hard for someone to steal her without being caught pink-handed. Sam and Bea also kindly offered to have two rather grubby tukkers staying with them in Brussels on the last leg of the trip.

Having had lunch with a world record holder on Monday, we were spurred into chasing up Guinness to see whether our journey would make it into the record books. The answer came back that upon completion we could well break the record for 'the longest journey ever by auto-rickshaw', currently held by Ken Twyford and Gerald Smewing, who drove an Indian auto-rickshaw 11 908 miles (19 165 km) between Hyderabad, India, and Great Harwood, Lancashire, England, from 17 December 1999 to 23 June 2000. The only slight caveat is that the rules stipulate that the vehicle must have 'no modifications'. Do roll-bars, a comedy horn and shocking-pink paintwork come into this category, I wonder?

Our wonderful web designer, Brian at Indrum in Brighton, has been busy adding all sorts of gadgets behind the scenes this week. We can now see how many hits we've had at www.tuktotheroad.co.uk and where our hits are coming from. You can imagine our excitement on seeing that in the past three days we've had over 3000 hits. Amazing! Who are all these people looking at our site? And no, it's not just us, although we might have added a few to the counter.

On the press side of things, *Marie Claire* is interviewing us for a feature on 3 May, and the *Mail on Sunday* has said it wants us to write a piece on our return. And then there was the journalist (who shall remain unnamed) who, in a brilliantly camp voice, asked Jo whether our 'luxurious' tuk tuk was equipped with a microwave. Dream on!

 **Thursday 13 April, Brighton, UK**

Happy Easter!

Ants has really put me to shame with her blogging skills. She had to remind me yesterday how to actually use our blog. So, this is the first post from me.

It's now only 35 days until we take off for Bangkok, but still this whole trip doesn't feel real. Ants has likened it to doing all the preparation and reading for your university dissertation before having to sit down and write the bloody thing. We are so involved in all of the planning and preparation that it is difficult to comprehend that in five weeks we will be flying out to Bangkok.

I went to see the nurse at my doctor's surgery today and was informed I will need to have four jabs before I go, including a polio booster, which I was most upset to learn is no longer given on a sugar lump. I have also been advised to have a meningitis jab and to consider jabs against rabies and Japanese encephalitis. So, next Tuesday I have an appointment with the nurse and will have the pleasure of two injections and my overdue smear test. I can hardly wait.

Before that, however, it is Easter – which means a couple of things: hot cross buns and chocolate. See, being made to go to church every day at school doesn't necessarily make one a good Christian. I am totally clueless about the Bible and its contents. Not that that makes me a bad person, does it? I think I am just one of the hundreds and thousands of young people out there who are not particularly religious and God-fearing. The closest I get to God is probably uttering the phrase 'Oh my God!' on a reasonably regular basis. The god on our trip will be Ting Tong, and I hope that she can undergo a blessing before we leave Bangkok. I will kiss her every day and worship her beautifully formed three wheels and pink bodywork. Actually, that reminds me that I probably need to read my latest purchase, *Auto Repair For Dummies*. Plus, I need to get intimate with my unloved motorbike and learn how to remove her front wheel, because on our trip we will need to change our front brake pads roughly every 2000 miles.

 Tuesday 18 April, Kelling, Norfolk, UK

 'Prozac Nation'

This was the headline of the *Independent on* (Easter) *Sunday*. Not exactly uplifting or Easter-Bunnyish but an extra reason why you should all sponsor us and help Mind fight the war against the depression pandemic that seems to be sweeping our green and pleasant land.

According to the article, 3.5 million Britons are popping pills daily. Fluoxetine, citalopram, paroxetine, sertraline, mirtazapine... you name it, we're on it. In the past decade, our collective misery has seen prescriptions of these pills rise by more than 120 per cent, costing the NHS £400 million a year. Alarming stuff. And not to mention that the World Health Organization predicts that depression will be the second biggest health problem globally by 2020. Mind and other charities campaigning for better mental health hence need all the support they can get.

 Friday 21 April, Brighton, UK

 Stress, depression and the twenty-first century

The article in the *Independent on Sunday* made quite shocking reading. Are that many people really suffering from clinical depression caused by a neurochemical imbalance? Maybe, maybe not. Unfortunately, there are no conclusive scans or blood tests that can be carried out by clinicians to diagnose mental health problems. Diagnosis is based on reports from the patient and observations from clinicians, friends and family.

Is the fact that modern life is so stressful the cause of so much unhappiness? A recent report in a scientific journal demonstrated that animals exposed to high levels of stress can exhibit depressed behaviours. This is not exactly a new finding, and extreme stress can lead to the development of a state called 'learned helplessness', characterised by apathetic behaviour.

I often feel stressed, but I usually feel stressed because I choose (or have learnt) to interpret situations as stressful. For example, when I am stuck in traffic and am going to be late for an appointment, there is little point getting stressed, as me being pissed off and uptight will not clear the motorway of traffic. I am sure that there are a lot of people out there who get stressed about things that they cannot alter. Over long periods of time, high levels of stress can eat away at one's physical and mental health. But are our lives today really more stressful and harder than those of people growing up 50 years ago? Are the causes of stress in modern society really the end of the world? No, they are not. I think in many cases we all need to re-evaluate our lives and work out what is important and what is not. Also, we need to remember that being a stress-head is generally not helpful and conducive to being a contented individual.

Another problem is that GPs are under huge pressure to treat patients within a finite period of time; it takes more than a ten-minute consultation to diagnose and treat mental health problems correctly. Unfortunately, the waiting times for non-drug therapies can be far too long – often months. While a patient waits for a referral for a talking therapy, is it better to just prescribe them antidepressants? Many people may be better suited to a talking treatment rather than medication, but what can GPs do with such long waiting lists for these psychological treatments? It also very much depends on the individual patient: some respond brilliantly to medication alone, some to psychological therapy alone, and some to a combination of both.

From personal experience, I honestly believe that antidepressants saved my life, although it took a while to find the one that worked best for me. I think the government needs to invest a huge amount of funds into NHS mental healthcare, because the problem is only going to get worse. It has been predicted that the cost of mental health problems to the country's economy already runs into billions of pounds. Surely that in itself is reason enough to increase funding?

I also believe that we need some kind of social revolution in this country. What has life come to when the majority of assaults are drink-related and 30-year-olds are being treated for cirrhosis? I think the media need to become more responsible to the young people in today's society, because many popular media aimed at young people are promoting superficial ideals. The majority of women are now dissatisfied with at least one part of their body, and many are just too caught up in our ever-expanding consumer society. We need to wake up to what is really important in life and get real.

 Wednesday 26 April, Kelling, Norfolk, UK

 Meetings with remarkable people

Aside from raising money and awareness for Mind, one of the best things about doing a trip like this is the people you meet. In the past few weeks we've met and spoken with a plethora of explorers, world record holders and all-round expedition gurus. Each of them has been truly inspirational. We've already recounted our meetings with Sam Rutherford and Hugh Sinclair, but since then we've had the pleasure of speaking with two more remarkable individuals, Simon Wilson-Stephens and Olly Hicks.

First up was Olly. Olly is younger than Jo and I – 23, I believe. On 28 September 2005, after four months at sea, he arrived at Falmouth having rowed solo across the Atlantic, the youngest person ever to do so. Mind-boggling: just him, the ocean and a pair of oars. And not a lot of food by the sound of things. My great-uncle won a bronze medal in the Olympics for rowing, and I was always pretty good on the rowing machine at the gym, but the thought of rowing all that way – on my own – defies imagination. Even more remarkable is Olly's next project – rowing around the world solo, due to lift off at the end of 2007.

Next in the line of remarkable people is Simon Wilson-Stephens. Simon had suffered from depression since the age of 15 or 16. His depression came to a head after the turn of the new millennium, when, as Simon says, his 'wheels came flying off' and he had a breakdown, his foundations crumbling as he tried to settle back into life in the UK after a stint in Africa organising safaris. Simon recovered and decided to go back to East Africa and follow one of Henry Morton Stanley's expedition routes by bicycle and kayak. He, with new friend Stanley the dog, completed the trip and in the process raised £16000 for the Charlie Waller Memorial Trust. When I spoke to Simon a few days ago, he had just run the London Marathon and Stanley the dog was off for a walk.

It's Simon's fault that we're now booked in to give a talk at the Royal Geographical Society on 12 December. The prospect fills me with more horror than a wrestle with a Ukrainian gangster.

And finally, Jimmy Goddard. I haven't actually met or spoken to Jimmy, but my friend Tom Townshend is in training for not one but two triathlons this year in order to raise money for Jimmy's Trust. Jimmy is in his late twenties and was paralysed from the chest down by a horrific climbing accident in 2004. Jimmy refuses to be beaten by his disability and is about to be the first paraplegic person to climb Mount Kilimanjaro. Hearing about people like this is a humbling experience and makes you regret those times you whinged about your own petty problems.

 **Wednesday 3 May, Kelling, Norfolk, UK**

 Sponsorship and naked marketing

Only 16 days to go until we leave for Bangkok, and there are still a million things to do. Our main tasks are fundraising and sponsorship. Letters have been flying out of Tuk to the Road HQ beseeching individuals and companies to part with their hard-earned cash. Subsequently I come down to breakfast most mornings to find a pile of cheques, which I rip open in anticipation – £790 came in one day last week, and over £200 arrived this morning. Mental health is something that affects so many people, and almost everyone we speak to about our trip and Mind has been affected by it either directly or indirectly. No wonder the cheques are flowing in. We're up to about £10 000 now, but I am sure that once we get on our way and show people that we are really doing it – really driving 12 500 miles in a pink tuk tuk – then more people will donate. They had better do, because otherwise Jo, being a naturist, is going to tour the country naked on our return. And 'they' thought the Naked Rambler was bad.

The past few days have been frustrating in terms of sponsorship. Although we have been consistently bowled over by the kindness of individuals, when it comes to dealing with big corporations the matter is very different. One particular company, which shall remain unnamed, has led us up the garden path. Over three weeks ago this company replied enthusiastically to a proposal to sponsor our flights, asking us what dates we wanted to fly, telling us they loved the idea, etc., etc. Now, 16 days before we leave, the company says no. Grrrr! But have no fear, for we've found some cheap flights via Kuala Lumpur on the afternoon of 20 May.

We have had some luck on the sponsorship front, however, with Liftshare and Activair. Both have kindly provided us with financial sponsorship in return for having logos on Ting Tong. The great thing about having

Liftshare on board is the fact that they tick the Big Green Box. The next thing to consider is how we can make our trip carbon-neutral – perhaps Future Forests could sponsor us by planting enough trees to negate the effect of our trip on the environment.

On a rather different note, Jo and I would like to send all our thoughts and love to the families of two very special people: Rose and Livs. Both girls were great friends of ours and tragically are no longer with us. I know that they would have approved of our madcap three-wheeled adventure, and we will be thinking of them often over the next few months.

 Tuesday 9 May, Kelling, Norfolk, UK

 The power of cyberspace

Only ten days to go until we get on a plane to Bangkok, and tuk tuk fever is setting in. I feel like I have written a thousand letters recently, telling people about our mission and asking them to support us and, more importantly, Mind. Luckily the response has been great and more and more cheques arrive daily. We've still got a massive amount of fundraising to do before we hit our £50 000 target, but I think a lot of people will donate when we are actually on the road. I guess our mission has to be begun to be believed. I still don't believe it's happening, so why should anyone else?

The past few days have been an astonishing testament to the power of cyberspace. A few weeks ago Jo got in touch with a guy called John who lives in Bangkok and runs www.khaosanroad.com. John put our story on his site's home page and within 24 hours three more potential sponsors and several travel magazines and websites contacted us. One of these is Travelfish (www.travelfish.org), a brilliant site all about travelling in South East Asia. Ting Tong is now going to be sporting a Travelfish sticker, and a story about our mission will soon be gracing their pages.

Gapyear.com (www.gapyear.com) also contacted us and is going to feature our blog on its site and help publicise the trip. Suddenly it feels like it's all happening.

Mind Week starts this Saturday and then it's our launch party on Wednesday. I'm vaguely terrified about the latter since between 6 and 7.30 p.m. Skype, one of our sponsors, has arranged a press launch at the Cobden Club for us and apparently there are journalists from the *Daily Mail*, the *Sun*, the *Financial Times*, handbag.com and various other publications coming along. Yikes! I used to find it hard enough to say anything at the *South Bank Show* departmental meetings, let alone open my mouth in front of an assortment of journalists.

 Friday 12 May, Brighton, UK

 I feel sad

I should be in bed getting a good night's sleep to prepare for the hectic week ahead, but I am feeling sad right now. The trip is starting to feel very real and this next week is going to be a rush of acquiring more kit, fundraising, Skype press conference, launch party, etc. I feel like there's too much to do and not enough time.

The reason I am feeling sad is because of my ferrets. The hardest thing for me is going to be leaving behind my 12 darling babies, knowing that if there is a problem I won't be there to kiss and cuddle them. You might think I'm crazy, but if you're an animal lover you'll understand. Two of them are unwell at the moment: Zac has kidney failure and Pebbles has suddenly lost the use of her back legs and can't go to the loo properly. It is quite likely that Zac will not be alive when I return, and Pebbles will probably have to be put to sleep next week if she doesn't improve. Just writing this is making me cry.

I am at my mum and dad's right now and am going to spend the day with them tomorrow, as it will be the last quality time I get with them before we leave.

Things seem to be taking off with regards to PR now, which is encouraging. I have done a couple of phone interviews today and was being asked loads of questions about my depression and self-harm and how it used to make me feel. It was strange to drag out old memories that I hadn't visited for years. Why would I want to think how I felt when I used to cut myself or how my depression might have affected my family and friends? I didn't expect it to bother me, but it has a little.

That's another reason why my ferrets are so special to me. When I was really depressed they honestly were my lifesavers. Mum said that if I ever did anything, i.e. attempt suicide, then she would give my ferrets to the RSPCA. I know that she didn't really mean it, but when I couldn't handle any human affection my ferrets were always there to lick away my tears and comfort me in the middle of the night when I felt so desperate and scared. God, this is probably the most depressing blog to date, but it is just how I am feeling right now.

Anyway, I hope it is a sunny day tomorrow so that I can take off all my clothes and indulge my naturist tendencies in the back garden.

 Monday 15 May, Kelling, Norfolk, UK

 In need of a holiday

Could things get any more hectic, I wonder? With five days to go until we finally leave for Bangkok, Jo and I are running round like headless ferrets. This morning we've been getting together the final things for our launch party on Wednesday: organising the sound-checks with Santi, the sound engineer, talking to the singers and bands, finalising the guest list. Then there's the Skype press launch to consider and the horrific thought of having to stand up in front of people and talk about what we are doing. I guess we had better get used to it.

Quite apart from the launch party, there's equipment to be ordered and bought, insurance of the satellite modem to sort out, embassies to be written to, travellers' cheques to be ordered. And to top it all, I've had a temperature for two days and have been lying in bed feeling utterly rubbish. Good timing, immune system!

With Mind Week and Lift Off just around the corner, it seems that the press are suddenly interested. Hannah, our PR guru at Skype, has been doing sterling work and it looks like our press launch on Wednesday might even have a few people there. Even the *Sun* is doing a piece (no, *not* Page 3, although I'm sure Jo would happily agree to any removal-of-clothing requests) in its health section, and Radio 5 Live apparently wants to do a series of interviews with us via Skype once we hit the road.

I hit Norwich yesterday in a bid to equip ourselves... and came back with tripods, digital cameras, a pink mobile phone, a cushty hoodie and some combat trousers. So lots more technology to get to grips with. Norfolk is looking so beautiful and verdant at the moment. I'm loath to leave. The cuckoo is out, the meadows are lush and the sky seems to get bluer by the day. It feels like the calm before the storm. In a weeks' time, Jo and I will be in the maelstrom that is Bangkok – a hooting, sweating, filthy mêlée of people and traffic. Norfolk will seem a million miles away.

Back to bed now for more echinacea and super-vitamins. I need to get my strength back for the rigours of the week ahead.

Friday 19 May, Jo's parents' house, Surrey, UK

 Technobabble

I'm sitting here in Jo's parents' garden while she deposits her 12 ferrets around various parts of East Sussex, tapping away on the web with the help of our new Inmarsat BGAN. That's a satellite modem in lay terms. All this technology is beyond me. Basically our BGAN means we can hook up to the net anywhere, as long as the unit can 'see the sky' and talk to the nearest available satellite. And to think that a few years ago I could hardly send an email.

Neither of us has really started packing properly and there is equipment strewn all over the house – GPS units, the BGAN, DV tapes, cameras, water filters, maps, guide books (I think we need a special bookshelf in Ting Tong to accommodate our fleet of weighty travel tomes), insect repellent, WD40, Ultraseal, solar panels... it's amazing all the weird and wonderful things we have to take with us. Luckily, Jo's pa Bob is coming to see us off in Bangers so we can give him some of our equipment and thus avoid being stung for excess baggage.

Wednesday was possibly the maddest day of my life – here's how it went:

7 a.m.	Drag ourselves out of bed. Jo and I are both rubbish in the mornings.
7.30 a.m.	Live interview with BBC Southern Counties Radio.
8 a.m.	BBC breakfast reporter and cameraman rock up to do a piece on us and Skype for the news.
10.30 a.m.	Meet Colin Cameron from the *Financial Times* for an interview. He's doing a piece in the November *How to Spend It* magazine on 'adventure philanthropists'.
12 p.m.	Haircut. Essential!

5.30 p.m.	Get to the Cobden Club for our Skype Press launch. Jo's forgotten to wear a bra and they want us to wear white Skype T-shirts.
6 p.m.	Press launch.
8 p.m.	Our Tuk Off launch party starts.
2 a.m.	Bed... yawn!

I'm still feeling grotty and have a filthy cold, which is not ideal.

Thanks again to everyone who has helped us so far. You're all amazing, and none of this would have been possible without you.

chapter 2
lift off

 Tuesday 23 May, Sawasdee Hotel, Bangkok, Thailand

Sawasdee ka **from Bangkok**

We arrived in Thailand on Sunday and it is all starting to feel a little bit more real, like we are actually going to drive home in a tuk tuk after all. It was quite sad saying goodbye to Mum and my brother Nick, because I knew I wouldn't see them for over three months and I love my family so much. Dad took us to the airport and I wasn't sad to say goodbye to him – not because I don't love him to death, but because he will be joining us in Bangkok in a few days.

Ants and I both had insomnia on the plane and I had really bad restless legs, which in the confines of cattle class is no fun. I purloined a selection of pillows and blankets and made myself a bed by the emergency exit. I had just settled down comfortably when a stewardess politely told me that I had to return to my seat. Instead, Ants suggested a novel form of sedative and after a few shots of Night Nurse we slept like babies for the rest of the flight.

We'd arranged to meet Anuwat at the airport and after a few phone calls found him outside having a cigarette. He and his wife Dow then drove us to our hotel and I started to feel seriously excited that we were in Bangkok. The bright lights, sounds and smells of Thailand welcomed us and there were tuk tuks everywhere.

The following morning we met Stuart from Travelfish, one of our sponsors. He spent a few hours with us to do an interview and take photos for his website. Anuwat picked us all up from the hotel and we drove to his factory to meet Ting Tong for the first time. We were both feeling full of nervous anticipation. When we first saw Ting Tong it was a bit of an 'Oh shit!' moment, because she had no wiring, no seats and no roof and we had assumed that she would be totally finished when we arrived. However, she is bright pink and absolutely beautiful and we have both fallen madly in love with her.

My friend Hannah is out here at the moment and we met up with her, her boyfriend André and her friend Jess on the Khao San Road. For those of you who have not been to Thailand, the Khao San Road is the traveller's ghetto in Bangkok, full of tourists, bars, restaurants, stalls and flashing neon lights. I think you either love it or hate it. It was quite fitting though, because I was with Hannah four years ago when I first came up with the idea of driving a tuk tuk back to England, and now here we are about to turn my crazy dream into reality.

We have got so much to sort out this week, and I still have no idea about tuk tuk mechanics. Anuwat is going to give me a couple of lessons in his factory later this week. God, I hope I pick it up quickly. It is really weird not being here as regular tourists, staying on the Khao San Road and going out partying every night. We've got too much on our plates to be doing any of that.

One of our big decisions at the moment is deciding where we want to start our adventure. Possibilities so far include the Khao San Road, the British embassy, Anuwat's factory and Pattaya, a resort over 50 miles away. I think the Khao San Road would be a fun place to begin, but it's really hectic and therefore may not be the best bet. We really ought to start from Bangkok, but then we would have to drive out of the city and neither of us has even driven TT yet. The traffic here is mental and the driving bordering on suicidal.

Poor Ants is feeling ill at the moment. She had a cold before we left home and now seems to have a nasty virus that is making her feverish. I hope that she feels better soon, because we are leaving in a few days... aaaagh!

 **Wednesday 24 May, Sawasdee Hotel, Bangkok, Thailand**

 The true meaning of Ting Tong

So much to write and so little time. It's 10 p.m. and Jo and I have just got in after another hectic day in Bangkok. I want to write a mega-blog but I also need to lie down and chill out... so I'll just include the highlights of today.

Today we had a very amusing lunch with Jim Short, the political secretary at the British embassy. Poor Jim was subjected to Jo's usual barrage of questions – How old are you? How long have you been here? Where is your wife from? Do you earn much? What size are your shoes? But he still managed to be a paragon of charm and British cynicism. Thanks, Jim, for your words of wisdom and amazing tolerance to the Spanish Inquisition.

Having had lunch with Jim, we eventually got in touch with Mrs Fall, the wife of British ambassador, David Fall. Mrs Fall and her husband have very kindly agreed to let the tukathon begin at the embassy on Sunday morning and Nuttanee, their press officer, is going to rustle up some press interest. We hope some of the Thai press people will have nothing better to do than wave off a pair of Ting Tong *farangs* (foreigners) in a pink tuk tuk.

Which leads me to my next point: we've discovered that Ting Tong in fact means 'crazy' or 'nuts' in Thai. Although we were careful to ascertain that it didn't mean some vile Mandarin obscenity, we omitted to check its Thai meaning. Oh well, it seems quite fitting really. Although, when our tuk tuk driver last night laughed, and exclaimed '*Ting tong!*' while gesturing at a blatantly mentally unhinged individual banging a stick against a tree, we did begin to wonder whether we might be creating the wrong impression.

As for Ting Tong herself – well, she's *pink, hot pink*! And she really is the most rocking tuk tuk in the world. We got a bit of a shock upon arriving at Anuwat's factory on Monday morning to find a bevy of Anuwat's workers swarming round her and no roof, seats or wiring. But they've done wonders and tomorrow she'll be ready for us to test drive. We learnt later that Anuwat thought we were leaving *next* Sunday, not this one, hence the uber-chilled approach to finishing her. Anuwat is a diamond though and has been giving me and Jo the five-star treatment, chauffeuring us around sticky Bangkok and kitting out Ting Tong to perfection, down to the latest MP3 player.

Tomorrow morning it's breakfast at the Four Seasons Hotel, then a visit to the Laos embassy to get our visas, and then mechanical training at the factory in the afternoon. We've managed to find a cameraman to come and help us out with the filming, so he'll be with us for the next few days capturing the action.

 Thursday 25 May, Sawasdee Hotel, Bangkok, Thailand

 Busy, busy, busy...

We are having quite a week of it here in Bangkok. The time is flying by and every minute is filled with things to do.

Ants' health took a turn for the worse today and Anuwat and I decided a visit to hospital was in order. They are not sure what is wrong yet so are keeping her in overnight to do tests. It's not ideal, since we leave on Sunday. Fingers crossed she makes a very speedy recovery. I am fine and seem to be in good health on my very poor diet of fags, Coke and the odd grasshopper. Grasshoppers are actually quite tasty – a bit like a greasy Kettle Chip – although yesterday I got a leg stuck in the back of my throat, which induced a little retching episode. I am happy to say that I did not throw up.

Yesterday we spent the afternoon in the tuk tuk factory and I learnt all of the mechanical skills that we hope will keep Ting Tong in tiptop shape. I also had a little drive, reaching a top speed of about 10 mph in second gear. Shit! If I go on like that, it's going to be a hell of a long journey back to Blighty. Perhaps the next challenge will be to do the trip in reverse – I am pretty nifty at reversing Ting Tong.

I went to the Laos embassy this morning on a double mission, first to obtain our visas and second to try and get special permission for us to cross into Laos at the Friendship Bridge. Currently the Laos government has banned Thai-registered vehicles driven by foreigners from crossing into Laos at this main border. This is a little bit worrying, because it is our intended route into country number two.

The traffic in Bangkok has got to be the worst in the world: think permanent rush-hour in the UK and you are still not even close. Coming back from the embassy this morning I opted to take a motorbike taxi, perhaps not the safest method of transport, but by far the quickest. I got back to the hotel in nearly half the time and was so happy that I was still alive I gave the driver a healthy tip.

Two days till Lift Off and my dad arrives from the UK today to spend a week travelling with us. It is very exciting, and having half a parental unit with us will certainly help to calm me down when we get lost or can't find the right gear, i.e. anything above second. Having said that, we will be travelling a little slower with Dad in the back!

Anyway, I'd better go now before a power-cut wipes this blog and sends me *ting tong*.

 Friday 26 May, Sawasdee Hotel, Bangkok, Thailand

 A night in a Thai hospital

Ugh! I have just returned from a 24-hour sojourn in the Samitivej Hospital in Bangkok. Not ideal two days before Lift Off. I am feeling too feek and weeble to write much now and need to get horizontal again and get my strength back before we start.

It was nothing serious – just a high fever, the shakes and sweats, a viral infection, throat infection, 'flu and pharyngitis according to the hospital medical report. I'm sure it's all been brought on by stress. What with all our final preparations, the launch party and arriving here, the past two weeks have been physically and mentally very challenging and my immune system caved in. We were at the factory yesterday learning mechanics and filming and I could feel myself getting hotter and hotter. By the time Jo and Anuwat took me to hospital last night I was a human radiator and my temperature had hit 104 °F. After a surfeit of pharmaceuticals, it's now down to normal. I'm feeling very weak though and not quite sure how I am going to get enough strength to leave by Sunday. Where there is a will there is a way...

Stage 1
Thailand ~ Laos

CHINA

Pak Ou · Luang Prabang
LAOS
Vientiane
Khon
Kaen
THAILAND
Ayutthaya
Bangkok

CAMBODIA

N

 Tuesday 30 May, Khao Yai National Park, Thailand

 Lift Off!

I can't believe it! The tukathon has actually begun. At 11.49 a.m. on Sunday morning Jo, myself and Ting Tong, under the watchful gaze of Queen Victoria's statue, turned left out of the British embassy in Bangkok and set sail for England. After so many months of planning, it's extraordinary to think we have actually embarked on our 12 500-mile journey and that for the next three months we will slowly be heading home, each day inching a little closer across the globe.

Having only come out of hospital on Friday I was unsure whether I'd actually be able to go with Jo for the first few days. But after a shaky day on Saturday and a few green, wobbly moments on Sunday morning we were off and I wouldn't have missed it for the world.

On Saturday night we took Ting Tong to the Khao San Road and got a taste of what the next few months might be like. Even in Bangkok, where tuk tuks are ubiquitous, people stopped, stared, laughed, took pictures and shook their heads in amazement when we told them we were driving our pink bomber all the way to England. Jo drove her into the Khao San and we parked her up for a few hours while we did a few interviews, people took pictures and Jo clambered on the roof-rack and risked her and Ting Tong's life for some photos. They'd better be good. Ting Tong went down a storm and, although we might be a little bit biased, she really must be the most supersonic tuk tuk this planet has ever seen. Everyone who sees her definitely goes a little green around the gills. Thanks Anuwat – you are a total star, and Jo and I are both very, very happy that we found you and your amazing tuk tuk factory.

Sunday morning was an early start as we had to load all our kit on to TT and be at the British embassy by 10 a.m. After a rigorous security check at the gates, we cruised up to the front door of the ambassadorial residence to find a pack of photographers and TV crews waiting for us. When Nuttanee, the embassy's press officer, had said she would be able to get some press along to the launch, we never expected such a good turnout. Maybe it was the lure of a morning at the ambassador's residence, where they do make exceedingly good cakes.

The next two hours were a blur of interviews, photos, smiling until it felt like our faces might crack, hanging off the side of Ting Tong for more photos, giving the ambassador and his wife a lift in TT, and hurried goodbyes to cousin Bert and Hannah, Jess and André. Then in we got and off we went. We could never have dreamed our launch would be such a grand affair, and we owe a very big thank you to Mr and Mrs Fall for their amazing hospitality. Even better – Mr Fall might get a tuk tuk from Anuwat to drive around Wiltshire in his retirement. Spread that tuk tuk love!

Since then, we've been speeding north in Ting Tong, eliciting smiles wherever we go. Jo was at the wheel for the first two days, cursing everyone's slow driving and bombing past astonished drivers at 60 mph in the fast lane. Despite the floods in the north of Thailand, the terrible Indonesian earthquake and all the strife in East Timor, we made it into seven Thai newspapers on Monday morning and onto two TV stations. We've heard back from Blighty that we've also been gracing the airwaves on Radio 2, XFM and Five Live, have been on BBC South Today and are on the BBC news website. Even weirder, Ting Tong also appears in papers as diverse as the *Indian Financial Times*, the *Deccan Herald* and the Pakistani *Globe* today. Why on earth would someone in Karachi want to read about a bright-pink tuk tuk?

We're in Khao Yai National Park now, where *The Beach* was filmed. Our hut is surrounded by jungle and I'm hoping we won't get eaten by a hungry tiger in the middle of the night.

200 miles down. Only about another 12 000 to go...

 Wednesday 31 May, Internet café, Phimai, Thailand

 Newsflashes

We drove from Khai Yao National Park to Phimai today, just over 125 miles, and have dived into the nearest Internet café to check our mail and update our blog. The drive here was fairly amusing. People were pulling up level with us on the freeway, winding down their windows and waving and taking photos. When we stopped for lunch at a tiny roadside café, the owner rushed out brandishing yesterday's newspaper with Jo and I and Ting Tong on the front page. More photos were taken, lunch was free and a crate of water was loaded on board before we waved and tukked off up the road.

The main purpose of this blog, though, is to highlight some of the press we have had in the last few days. Thanks to giving an interview in Bangkok to international news agency Associated Press, the tale of our tukathon has reached some most unexpected corners of our planet. We were thrilled to see an article on the BBC news website entitled 'Two in a tuk tuk for 12,000 miles'. Our story in the *Deccan Herald* is sandwiched between articles about a dog show in Bangalore and honour killings in Pakistan. Spot the odd one out.

Last but not least, Jo and I have been giggling inanely at a blog we found that takes the piss out of our venture. For cheap laughs you really must read it: www.armedtechnician.blogspot.com.

I've no idea how the Armed Technician heard about our story, but on 28 May he wrote a blog entitled 'Mental patients make break for it'. Under a picture of Jo and I in Scott Wallace's tuk tuk, he continues: 'Two mental patients have escaped from hospital and are being pursued by police as they flee in a rickshaw they constructed... A doctor at the hospital told reporters that the pair watched the movie *Thelma and Louise* at least three hundred times prior to their escape.'

The Armed Technician then followed this up today in a blog entitled 'Mental update'. According to this we have now assumed the identities of gay nuns in order to elude the authorities and are believed to be heading to Thailand on our 'dyke-bike' in order to rescue ladyboys from the sex trade. Oh, and we're also armed with ten-inch black mamba dildos with which to beat off any assailants.

Thanks Mr Armed Technician, whoever you are. You are keeping two grubby tukkers highly amused. Ting Tong's a bit upset at being called the 'dyke-bike' though. I think you owe her an apology.

One final point: Jo is currently reading an email from her ferrets.

Wednesday 31 May, Internet café, Phimai, Thailand

 Life on the road is hot and happy

It's day four and I apologise that my blogs have been slightly lacking recently. We are now in Phimai and I really need a good wash. Because Ting Tong is exposed to the elements on three sides, you get full access to the environment, i.e. dust, sand and copious exhaust fumes from other vehicles. Hence us being grubby all over, particularly my feet, which gather dust as we zip down the highway at 60 mph (yes, Ting Tong is very fast).

We've just arrived here from Khao Yai National Park, which, although pretty chilled, had the worst food I have ever tasted. Last night our supper consisted of inedible cuttlefish crisps, raisins and beer. We also visited the waterfall where the scene from *The Beach* was filmed, although it looked far bigger in the film and was nothing to get excited about.

 Saturday 3 June, Setta Palace Hotel, Vientiane, Laos

 A five-star celebration

Yesterday, Jo, Ting Tong and I tukked over the Friendship Bridge linking Thailand and Laos and breathed a collective sigh of relief. Ever since we arrived in Thailand two weeks ago, crossing into Laos has been our biggest perceived obstacle, thanks to a recent ban on Thai-registered vehicles driven by foreigners entering at this main border. There was also the *carnet de passage* issue. We decided months ago against getting a carnet, since they are not legally necessary for any of the countries we are crossing and are complicated and expensive to organise. Since arriving in Bangkok, however, we'd heard that we would have a better chance of getting into Laos if we did have one. Great. So, it was with bated breath and butterflies in our stomachs that we eased down the gears and drove up to the border yesterday afternoon.

Jo has been in charge of organising all the paperwork for Thailand, Laos and China, so as she disappeared into the ominous-sounding 'Room 6' at Laos customs I selected Leftfield on my iPod and waited nervously. Leftfield was short-lived, however, as a bevy of tourist police, customs officials and passers-by were soon crowded round Ting Tong. 'Where are you from?' 'Where are you going?' 'How much was your tuk tuk?' All the usual questions were fired at me, followed by the familiar raised eyebrows and looks of 'Are you crazy?' upon learning of our destination. One lady spoke good English and warned me that Route 13 is very mountainous and that we should avoid driving at night due to the Hmong rebels in the north. All things we have been told before. More interesting was her revelation that there is only one psychiatrist in Laos and that depression doesn't really exist here.

After about an hour, Jo emerged triumphantly: we had been granted special permission to enter Laos, but had to wait until Monday in Vientiane in order to get permission to drive through the other provinces. It seems that the Thai press cuttings Jo had shown Laos immigration had worked their magic and, rather than facing an unpleasant diversion, all we had to do was endure a weekend of city arrest in the Laos capital. Not exactly a hardship.

We hadn't even thought about where we were going to stay in Vientiane, so we turned to the accommodation options in the Laos Lonely Planet for some guidance. Overjoyed at being allowed across the border, we decided to celebrate and head straight for the best joint in town, the Setta Palace Hotel, lauded in the Lonely Planet as '*the* place to stay in Vientiane'. The poolside bar and Venetian marble bathrooms sold it and off we tukked, realising as we turned off the bridge that they drive on the wrong side of the road here. Not until England will we drive on the left again.

Crossing borders is a strange experience. How in the course of a few hundred yards can everything be so different – language, faces, roads, food, smells? We had got used to the rampant westernisation that has invaded Thailand, where the roads are nearly perfect, the cars are new and shopping malls litter the roadsides. Yet the instant we crossed the mighty Mekong into Laos, the cars got more battered, the tarmac more potholed and the driving more chaotic. The driving philosophy here is definitely 'there's room for three'. Cars, jumbos – the Laos equivalent of tuk tuks – motorcycle taxis, bicycles and stray dogs all jostle for room, and our two mile tuk to Vientiane was not without a few squeaks from me.

So, here we are at the aforementioned Setta Palace, where the pool is divine, the breakfasts delicious and the beds worthy of staying in for extended periods of time. Jo and I were also a little grubby after a week on the road so in need of hot showers and a good scrub.

A few brief notes on Laos: I can't believe Vientiane is a capital city, because apart from jumbo drivers and the odd *farang*, the streets are practically deserted. The pavements are lethal and too much Beer Lao could result in an ignominious descent down a vast uncovered drain. The cakes are plentiful, the massages are excellent and the people are lovely.

On Monday morning we head north up the (slightly) dreaded Route 13, stopping at Vang Vieng, Luang Prabang and Luang Nam Tha en route to the Chinese border at Boten.

One final thing: I forgot to mention the food market we stumbled upon at Phimai the other night. Among the gastronomic delights on offer were crispy fried frogs on skewers, toad-in-a-bag, still-gasping fish and, best of all, pigs' willies. While I recoiled and retched violently at the sight of the last, Jo whipped out her camera and zoomed in for the close-up. Delightful.

Over to Jo...

So, here we are in our luxury hotel, with the most comfortable beds outside of England. Breakfast this morning was an interesting experience. I was just about to tuk in to my plateful of pastries when I noticed that my plate was moving ever so slightly. I was sober and not high on Coke (the liquid variety) at the time and the motion was caused by some ants – not the one sitting at the table, but the small black ones with lots of legs. I went back to examine the pastry plate more carefully and found there to be quite a few ants. I then decided to add some sugar to my cup of rather tasteless Lipton Yellow Label tea and found a little critter in the sugar bowl as well. I avoided the ant and added my sugar, before I informed the hotel staff. Is this really the sort of thing one expects from a five-star establishment? Anyway, breakfast was quite a feast and made a pleasant change to rice and American pancakes.

I will now backtrack to recap on the past few days.

We left Phimai and its historical park, containing a Khmer temple complex that predates Angkor Wat, and headed north to Khon Kaen. Ting Tong has us wrapped around her little wing-mirrors and, after arriving at our hotel, we unloaded and got her ready for bed, i.e. unrolled her rain covers and put on her silver nightie (tuk tuk cover). Dad and I shared a room and left Ants to have her own room. This is for a few reasons: I snore, I like to watch TV, I like to stay up and ferret around, I like to smoke in the bedroom and I like air-conditioning. All of these habits are a little unsociable and I do not practise them when sharing with Ants. If I want a cigarette, I will have it in the bathroom; I will go to bed at a sensible time and not watch BBC World after lights-out; and the temperature of the air-con will be decided after a bout of Thai boxing. However, I still snore.

Our night out in Khon Kaen was a little bizarre. We went out for a meal and decided on a street stall where we were all given a plate of spicy salad, which was flavoursome but ultimately unsatisfying. We then went to a restaurant complete with a live band. Musically they were good, but they chose to sing a collection of old country-and-westerns, which Dad found quite odd. We ordered some snacks to share and, because the waitresses did not speak very good English, we were presented with the wrong order. I don't like to make a fuss and would have just eaten them, but Dad asked them to change the order. I think I am paranoid about complaining about food in restaurants after seeing a programme in England where people spit in your food if you complain. The band ended and then came a couple of Thai comedians. I didn't understand a word but still found them funny. They called us *farangs* and said a joke that made everyone who spoke Thai laugh. I think the joke was probably on us. This was followed by a couple of dwarfs of varying sizes who proceeded to beat each other over the head with plastic objects. To make it stranger, the larger of the two dwarfs wore a Batman suit and had hearts painted on his face. As if things couldn't get any odder, a very thin old man climbed on to the stage in a nightie, which he took off to reveal the shortest skirt I have ever seen, before bursting into song and being hit on the head by the two original comedians. Very weird. We decided to pay up and leave.

The following morning it was time for Dad and us to go our separate ways, he back to England and us on to Laos. I started crying and I think I upset Dad too. Ants and I both had butterflies in our stomach for the first time on the trip. Having Dad around had been comforting and had given us confidence, even though we can now drive about 5 mph faster. Now suddenly we were on our own, with 12000 miles to go until England.

The Thai side of the border was a mere formality and they let us cross the Friendship Bridge without any problems. Although we had technically arrived in Laos, I knew that we could easily be retracing our steps back to Thailand at the discretion of the Laos authorities. I went from counter to counter before being sent up to Room 6, the place where they decide whether a vehicle can enter Laos. I provided our documents and a selection of press cuttings of us and TT from the Thai press and prayed to a non-specific God. Luckily, we were given special permission to enter, although as *farangs* driving a tuk tuk we should have been turned around and sent back to Thailand. After organising insurance (£3 for ten days) and having more papers signed and stamped, we were allowed to pass. I suddenly realised that we were meant to be driving on the other side of the road and hastily changed lanes. I have never driven on the wrong side of the road, but I better get used to it as we have a long way to go before being back on the right side.

So, today we were up and breakfasted before an interview via Skype with Five Live in England. I did the last one and so Ants had the honour this morning. We have decided to alternate interviews and I hope that we increase awareness about the trip and raise some more money for Mind.

In a rather large nutshell, that is it to date. Tonight we will go out to eat and spend a relaxing evening in probably the most chilled-out capital city on earth. Tomorrow I will indulge in some minor tuk tuk mechanics, i.e. tightening the bolts that affect our steering as our suspension continues to be worn in. For those technical geeks out there, this needs to happen when the steering bars start involuntarily having spasms, i.e. moving left to right without our input.

 Monday 5 June, Vang Vieng, Laos

 A surfeit of cake

Jo and I are sitting in an Internet café in Vang Vieng, tapping away with geckos and grasshoppers for company. I'm not feeling particularly verbose tonight so I will keep it brief.

After five hours' driving today, punctuated by cake, beer and noodle stops, we tukked into Vang Vieng. Laos could not be more different from Thailand and, as we wound into the mountains, leaving the capital Vientiane behind us, I was struck by how incredibly bucolic this country is. Pigs, turkeys, cows and various other livestock roam the villages, and the road – Route 13 – was flanked all the way by rice paddies and tree-covered mountains – very beautiful and a far cry from Thailand's shopping malls and day-glo buses.

VangVieng, however, is unfortunately a violent deviation from the rural idyll I have just illustrated. If you have ever been to Haadrin in Thailand, then this is its Lao equivalent. Grotty guesthouses and TV bars cram the streets, and everywhere there are signs of yet more grotty guesthouses being built. Yet the surrounding countryside is stunning and tomorrow Jo and I are going to kick back and spend a day tubing, imbibing – Beer Lao of course – exploring caves and eating cake, of which we seem to have done quite a bit lately. My visions of us returning lithe and brown after three months on the road are slowly dissolving and, although I keep threatening to go running, I haven't quite made it yet.

Jo will fill you in on the rest. She's been beavering away on the next-door computer for a while, so I assume a masterpiece is in the offing.

 Ting Tong's first real adventure

We are about 100 miles north of Vientiane. Our driving speed has dropped to an average of about 30 mph due to the copious potholes and winding hilly roads. Ants and I were both knackered today and were trying to get each other to drive. I think that we both ate too many cakes over the weekend and as a result were feeling pretty sluggish.

Now back to the past few days.

On Saturday night we headed out to supposedly one of the best restaurants in Vientiane, where the mediocre food was made up for by the interesting company. As soon as we sat down we were joined by a very drunk local, who I assume had had too much Beer Lao. He repeated himself frequently, as drunk people often do, fell off his chair every couple of minutes and came out with the classic comment 'I love you Mr Ant'. I have now taken to repeating this phrase far too often.

Our drunken friend was asked to leave by the waiters, so we finished the rest of dinner in peace, only to find him waiting outside for us on his moped. We couldn't find a tuk tuk and so had to walk back to town, followed all the way by 'I love you Mr Ant'. The guy could hardly walk straight and I was horrified that he was on a bike. If you want to drive me mad, then drink-drive. I think drunk people are pretty uninspiring company at the best of times, but to take charge of a car/bike when wasted is unbelievably selfish and stupid. We tried to ask him to leave and maintain a straight face, but when he kept saying 'I love you Mr Ant' it was hard to stop ourselves from giggling. After about one mile he finally got bored and went away. The situation did not feel remotely threatening, merely slightly irritating after the best part of an hour. In England I would have called the police or been more aggressive, but that isn't really an option here. I find that the best thing is to not get aggressive and potentially antagonise a situation.

Sunday: awoke and had breakfast with more ants in it, which was charming. I didn't need to eat sausages as I had enough protein from the little critters. We then went to see the beautiful Pha Tat Luang, the most important temple in Laos. I don't wear sunglasses and therefore might have sustained slight damage to the innards of my eye thanks to the blinding golden glare from the temple. We did a bit of filming and then in the afternoon went for a herbal sauna and massage.

What better way to finish off the afternoon than with a sandwich and chocolate eclair? The sandwich was good, but the chocolate eclair contained the wrong sort of cream and, to add insult to injury, they had added custard. I ate it all the same, but was none too impressed.

This morning we split up. Ants went to sort out our permits for driving through the rest of Laos and I did some minor tuk tuk mechanics, i.e. checked the oil, water and tyres and tightened the big bolt on our steering column as our suspension keeps dropping.

At 10.30 a.m. we hit the road and I tried to drive down a one-way street the wrong way. Well done Jo! As we headed out of town, we pulled in to get the tyre pressure topped up. They were each three psi down and I wrote down the required pressures on my hand for the woman with the air gun. She nodded and squirted some air into TT's tyres. I wondered how she knew the correct pressure as there didn't seem to be a gauge visible. Still, I assumed that as she filled up tyres all day, then she knew what she was doing. I didn't realise until later that she had doubled the suggested air pressure. I will never let a random person violate poor TT again. We are lucky her tyres didn't burst from the excessive air. Tomorrow we will get our digital tyre inflator thing from the roof and do our own air in the future. The vehicles in Laos must all have the most pumped-up tyres in South East Asia, and this is a risky thing if riding a motorbike or a three-wheeler.

Next stop was lunch, which was cold and had unidentifiable objects floating in it; however, it tasted pretty good. As we neared Vang Vieng we passed what looked like a café and pulled in for a cooling drink, assuming that the guy who welcomed us was the owner of the shack. In fact, he was just a local who was – guess what? – wasted on Beer Lao and proceeded to fill our glasses, slobber all over my cheek and grab my boobs. Of course, Ants caught it all on camera.

Enough waffle from me now. Good night, and good afternoon to those in the West.

 Tuesday 6 June, Vang Vieng, Laos

 Tubing and Beer Lao

It's our second night in tourist-tastic yet beautiful Vang Vieng, where there are definitely the most white people I have seen in one place since England.

Today we both woke up feeling exhausted, even though we had had plenty of sleep, and opted for a leisurely day's sightseeing. After a huge pineapple pancake and cup of tea (or yoghurt and rabbit food for Ants), we pottered into town and found a tour operator and, within a few minutes, had sorted out our day's entertainment.

Our first adventure was kayaking. I was put in the back and given the task of steering. I lost all knowledge of left, right, forwards and backwards and before long was sitting on a rock in the middle of the river and Ants had jumped ship. I was then told to paddle rather than steer, so I swapped to the front of the kayak. I am not particularly fit at the moment, but I managed to propel us down the river at a sort of doggy-paddle speed. Ants was much better at steering and there were no more rock incidents. My arms started to get pretty tired and I was glad when we stopped for our next adventure, which consisted of putting our butts in two large tractor-tyre inner tubes and pushing off down river. This was a far more relaxed way to see the mountains. Luckily we had a wonderful guide with us called Pon, who told us which way to go to avoid the rocks. We stopped for lunch at a riverside shack and had beer and spring rolls. There were lots of other tourists there, and we had a nice chat. We explained about our trip, which some other Brits had read about on www.gapyear. com. It's strange how many people we meet have already heard about our trip one way or another.

After lunch we carried on tubing and stopped at a place called the 'sleeping cave', where about 200 people hid from the invading Japanese during the Second World War. We didn't have torches and so swum in only a few yards. It was pretty amazing, but I get a little scared in deep water and Ants and I asked Pon repeatedly if there were any snakes, spiders or alligators. He assured us there were none.

Just as we were tubing into Vang Vieng, the skies opened and we got drenched. I found the experience very beautiful and refreshing – high tree-covered mountains surrounding a river valley with no sign of modern life. It was one of those very peaceful and special moments.

Tomorrow we are off to Luang Prabang and we anticipate a good seven hours on the road, providing we get TT up the muddy, stony, steep slope from our guesthouse.

Goodnight.

 **Wednesday 7 June, Sayo River Guest House, Luang Prabang, Laos**

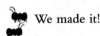 We made it!

Another hurdle was crossed today by the three-wheeled trio, for Jo, TT and I are now in Luang Prabang, in three whole pieces.

Today was a perfect example of how the fear of something is so often much worse than the actual reality. After all the rumours of rebels and treacherous roads, Jo and I set off this morning feeling very unsure of whether we would make it here. The road from Vang Vieng to Luang Prabang is, as we have mentioned before, notorious for a number of reasons, namely hairpin bends, armed bandits and landslides. Since the public bus takes eight hours to climb the 140 miles to Luang Prabang, we banked on taking about the same time. TT may be supersonic, but we weren't quite sure how she'd handle them there mountains. Spiffingly is the answer.

For three hours we climbed and climbed, until stopping in a random town for Coke and *foe* (noodle soup with many unidentifiable things lurking in its depths). We had read that the road after this was particularly dangerous and a favourite haunt of Hmong rebels, so when I tuk to the wheel I put my foot down and headed further into the mountains as fast as was safely possible.

As we drove I was struck by the fact that this is Laos's *main road*, the superhighway linking Laos, Thailand and China. Yet all along its route are tiny hill-tribe villages populated with scruffy children, piglets, goats, chickens, wandering water buffalo, cows and bent old women. As we tukked through each settlement, gangs of children screeched in delight at the sight of the peculiar pink vision whizzing past, and livestock scattered from the road. I am now convinced that the average age in Laos is about five years old, as the number of tiny children far outnumbered adults. Where have all the oldies gone? Maybe they were all watching TV, since many of the rickety bamboo huts sported vast, incongruous satellite dishes.

So, at 5.30 p.m. we made it to Luang Prabang. Phew! No rebels, no mudslides and no toppling off the edge of the mountain. We did see several people wandering along with rifles slung over their backs, though, and some bored policeman decided to pull us over simply to see who we were.

Tomorrow we've got a day off – yes, another one – and then we head for China on Friday. Strange to think we are so nearly through our second country. Poor Jo is missing her ferrets terribly and shed a few ferrety tears last night.

 Relieved, tired and missing my furry friends

I am so relieved we made it to Luang Prabang. As Mr Ant has said, having heard so many stories about Route 13 we had no idea what to expect, but it didn't live up to its frightening reputation. The road was mountainous and bendy but also a lot wider than I thought. The precipitous drops I had imagined were few and far between, we were not jumped by Hmong rebels and the potholes were navigable.

TT performed like a true superstar, although towards the end of the journey her backside started to make a noise (that's TT's, not Ants'). We thought it might be the rear suspension, but after pulling over and getting down on the ground we have concluded that she probably has a small hole in her exhaust, which we will get checked tomorrow. It possibly happened when I sent her shooting up the drive from our guesthouse this morning.

Oh yes, I miss my ferrets and last night had a really good cry into my comfort blanket (sad that I still have one at 27). I am sure that this will not be the first time that I cry because I miss them, but I hope that I don't get upset too regularly.

Thursday 8 June, Luang Prabang, Laos

Ting Tong's backside

This morning has been spent flat on my back in the middle of the road, fag in mouth and can of Coke within reach, inspecting TT's undercarriage for any obvious signs of an exhaust hole. I found nothing out of the ordinary, and the exhaust and its various nuts and bolts all seemed OK. The exhaust manifold (I think that's what it is) looks a bit rusty and so that may be the cause of the random noise on Route 13. Perhaps we had just picked up a stone or something on the drive and it has now gone. Anyway, we will be keeping our ears peeled. I did the usual tightening of the bolts under the handlebars as we break in TT's suspension further. If it keeps going on like this, then we will be driving into Brighton on our nose. I am a pretty useless mechanic, but I look like I know what I am doing when armed with a two-foot-long wrench, covered in dirt and oil and lying flat on my back under TT.

Anyway, enough about TT and more about us. She is getting all of the attention on this trip and is in danger of becoming a bit spoilt and pampered. We will come back to England driving the Paris Hilton of tuk tuks and will have acquired a ridiculously small dog that looks a bit like a rat and wears a diamanté collar. Soon she will be deciding what we listen to on our sound system and start flirting with other tuk tuks. This type of behaviour is totally unacceptable.

So, today was our first and last full day in Luang Prabang, which is a shame as it is such a great place. The town itself is a World Heritage Site and is crammed full of temples, as well as being situated on the banks of the mighty Mekong. Although it is well developed for travellers, it is not brash and unattractive like Vang Vieng. It has an air of France about it, with baguettes, coffee, and quaint houses with colourful shuttered windows. There is a real atmosphere about this place, something that is difficult to put your finger on but that draws you to stay for a while. We don't have the option to stay and explore, and so today we jumped in a boat and travelled up the Mekong to visit Pak Ou caves. As far as caves go they weren't mind-blowing, but what was interesting about them is that they were full of stone, metal and wooden Buddhas. The signs in the cave said that it is against the law in Laos to take images of Buddha out of the country, so that was a random fact for the day.

The boat journey took two hours upstream and half the time downstream. There is something very relaxing about journeying down the rivers here, surrounded by mountains, trees and the odd small settlement. It certainly beats a cruise down the Thames.

Now I am going to phone our tuk tuk guru Anuwat to try and do some more troubleshooting. We don't have a day off now for over two weeks until we reach Xian in China, and we can't afford for TT to be misbehaving.

A quick final point: for some reason, Ants and I have been feeling a bit mentally flat. It is strange doing this trip, because we know that it is probably going to be the most amazing thing we do in our lives, but right now we are not appreciating the experience as much as we should. Emotions are a funny thing, and this trip is quite an emotional rollercoaster. I hope we feel better soon.

Goodnight from Laos.

chapter 3
the dragon's den

 **Saturday 10 June, Green Diamond Hotel, Meng La, Yunnan Province, China**

 Welcome to China!

It's less than two days since we left Luang Prabang and yet already it seems like aeons ago, so much have we seen and experienced since then. Luang Prabang beguiled us both, and it was with dragging heels that we left Sayo River Guesthouse and turned north up Route 13 yesterday morning. Next stop Udomxai.

Having conquered the worst stretch of Route 13 the day before, we set off with increased confidence in our new-found mountaineering skills. Udomxai was only 100 miles away and we had been assured that the road was good. Slightly baffling was the fact that public buses take over four hours to cover this relatively short distance. Yet rather than making us suspicious of what lay ahead, we just put it down to the spluttering, bronchitic old buses and not the road conditions.

The first 60 miles flew by. I lounged in the back and admired the beautiful country slipping by, and Jo skilfully navigated the road north. We'd practically be in Udomxai for lunch at this rate. But in the blink of an eye everything changed: the corners got sharper, the hills steeper and the potholes more prolific. And the road signs disappeared completely. As we rounded one particularly fearsome bend, we were met by huddled groups of people sitting in the road – monks, women, children, old men. Behind them was the bus that was supposed to be taking them to Vientiane, clinging to the edge of the mountain, miraculously held there by a tangle of plants and trees. Only 20 minutes before the driver had lost control on the corner and narrowly escaped killing all. Terrifying. I should think those monks said a special prayer to Buddha last night.

After stopping to see whether everyone was OK and whether there was anything we could do, we tukked off, driving even more carefully than before. In the end we didn't tuk into our destination until 4 p.m., over five hours after we left Luang Prabang. We had covered 130 miles and, having had no lunch and little water, felt totally exhausted.

If you're contemplating a holiday to Udomxai, think again. It really is the armpit of Laos, a strange Chinese–Lao trading post teeming with Chinese construction workers and half-finished buildings. Rain, bedbugs, a plague of mosquitoes, extreme tiredness and then insomnia made for a wholly unpleasant night, and in more driving rain we set off for the Chinese border this morning.

We thought the roads yesterday were bad. As we drove the last 60 miles to Boten, I found myself thinking repeatedly, incredulously, that this was Laos's main artery, the principal thoroughfare linking it with China and Thailand. Yet a few miles north of Udomxai the road almost disappeared altogether. It took us over four hours to reach Boten in conditions that would test the most hardy 4×4. Once again, Ting Tong excelled herself. We love Ting Tong.

About five miles before the Chinese border, the road suddenly improved, an omen of things to come we assumed. At the border we were met by Sam, our guide from the CSITS. TT had her Chinese plates attached, we underwent a health check to ensure we were fit to enter the country, and we were in. Sam seems lovely, really relaxed and helpful. Thank goodness, as the three of us are going to be coexisting in very close proximity for the next few weeks.

Laos – what an amazing place. We spent a mere six days cutting a hot pink swathe through its middle, but it is definitely somewhere we both want to return to. The Hmong, whose much talked-of 'rebels' stalked our imagination up Route 13, turned out to be one of the most fascinating aspects of the country. Their remote mountain villages were incredible, and at the risk of sounding occidental and patronising it was extraordinary to find bare-breasted women in tribal garb wandering down the main road of the country. I was so curious about these people of whom I had heard so many rumours that I did some research and discovered that Hmong means 'free' and that for hundreds of years these fiercely independent people have fought to preserve their autonomy – hence, their isolated mountain dwellings and warlike reputation. Such brave fighters were they that the USA enlisted their help in the Vietnam debacle, with the Hmong providing 99 per cent of their ground forces in Laos. In return for their efforts, they were promised a homeland. Of course, this never materialised and after the fall of Saigon the USA abandoned their brave allies to face the revenge of the winning communists. Out of an estimated pre-war population of 3 000 000, fewer than 200 000 made it to safety across the Mekong.

The persecution persists today, with the Laos government forcing the Hmong people from their mountain villages in order to police them more closely. I recommend everyone to visit a Hmong village and hang out with some of these 'rebels' before they are assimilated entirely.

So here we are in China, in some random town 40 miles north of the border. Jo and I are so flummoxed by the whole place that at supper we just sat and gawped at the otherness of it all. Even the Coke cans are weird. Thank goodness we've got Sam with us, otherwise we'd get very confused and probably end up starving and very lost.

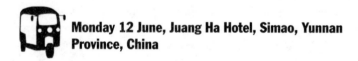

Monday 12 June, Juang Ha Hotel, Simao, Yunnan Province, China

The very long way round

China, it seems, has been sent to test us. The past two days have been, to put it mildly, challenging. When we left Laos we felt sure that we had just conquered the worst roads we would encounter in our entire tukathon. The gleaming tarmac of the last five miles to the Chinese border seemed an omen of things to come. How wrong we were. As soon as we were over the border, the roads deteriorated once again. This time there was a total absence of solid surface, and what was supposed to be a road was in fact a filthy quagmire.

We were scheduled to drive 125 miles that night to Jinhong, but instead we made it only 40 miles to Mengla. Yesterday was even worse. The 85 miles to Jinhong took us an excruciating six hours. By lunchtime, Sam, a non-smoker for the past three years, was cracking into a packet of cigarettes. By mid-afternoon, the packet was nearly empty and a stream of English expletives was emerging from his normally clean mouth.

It's hard to describe quite how bad the roads are in Yunnan. They make Laos's Route 13 seem like the M25. Not only that, but we have to fight with literally hundreds of vast construction lorries, all of us after the narrow sliver of passable road on each stretch. I was so frustrated yesterday I wanted to jump out and pummel the potholes with my bare fists in fury, shout, scream and stamp my feet. Not that this would have achieved anything... but it might have made us feel better. By the time we arrived in Jinhong last night, we were filthy, tired, hungry and in need of a mechanic. Ting Tong's leaking front suspension had got significantly worse, and Anuwat had advised us to go and get the front shocks replaced.

So, rather than having the relaxed evening we were desperately in need of, we spent seven hours sitting on the pavement outside a mechanic's, Ting Tong resting her muddy haunches on jacks, while five men battled with fitting her new suspension. At 1.30 a.m. they finally won the battle and we tukked back to our hotel, safe in the knowledge that this morning we would be cruising along the expressway to Kunming.

But oh no, such was not to be. Our arrival at the shiny new tollgates of the Kunming expressway was met with shaking heads and a flurry of men in uniform. We were ordered to turn round and go to the police station, where no end of persuading, pleading and stubbornness could change their minds. Three-wheelers and Chinese expressways are mutually exclusive concepts, and it seems nothing we could say was going to change that. Dejectedly, we turned round and turned on to the old road. What should have taken us one hour today took us six.

The implications of not being allowed on the expressways here are massive. We have 28 days to travel 4375 miles across China, and our £6500 itinerary was arranged by the CSITS on the premise that we would be speeding along throughout on these perfect new roads. The alternatives are old, disused, windy mountain roads, littered with rocks and potholes. Enough to make any tuk tuk turn a funny shade of green. Of course, we are not going to accept this without a fight, and we are trying to mobilise the powers that be to give us special dispensation. But China is the worst place in which to attempt any bending of bureaucracy, and we could be facing up to double our planned tuk across China. Unbelievable! This makes both our Kazakh and Russian visas invalid and causes a whole host of problems. Jo and I have both been devising plans to give Ting Tong an extra wheel.

Sam not only is smoking again but also has developed a gallbladder problem and a total loss of appetite. Then again, we never thought this would be a glitch-free adventure, and Jo and I are both determined to succeed. The more challenges we face, the more determined we become.

Just to top it off, our satellite modem refuses to work, as does our mobile phone. But at least Sam is a total dude and China is an endlessly, fascinating, utterly weird place.

Over to Jo...

 Despite the hardships of the past few days, I really do love China. The people are friendly, the food is good and the scenery that we have got to appreciate at about 6 mph has been spectacular. Before we got here, I had an image of China in my mind and our experiences so far have been that image to a T – terraced paddy fields and vast tea plantations, punctuated by rolling green hills. One advantage of the roads we have been forced to travel down is that we are going the scenic route. I have learnt to appreciate this from my childhood: given a choice, Dad would always choose the scenic option. The consequences for us are that each day takes five hours longer than it should and leaves us two days behind schedule. At this rate we will be driving through China for at least the next year and should be fluent in Mandarin and about £60 000 in debt.

I am a strange creature: if something small happens, I go off the handle, e.g. if I lose my cigarette lighter or miss a programme on TV. However, if something big happens, then I tend to be far more calm and rational, e.g. this whole China business. I tend to compare a big situation in my life to a big situation in the life of someone else who is less fortunate than myself, e.g. people in the world who are hungry because they don't have enough money to eat. Yes, our current situation is very frustrating, but we are alive and well and it is not the end of the world. We will still make it back to Brighton and raise £50 000 for Mind, and this slight delay will not affect that outcome. Anyway, Ants is on the case with her contacts, and we may yet get to drive down the glistening, smooth, beautiful black tarmac.

I honestly didn't believe that the roads could be worse than in Laos, but they are. At one point today, I really wasn't sure whether we could make it through a particularly rough patch of rocks (we have upgraded from stones to full-on rocks). What made it even more irritating was that our route ran right next to the expressway – you could almost smell the smooth tarmac. This form of torture happened intermittently throughout our six-hour drive, as we would often cross or drive next to the expressway. Still, if you don't laugh you cry, and we certainly had a few laughs along the way. PMA (positive mental attitude)!

Sam assures us that the roads will improve as we tuk north. We can only hope this is true. Thank goodness for the presence and company of Sam, who is an absolute legend. He has been very patient, level-headed and constructive since we met him, as well as being a really nice person with whom it is very easy to spend time. I only hope that this trip is not causing him too much stress, although his smoking and lack of appetite seem to suggest that he is feeling the strain a bit. He has assured us that this will be the first and last time a tuk tuk travels through China driven by foreigners.

As I mentioned previously, we are now two days behind schedule and tomorrow we need to try and cover 350 miles north to Kunming, capital of Yunnan. This would be possible on the expressway, but on our proposed route I think it is about as likely as me physically sprouting whiskers.

Last night was an interesting test of endurance, as we watched the wonderfully persistent mechanics struggle with TT's front shocks. We are so grateful for their persistence, otherwise Anuwat might have had to fly out here to sort out TT himself. She now has her new shocks and springs and is no longer leaking hydraulic fluid. As we were driving today, the new springs made us bounce around the driving seat like we were sitting on a pogo stick, which looked very amusing from the back seat.

An interesting and surprising fact that I gleaned today is that, in China, men are phoned up in their hotel rooms and asked if they want a special massage. My mouth dropped to the floor when I found out exactly what a special massage involves. Personally I think it is a bit sexist, but we now unplug our phone every night, so that we are not awoken from our much-needed beauty sleep and offered the special treatment.

 **Thursday 15 June, Camellia Hotel, Yunnan Province, China**

 Testing times

The past few days have been a blur of bad roads and blue construction lorries. Yesterday we covered 200 miles in 11 hours, and the day before 175 miles in ten hours. Even if you are as bad at maths as I am, you can work out that that is a painfully slow average speed. With another 3750 miles to go in China, we could be here a very long time.

Despite the British embassy's help, the transport office has said a big fat 'no' to Ting Tong using the expressways. We have heard from several sources that the Chinese government is terrified of anything happening to foreigners, hence their refusal to bend the law. Apparently a lot of accidents happen on these roads – Sam said that last month there was a pile-up killing 30 people. Who knows? Maybe it is for the best and the expressway would have been dangerous, but at the moment it's just frustrating. While we crawl along in second and third gear on roads used only by water buffalo, goats, mule carts and the odd tractor, streams of blue Dong Feng lorries speed past us on the adjacent expressway. The mothertruckers.

The solution is uncertain at the moment. Put bluntly, we are in China and we've got to get to Kazakhstan, by 7 July if possible. The CSITS is proposing that we drive in excess of 200 miles a day for the next 24 days straight. Given the evidence of the past few days, this isn't going to be possible. So we find ourselves in a sticky situation. And no, we are *not* going to put TT on the back of a train or lorry. That would be cheating.

Jo and I are still in shock at the condition of the roads in China – well, in Yunnan Province anyway. Yesterday we arrived in Kunming, 'the city of eternal spring' and capital of Yunnan, home to five million people and one of China's largest cities. Yet only three miles from the centre, the road was no more than a dusty track, riven with deep holes. Trucks, pony carts, tuk tuks (or 'bom boms', as they call them here), motorbikes and bicycles all bumped along at 10 mph in a cloud of dust. You should have seen the state of us and TT when we arrived at our hotel. Grubby doesn't even begin to describe it.

However, it's certainly not all bad. Yunnan is absolutely breathtaking, a magic place. The roads may be bad, but they are flanked by awe-inspiring scenery: mountains wreathed in tea and rice terraces, banana plantations and pine forests. If we weren't under such time pressure we would be delighted to be taking these roads and not the expressway – you see much more of the real China this way. We also have the endless amusement of people's reactions to not only westerners driving past, but westerners in a pink tuk tuk. Reactions range from bewilderment to hysterical screams and gaping mouths. We even had one lorry full of construction workers hollering 'I love you!' at us.

Sam, on the other hand, is finding the whole experience mortifyingly embarrassing. His most frequent expression is 'Preease, save my face'. In other words, stop embarrassing me. This is normally provoked by our mid-afternoon outbursts of hysteria, when we start singing ('Ting Tong merrily on high' is a current favourite) and generally behaving in a puerile manner. There have also been a few occasions when, erm, nature called and we simply had to pull over by the side of the road. Sam was appalled, but when you gotta go... The fact that we are travelling in a tuk tuk is also a source of constant humiliation for him. In China everyone wants brand-new SUVs – a tuk tuk is something reserved for poor rural areas and he cannot understand our choice of vehicle. Even worse is travelling in a *dirty* tuk tuk, and most mornings we find him, sponge in hand, fervently washing the layer of mud and dust off TT. Poor Sam: I think he might be in a straitjacket by the end of his two weeks with us.

So, times are hard but all is OK and the adventure is truly in full swing. The past few days have been very, very tough but we never expected it to be easy. We're off to the Stone Forest at Shilin today, and we hope that in the next day or two the CSITS will come up with a solution.

Happy Thursday everyone.

 Friday 16 June, Shilin, Yunnan Province, China

 The Stone Forest

The past three days have consisted of driving, sitting in the back of TT and sleeping in hotel rooms. For me, the days seem to blur into one long drive punctuated by different but same-same Chinese cities. The advantages of this are twofold: we get to see some amazing scenery rather than flying down the expressway and we get to stay in cities that are very Chinese and not frequented by foreigners. The disadvantages are that we are very tired and under constant pressure to make up the time that we have lost from driving at an average of about 20 mph. We are currently three days behind on our proposed itinerary.

We now know for definite that we cannot drive on the expressways during our time in China, which is pretty soul-destroying. Consequently, our average speed is reduced by at least half. We are hoping that the CSITS will give us a ten-day extension on our Chinese permits, as driving for 11 hours a day is not practical or safe.

Today we tried to pull a slightly cheeky one and sneak on to the expressway. We stopped at the tollgate and a queue of vehicles pulled up behind us. The lady at the toll booth was unsure of what to do with us and immediately called her managers. The cars and trucks behind us started beeping frantically and one driver looked at us with pure fury in his eyes. After about five minutes, they all started to reverse and enter at a different entrance. In the end we were told that our ploy had failed because there were some police just down the road and we would get in serious trouble with them when spotted. So Ants had to reverse TT back into the flow of oncoming traffic and we had to carry on and find the old road. Oh well, at least we tried.

At about 4 p.m. we arrived at our hotel at the Stone Forest, unloaded and then actually had time to go for a walk and be proper tourists. The Stone Forest is a huge area filled with amazing natural karst limestone rocks and trees, like nothing I have ever seen and quite spectacular. The rocks have been there for 270 million years and their structure (jagged, narrow and spear-shaped) has resulted from millions of years of natural erosion, the retreating ice age and earthquakes. The earthquakes have made some of the rocks look like someone has glued an extra piece to the top, where the rock has fractured. There were quite a few other tourists, all of whom were Chinese. We took some very cheesy photos (well, I did) and ended up buying some authentic handmade articles from the local Yi people, a minority in China to which our guide belongs. A very weather-beaten old woman wearing local dress offered us some aprons and bags for sale. I bought an apron and have been proudly wearing it all evening. I think the locals think it is a bit strange.

We then spent an hour tasting teas unique to Yunnan Province and purchased two different varieties, one that is good for digestion and the other for the liver and general wellbeing. Then we went out for a meal with Sam and the lady who had sold us the tea, and we enjoyed the best meal we have eaten in China. It was absolutely delicious. I honestly believe that some of the best food you will eat in a country like this is not in posh restaurants and five-star hotels but at small local restaurants.

Today has been the best day so far in China, apart from the fact that I feel sad, as one of my ferrets had to be put to sleep. Pebbles had been poorly before I left and I hadn't expected her to survive while we were away, but of course I hoped that she would be OK. Her adopted mother Lara did a great job, giving her a happy extra month of life, and I am so grateful that she took the decision not to let Pebbles suffer. There have been a few tears shed, and last night my snuggle blanket and Ants got well and truly cried on. I feel guilty that I wasn't with Pebbles when she most needed me. Mum and Dad have arranged for her to be cremated and they will scatter the ashes in the back garden between where Zed and Amber (two that died last year) are buried. Death is very strange and is one of my biggest fears. I am not scared so much of my own death but of the death of the people I love, particularly my parents and my brother. I feel like if they died my life would be over. Whenever anyone I love dies, whether it is a human or animal, I think a small part of me dies that will never be replaced. Anyway, enough misery, because I am going to start crying again. A lump has developed in my throat and I don't want to cry any more.

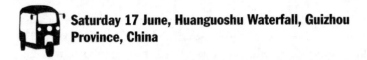 **Saturday 17 June, Huanguoshu Waterfall, Guizhou Province, China**

 'Welcome to China – country under construction'

We are now in a hotel in Huanguoshu, where there is a very large waterfall that is supposed to be one of the key highlights of this province, Guizhou. We arrived too late to enter during daylight and were lucky enough for them to be doing a night lightshow. So we had some supper and descended 559 (Ants counted them as we ascended) steps to see the waterfall illuminated by green floodlights. I have never seen a waterfall by night and it was quite impressive – I actually think we enjoyed the experience more than we would if we had seen it during daylight.

Back to the past two days of driving.

The roads seem to have improved since we left Yunnan. Rather than being bad all of the time, they are now just bad some of the time. Today's drive had mostly good tarmac, but we were slowed down by the steep and windy mountainous roads. TT has a front disc brake and back drum brakes. The disc brake is a motorcycle brake and is used for the majority of our braking power. This is not ideal when we are descending steep windy roads. Rather than speeding up between corners, we have to keep TT in third gear and use the engine as our main brake. This is not a criticism of her construction, because it is the only way that she could be built.

Yesterday was possibly our most challenging day, although I didn't find it as mentally tough as the driving last week. Our accelerator pedal had been feeling increasingly stiff and we were worried that it may snap. Lo and behold, I was driving down the road, the cable snappped and we ground to a halt. We were right out in the sticks, with the nearest form of civilisation 20 minutes away. I phoned Anuwat in Bangkok and he told me it was really easy to fix and that we needed to find a spare cable, unscrew the front seat and get access to the engine. Thank goodness Anuwat had sent us on our way with two full boxes of spares. We located the cable and Anuwat then told me that I needed to find the carburettor, to which I replied 'I don't know what the fucking carburettor looks like', which he found absolutely hysterical. We toyed with the idea of hitching a lift to the next town and getting a mechanic to come and help us, but because Anuwat said it was easy to fix I was determined that we should try without help. The next two-plus hours were spent on our hands, knees and backs removing the old cable and putting in a new one. We then had to make sure the tension was correct and cut it to size, so that it did not dangle on the floor. Eventually we succeeded, a combined effort from Ants, myself and Sam. It was with great trepidation that I started the engine and drove off, unaware whether the tension would be OK. To our great relief TT was driving like a dream. In the next town we asked a mechanic to check our handiwork, and he said it was fine. I cannot tell you how satisfying doing our own mechanical repairs was, even though it left us with many hours still to drive. If we had to do the same job again it would probably take just 20 minutes.

Our day ended with a tropical downpour. The rain was like nothing we get in England – it was like having buckets of water thrown at you from all angles. I hate getting wet. When I was a child I would cry if my feet got wet. When the rain started, Sam and I got out and put down the back rain covers, with me holding a limp and useless umbrella over my head. We hoped the rain would pass, but it got stronger and stronger, until everything in the back was soaked and I decided to get out again and put down all of the covers. I screamed at the top of my lungs and got soaked to the bone. Ants was driving, and it was dark, pissing with rain and really windy. We eventually made it to the hotel at 9 p.m. It was a town that I doubt sees any westerners. We parked TT, emerged sopping wet and staggered into the hotel. I think they could hardly believe their eyes.

I have decided to get a T-shirt made that reads 'China: Under Construction'. It seems like most of the roads and buildings here are undergoing some kind of structural alterations.

Over to Ants...

 This country really should welcome all visitors with a sign saying 'Welcome to China – country under construction'. Everywhere you go a plague of blue Dong Feng lorries blights the countryside, the beginnings of new expressways march across the mountains and piles of rubble litter the roadside. You cannot drive more than ten miles without being met by queues of honking traffic waiting to pass a motley crew of roadworkers, smoking cigarettes and ostensibly improving the roads. It gives true meaning to the phrase 'developing country'.

The past few days have, as Jo has aptly illustrated, been incredibly tough. We covered 170 miles in eleven hours yesterday, and 150 miles in nine hours today. Yesterday was hellish: not only did we have to deal with fixing the accelerator cable (when Jo yelled down the phone to Anuwat, I thought we were in deep trouble), but also we got totally drenched by the most violent tropical rainstorm I have ever had the misfortune to encounter. So suddenly was it upon us that by the time Jo had bravely leapt out to put down the rain covers, we, and all our stuff, were drenched. All I cared about was the DV camera, which we wrapped in my tropical poncho and saved from a watery grave. You should have seen the faces of the people at our hotel last night as a pink tuk tuk pulled up and three sodden individuals crawled out. Jo's T-shirt slogan, 'What the fook fook is a tuk tuk?', summed up the situation perfectly. However, the comically bad karaoke – a feature in every hotel here – soon had us laughing hysterically and forgetting the hardships of 11 hours on the road.

We now find ourselves in Guizhou Province. A traditional saying states that here there are 'No three days without rain, no three hectares without a mountain and no three coins in any pocket'. They also have a predilection for eating dog, which has me looking at every dog wondering whether it is dinner or a pet. We've already experienced some of the region's famous karst landscape, and the roads today have taken us through some incredible mountains, rice terraces and lakes dyed electric green by the limestone. As for the roads, they are definitely better than Yunnan's but still hard work. The potholes are smaller but the S-bends just as challenging. Having said that, we did encounter a stretch of road this morning where I had to hang off the side of Ting Tong to balance her as Jo navigated some particularly deep rain-filled potholes.

The roads may be better, but the driving is still totally bonkers. Our 'best' stretch of road yesterday was perhaps the scariest we have encountered: buffalo carts doing U-turns on to the carriageway, trucks coming straight at us down the wrong side of the road, and upturned nails where temporary speed bumps once were. You can't afford to lose concentration for a nanosecond. I still can't work out why so many people here seem to favour driving the wrong way down dual carriageways or going round roundabouts backwards.

One final thing: the loos here are the worst I have ever encountered – think Glastonbury, day three, and you are almost there. I nearly vomit every time I have to use one, much to Jo's amusement. She certainly has a stronger stomach than I have.

 Monday 19 June, Louzhou, Sichuan Province, China

 Grubby tukkers

Another day, another 200 miles covered, and after eight hours spent tailing Dong Fengs belching black smoke we are absolutely filthy.

War nearly broke out between the mothertruckers and the mothertukkers this afternoon. We've almost become accustomed to the driving here, the penchant for overtaking round the blindest corners, the neither-a-look-to-the-left-nor-to-the-right before pulling out, the constant near-misses. But one Dong Fenger today really took the biscuit. As he roared past us, nearly sending Ting Tong and contents off a rocky precipice, I made the error of giving him the finger. The sight of an angry white arm appearing out of a mobile pink Wendy house obviously riled him for as soon as he passed us he, while driving, opened the door of his truck, leant out and shook his fists in fury. Unluckily for us, a tollgate appeared one mile later and, as we pulled up, the still-seething trucker leapt out of his lorry and marched over to Ting Tong, gesticulating wildly and shouting what I can only assume wasn't 'Welcome to China, have a nice day'. I seriously thought he might punch me, and he probably would have done if a burly security guard hadn't restrained him. He did, however, manage to unzip his trousers and reveal a pair of red Y-fronts and all therein before Jo finally paid the toll and we zoomed off. I spent the next 40 miles quaking with fear, remembering that film *Duel*, waiting for the offended trucker to appear on our tail and force us off the edge of the mountain. I guess it's all down to cultural relativism – driving that is totally acceptable here would lose you your licence in the UK in two minutes. So he probably thought my finger was unjustified, while I saw our lives flashing before my eyes.

We're in Louzhou tonight, which is big, polluted and very hot. Sam has left us to our own devices so we're off to explore and, we hope, not get lost or fed dog by accident.

 Monday 19 June, Louzhou, Sichuan Province, China

 China rocks

Things I like about China:

- the people
- the food
- the scenery

Things I dislike about China:

- the driving conditions
- the public lavatories

So, overall, China gets a big thumbs-up and we seem to be settling into a routine of getting up and driving for long hours without too many grumbles. It would be nice to have a day off at some point in the next three weeks, but if we don't it won't destroy us. What doesn't kill you makes you stronger, and if you don't laugh you cry. Oh, how I love clichés.

Yesterday we visited Zhijin caves, which were absolutely breathtaking. They must be one of the most impressive cave systems in the world. The caves are eight miles long, although I think we covered about half that distance. I have never seen such large stalactites and stalagmites – some must have been about 60 feet tall. I also learnt a new thing about limestone rock formations created by dripping water: when a stalactite and stalagmite join together, it is called a stalacto-stalagmite. The rocks were amazing shapes, with many looking like large jellyfish. We passed through different levels of the cave and eventually came upon the huge main cavern, which was at least the size of a football pitch. I worried about a stalactite falling from the roof and causing an ignominious death for us both. I informed Ants that I thought it would be a very painless death and that it would make a good article in a newspaper. I then put on Ants' iPod, which inspired me to start cave dancing in a rather peculiar manner. What I had failed to realise was that a security guard was walking right behind me as I shook my little booty.

I thought I smoked too much, but the Chinese really put me to shame. I am not sure how the roads ever get built as there always seems to be someone having a cigarette break. They also smoke while riding motorbikes, which I am sure is quite dangerous as it wouldn't be hard for the ash to go in the biker's eyes, making them lose concentration and end up under the wheels of one of the Dong Feng army. You seem to be able to smoke everywhere in China – apart from the lifts. There are notices in all hotel rooms advising against smoking in bed, for obvious reasons. That reminds me: in our hotel room today, it is possible to buy a packet of blue pills, which I am sure must be the Chinese equivalent of Viagra. I suppose the population didn't reach over a billion for no reason.

Today we were on the road for nine hours, which included an hour for lunch. We must be getting used to the long hours, because it was OK. Apart from Ants' incident with the rather cross Dong Feng driver, there were no problems. Two strange things we saw today included a dead foal strapped to the back of a motorbike and a dead dog being dragged along the road by a small child – pet or lunch?

Tomorrow we are getting TT serviced. I will watch carefully so that I learn how to do the oil filter and air filter myself. I will change the front brake pad but get a motorcycle mechanic to check my handiwork. Changing the oil is something we will let a mechanic deal with, because they can dispose of the old oil safely and we cannot. Also, we think her accelerator is starting to stiffen again so will get the mechanic to check that too.

That's all folks. Time for bed, as another long day beckons and the tired tukkers need their beauty sleep.

 Tuesday 20 June, Leshan, Sichuan Province, China

 Giant Buddhas

A real quickie from Leshan, where we've got five minutes in an Internet café to try and sort out our revised itinerary with the CSITS, before hitting the road to not-sure-where. We're supposed to be going to a holy mountain called Emei Shan today, but we are both in need of a sleepathon, not mountain climbing, so are going to see where we get to. Jo said the other day that the tiredness is cumulative, and she's right: every day you feel just a little bit less like getting up and a little bit more like sleeping for a week or two. Caffeine and cigarette intake is on the increase in a big way.

Leshan is home to the biggest stone Buddha in the world. He's pretty impressive and the mind boggles as to how they made him back in 820.

Jo bought an apron off an old Yi lady in Shilin the other day and is insisting on wearing it most of the time. Sam's embarrassment is complete.

 Friday 23 June, Pingwu, Sichuan Province, China

 Pingwu the Penguin

Yesterday we had a day off (whoohooooo) in Chengdu, but we were both too exhausted to appreciate it fully. We were planning on going to a Chinese opera/martial arts/drama show in the evening, but Ants put herself to bed and I got lost for an hour and wandered the streets looking at my Rough Guide for clues as to my whereabouts.

We left Chengdu this morning and TT had her front brake pad changed, which cost a measly 70 pence. I watched closely and will perhaps do them in the future.

Tonight we are in Pingwu, which we insist on calling Pingu, like the penguin. It is very Chinese and I doubt they get many tourists here. The roads today were brilliant – pure tarmac – and our average speed has increased to just over 25 mph. It doesn't sound much, but it makes the driving so much more bearable.

We are off to the hotel now for an early night. Ants and I are sleeping in separate rooms tonight because neither of us is sleeping well and apparently I snored like a real man last night. My mother would be proud.

Tuesday 27 June, Lanzhou, Gansu Province, China

 Linjian's little surprise

18 days into our Chinese tukathon and we've reached the halfway point in this never-ending country. As you can probably tell by the absence of blogs in the past week, we've had our foot flat to the floor, driving on average ten hours a day. If we didn't have a logbook, I would find it very hard to remember where we have been or what day or date it is. It all melds into one long bumpy road.

After our encounter with the giant Buddha in Leshan, we headed for Chengdu, capital of Sichuan Province and home to around ten million people. We gave Emei Shan, the holy mountain we were supposed to climb, a swerve and opted instead for a much-needed day off.

Some day off. The CSITS insisted we went to extend our visas, saying it would take an hour. So we hung around, filled in forms and waited some more, only to be told after wasting about four hours that in fact we would have to wait five days to get our passports back. We were not amused. It was our first day off in 12 days, we were desperate to explore the city and just chill out. Our plans had been scuppered once again by the CSITS. And guess what? Chengdu's *pièce de résistance*, Tianfu Square, looked upon by a towering statue of Chairman Mao, was a pile of rubble, apparently due to the construction of a new metro system.

For the next few days we headed further north through Sichuan. The beautiful mountains of Yunnan and Guizhou were replaced by a stream of filthy towns, shrouded in a noxious cloak of pollution, some places no more than mountains of bricks and half-knocked-down houses. I feel so sorry for the people who live in these towns, victims of China's frenetic quest for development, living in places that looked like they have been caught in a blitzkreig.

After the pollution and filth of central Sichuan came Gansu, where we currently are. Traditionally viewed as a buffering zone between China and the barbarians beyond, Gansu is a huge province that goes from Lanzhou in the east to Dunhuang in the west.

Driving into Gansu felt like entering a different country. The manicured hills of Yunnan and Guizhou were replaced by rugged, scree-laden peaks. Hints of Muslim culture began to appear, and the air became dry and stifling. And Gansu had a special surprise in store for us.

On Friday evening, after 11 hours on the road, the afternoon tuk fever and hysteria set in. With me at the wheel, Jo launched into singing '*nee hao*' ('hello'), in perfect operatic tones, to all lucky passers-by. Whether toiling in the fields, selling watermelons by the side of the road or just strolling into town, they all got treated to Jo's dulcet tones. Sam hid under his map in embarrassment, trying unsuccessfully to contain his laughter, and I tried to drive straight while weak all over from laughing. It really was hilarious. The zenith came as we drove slowly through a small town called Linjian. Tens of Dong Feng trucks were pulled up by the roadside and crowds of people milled around. We assumed it was dinnertime and everyone had stopped for their rice and noodles. Jo continued her operatic offerings, safe in the knowledge that we would never see these people again. As we rounded a corner, we saw the cause of the crowds – a vast landslide blocking a 100-foot section of the road. We soon discovered there had been not one but two earthquakes, causing the landslide as well as destroying some houses. There was no escape. It was 8 p.m., all the hotels were full, everyone had abandoned their houses for fear of an aftershock, and the only other road to Wudu – which lay tantalisingly close at 30 miles away – was a 200-mile diversion along dirt tracks. The only option was to wait until they cleared the path. It could be the next day, it could be in two days.

What followed was by far the funniest night we have had in China so far. Ting Tong and her inhabitants became an instant source of amusement for the locals, and we spent the night at a karaoke bar, drinking far too much beer with the local lads. Sleeping on the pavement wasn't quite so much fun, but hey, it's all part of the adventure. Amazingly, by noon the next day, one ancient digger and some dynamite had cleared the road and we were off again.

Yesterday was another massive day of driving – 12 hours on the road, 230 miles covered. The long hours were alleviated by the incredible beauty of the country we were passing through. Magic. Mountains rose up on either side of the road, so perfectly green it was as if some ancient being had cast a giant velvet cloak over their shoulders. Funny yak-like creatures, wild horses and goats grazed in flower-strewn meadows. And to top it all off, we ended the day by driving into a perfect sunset. However long and tiring the days are, scenes like this cannot help but lift the spirits. That's not to say I didn't feel slightly deranged by fatigue by the time we arrived in Lintao last night.

So now we are in Lanzhou, where after 3500 miles of tukking north we turn Ting Tong west and head along the Silk Road for Central Asia and home. Our visas are being extended today and we are changing guides. Sam is being replaced by Jack, who hails from Urumqui. Sam was so relieved to make it through his tukathon he leapt out of Ting Tong this morning and embraced Jack like a long-lost brother. Sam's been a funny one, oscillating between perfect charm and vile sulks. We hope Jack is a little less moody.

As for our Chinese solution – well there isn't one. The CSITS can't extend our permits and we can't drive any harder than we currently are. There is no way we will make it out of China by 7 July, so we'll just have to pray we don't get whipped and sent to prison at the border.

A few random observations about China: at least 20 per cent of the cars are VW Santanas, ankle socks are all the rage, perms à la 1980s are the height of fashion, and the biggest crowd TT has pulled so far is 46. That was at a five-minute ice-cream stop yesterday. It is the most bizarre country and, although an endurance test, it's been our favourite so far. Every day something makes us really laugh.

Earthquakes, congratulations and get well soon

The past week has been filled with lots of driving, but overall the road conditions are improving, with longer stretches of pure unadulterated tarmac and an average speed of 20 mph. When we occasionally get the chance to drive over 30 mph, it feels like TT is taking off, which is very strange.

TT is behaving herself but has developed a few little sounds – whistles, squeaks and groans. I interpret these as a form of communication and I think she is trying to sound like all the other Chinese vehicles. She had a good service and several mechanics have checked her over and assured us she is fine.

The highlights of the past few days include being stranded by an earthquake. We had been on the road for a good 11 hours and were within easy striking distance of our next town. Ants and I were both experiencing our silly hour and, as Ants has mentioned, I was singing *'nee hao'* to every living creature we passed. I think the combination of this and two foreign girls in a bright-pink tuk tuk was too much to take in, and many jaws hit the floor. We passed through a town and I continued howling at crowds of locals, only to find our exit blocked by a landslide. There was no escape and the locals gathered around for a good look. I was slightly embarrassed that I would have to look people in the eye after singing to them.

Before bed, we met the local youths and enjoyed beer and karaoke with them. I agreed to do karaoke and was hoping for a Chinese song to sing *'nee hao'* to. Unfortunately, they found me a famous Chinese love song sung in English, which I had never heard before. I stood there like a total lemon, bum-bag strapped to my waist, and tried to sing the chorus. Amusing and confusing for everyone there, and horribly humiliating for me.

Bed for the night was the back of TT for me and the pavement for Mr Ant. Mr Ant was in a deep sleep but was awoken at 4 a.m. by one of the guys we had met at karaoke. He rapped on her head hard and then blabbered some Chinese nonsense to her. I found this highly amusing in the morning and Ants also managed to see the funny side.

I would like to say a big congratulations to my brother on getting a 2.1 in his media degree (he is the future Nick Broomfield) and get well soon to my darling ferret Shrimp, who has had a growth removed from his fat tummy.

 Wednesday 28 June, Wuwei, Gansu Province, China

 The first pink tuk tuk on the Silk Road?

Today we finally turned west and headed for the plains of Central Asia along the fabled Silk Road. It's good to feel that we are, after five weeks of tukking north, finally heading for Europe and home.

We said goodbye to Sam this morning, who flew back home to Kunming to sleep for a week and celebrate his survival. So now we are in the capable hands of Jack, aged 26, from Urumqui. After a day with him we feel sure he is going to be lots of fun. Rather than cringing with embarrassment when we sing, or when Jo sprung into an impromptu Cossack dancing display in the middle of a quiet mountain road today, he joins in. Several cars stopped to view this latter strange scene, I whipped out the camera as per usual and then off we went. Now we are in Wuwei and tomorrow it is 150 miles to Zhangye.

Very amusingly, Jo just got an email from Mind saying we have been short-listed for *Cosmopolitan*'s Fun Fearless Female award, which is hilarious. Great for boosting our fundraising though – we are currently almost at £20000 and so still have another £30000 to go until we reach our target.

I was just thinking as we were driving today how wonderful it is to be travelling with Jo. Ever since an, erm, eventful five-day caravanning trip in Norfolk aged 17 (had a car crash, went to hospital, nearly blew up the caravan, evicted from the caravan park), we have wanted to go travelling together. University, jobs and Jo's illness delayed us by ten years. I couldn't wish for a better person to be doing this trip with. Jo makes me laugh hysterically every day, rarely gets crotchety and always makes me wear sunscreen. What more could I wish for? So thank you, ferret.

That's all for today. Gansu continues to fascinate with its curious meld of Chinese and Muslim cultures, the mountains get more beautiful by the day and the fruit is incredible. Jack ate chicken's feet for dinner, which he says are quite delicious. I'm not sure I agree.

 North west for the British penguins

We are now heading westwards with our new guide Jack. He is a total dude, dances with me in the middle of the road and doesn't mind us singing in public – in fact, he joins in. The only drawback is his fondness for chicken's feet. They appear more meaty than I imagine, and Ants has dared me to try one. Not tonight, though, as I would like to keep my tasty supper in my stomach.

I will now explain the title of this blog. In Lanzhou, a couple of nights ago, we went for a wander in the rain, both sporting green ponchos to keep dry. The pavements here are very slippery when wet and our foot attire – flip-flops – didn't have much grip. We both nearly went arse over tit a few times and realised that the only way to stay vertical was to shuffle along like a couple of penguins in single file. The thought of either of us suffering a broken limb was enough to reduce our walk to the pace of a crawling baby, because if one of us breaks a bone, the other would have to drive the whole way back to England – I can tell you that this is our idea of a nightmare.

The highlight of today was driving alongside a ruined section of the Great Wall. It is not how you might imagine it, since for the most part it is in a pretty tatty state. Sometimes it continued undamaged for a mile and there were watchtowers (I assume) at quite close intervals. But it was still an imposing sight, and so tall and wide that old Genghis Khan must have found it a challenging obstacle. A special day.

 Friday 30 June, Jiayuguan, Gansu Province, China

 My new favourite food

Another day, another pair of underpants (as my friend Sarah Craig used to say at school). Today was a really good day. Not only were the roads brilliant, but also we visited the last fortress on the Great Wall, here at Jiayuguan.

We set off this morning at the leisurely hour of 9.30 a.m., which is a very late start for us. The tarmac was beautiful (Ants and I are keen tarmac enthusiasts) and we covered 62 miles in less than two hours. This kind of distance has not been covered in such a short time since Thailand. I felt quite euphoric and we stopped for a cup of coffee in a petrol station to celebrate. The roads became slightly less smooth when Ants took over, but we were still travelling at 35 miles, which is the speed limit here in China for a three-wheeler.

The beauty of not taking the expressways has become apparent to us, and we now look down on those poor people who are stuck travelling at speeds in excess of 60 mph. Well, occasionally we are a little envious. The advantage of travelling on the older, slower roads is that we can stop whenever we want to take photos or have a short break. We travel through completely untouristy villages and towns, where we can stop and eat lunch. The local people are interested in TT and we are interested in them. It is a mutually beneficial relationship. However, we aren't always impressed when they shake TT to test the suspension or get in the driving seat and start changing gears. We have a remote control that can start and stop the engine within a range of a couple of hundred feet. Sometimes we start the engine while we are eating lunch to give the assembled crowd a shock – it is quite funny watching 30-plus people jump – although not in a nasty way, and they always find it funny.

The title of this blog indicates that I have found a new favourite food here, and to celebrate I ate about one pound of it at supper. In Chinese restaurants in England we have toffee banana or apple; here, they have toffee potato. It sounds a strange combination, but it is delicious and great energy food. I think I could do my Cossack dancing for at least an hour after a plate of this stuff, although I haven't tried yet. That reminds me: supper tonight was very amusing. We brought in our own beer and were drinking it from tiny teacups. The waitress came over and poured Chinese tea into Jack's beer, which made us giggle. Then our food arrived – coriander salad (devil's herb), cooked celery (double yuck), my new favourite food, a tofu dish and a fish Jack had chosen from its tank. Jack asked Ants whether she liked wasabi (Japanese mustard-based rocket fuel for the taste buds). She said she did, and so Jack poured the whole bowl of wasabi over Ants' coriander salad. Ants took a large mouthful, went red and nearly choked, and tears poured from her eyes. We all collapsed into laughter and the waitress must have thought we were bonkers. The toffee potatoes had totally set, and we tried to prise them apart with a combination of chopsticks (useless), fingers (a little better), toothpicks (the best) and a knife and fork (success). Bits of toffee started flying everywhere... the table, the floor, on us. We laughed again and ate more toffee (i.e. pure sugar) than is probably good for us.

Our new guide Jack just highlights the differences between him and Sam. Jack is the sort of person with whom we would be mates back home; Sam was grumpy and somewhat uninspiring company. Jack always asks whether we slept well, what food we would like, etc. Sam never did any of this and would often keep us waiting ten-plus minutes in the morning because he was still asleep. Jack sings, dances, is funny and charming, and is a great person to be around. He is not as good at map-reading as Sam, but who cares? He is such a wicked guy and we hope he can come with us to the border. Currently, his boss is due to escort us out of China (I think to make sure we leave), but it is unsettling changing guides and why would we want someone new for two or three days when Jack fits our threesome so well?

Jiayuguan Fort was impressive, with incredibly steep walls that I am sure would have been very difficult for any enemy to penetrate. The views were inspiring in three directions: mountains, snow-capped peaks and desert. In the fourth direction you could see the town of Jiayuguan and four ugly power-plant chimneys. We finished our touristic duties with a trip to the Great Wall museum, which provided a detailed history of the Wall and various battles that were fought over the ages. By comparing notes with Jack, we realised that they had accidentally put the wrong length of the Wall in Chinese. Jack pointed this out to the museum staff and now it will be changed.

So, life is good with the tukkers. We still drive long days, but we have got used to it and six hours of driving feels like nothing. China has been an experience from day one, and I wouldn't rather be anywhere else or with anyone else (Ants, I love you).

 Tukking the Great Wall by storm

It's funny to think that when Jo and I first got our Chinese itinerary from the CSITS we balked at the sight of a 350-mile day, imagining the horror of driving for eight hours. Now here we are, 21 days into China, and today, at six hours, was far and away our shortest day on the road. Even eight hours falls into the short-day bracket now, so used are we to arriving at our destination each night after upwards of ten hours' tukking.

Since we left Lanzhou a few days ago we have been heading west, along the old Silk Road, more used to carrying precious caravans of silk and spices than Ting Tongs. Our route has taken us along the Hexi Corridor, a 600-mile stretch of land sandwiched between mountains to the south and the Gobi Desert to the north. For centuries this was the trading route between China and the West, the only way for goods and people to cross the cultural and geographical divide. Today, spanking new expressway stretches across the wilderness, a far cry from the camel caravans of ancient times, and Dong Feng trucks carry coal and other goods to Xinjiang and beyond. The Hexi Corridor is also famous for being the location of 625 miles of the Great Wall, which we saw yesterday for the first time.

This mythical wall, often incorrectly lauded as the only manmade structure visible from space, is always something I have imagined as a vast brick edifice. But the wall we encountered yesterday is no more than crumbling mud ramparts, barely distinguishable from the desert engulfing it. For most of the road between Wuwei and Zhangye, we tukked along beside this historic remnant, evocative even in its advanced state of disrepair. I feel sure that Ting Tong is the first pink tuk tuk to follow its path.

Today was equally impressive driving, the road continuing west through vast treeless expanses. Rearing up in the distance on our left were the snow-capped peaks of the Qilian mountains, to our right the endless horizon of the desert. Never before have I been somewhere so remote. It felt like driving to the edges of the universe. Which, to the Chinese, it is almost.

Jiayuguan, where we are now, has always been synonymous in Chinese culture with grim desolation, comparable to the outer edges of Siberia in the Russian psyche. Here lies the last fortress of the Great Wall, built in 1372 by the Ming dynasty. Looking out over its ramparts this afternoon, it was easy to imagine why this place has such connotations. Sand and snow-capped mountains filled the horizon and although the temperature was a scorching 34°C today, in winter the thermometer plunges to 20 below zero.

Thanks to Jack's encouragement − Jo and I were both feeling tired and idle − we also took in the Great Wall museum. Did you know that the wall was begun in the seventh century BC, took over 2000 years to build, and during the time of the Ming dynasty needed a million men to guard its 15 600-mile length? No, neither did I. Quite amazing.

Tomorrow we continue further west, to Anxi. We've got to leave very early as for 150 miles of the 200 miles route there are roadworks, surprise, surprise! Then we hope to have a day off paragliding or dune-surfing in the desert. Double whooopeeee!

 Sunday 2 July, Dunhuang, Gansu Province, China

 Ting Tong hits the desert

At last, after 24 days of tukking, Jo and I are having a proper day off. Bliss. Moreover, Dunhuang couldn't be a better spot to have it at. An oasis town, teetering on the edge of the Gashun Gobi Desert, Dunhuang is famous largely for the Mogao caves. Unless you are an aficionado of Buddhist art or the peregrinations of Aurel Stein, you probably won't have heard of these. And I am slightly ashamed to admit that since the caves need the best part of a day to see, we've opted instead to go paragliding, sand-dune tobogganing and sun-lounging. I know: total philistines, the pair of us. If you want to know more about the Silk Road, Stein's looting of the Mogao Treasures and the understandable chagrin of the Chinese, then I highly recommend Peter Hopkirk's *Foreign Devils on the Silk Road.*

In a nutshell, the caves are one of China's most important archaeological sites and house a vast collection of ancient Buddhist art and manuscripts. When the trading routes along the Silk Road dried up in the fourteenth century, the caves were sealed and it wasn't until 1907 that Stein, a Hungarian secret agent/explorer in the employ of the British government, heard rumour of these newly rediscovered caves and brought over 7000 manuscripts back to Britain, where they still remain, languishing in the vaults of the British Museum. Anyway, I won't waffle on about somewhere we haven't even been.

Yesterday was an incredible day on the road. We got up at 6 a.m. (ugh!) and left soon after. Jo and I are both rubbish at getting up, and rising at such an ungodly hour was a feat in itself. Bleary-eyed, we packed up Ting Tong and headed for Dunhuang. The spectre of 150 miles of roadworks was large in our minds, but, thank God, Jack had got in with the locals the night before and heard of an alternative route. So, after only ten miles of construction, we turned left and headed into the desert. Ting Tong once again proved her super-tuk powers, trundling through deep sand and along gravel roads and dodging potholes. The miles ticked by... 50, 100, 150... until finally, after 200 miles, we hit the most perfect bit of tarmac you could ever imagine. Not in my wildest dreams could I imagine that such a road existed in China. Perfect, black, smooth and straight as an arrow. So for the last 75 miles we sped through the desert, sand engulfing our vision on all sides, whooping with excitement at the state of the road. At 9.30 p.m. last night, after more than 14 hours' tukking, Dunhuang loomed out of the desert sunset: we had arrived – 275 miles and 14 hours later. Although fairly tired, Jo and I felt strangely elated at having completed such a huge distance, across such breathtaking land. There's something about such wide open spaces that really lifts the spirits. We wondered, being as we felt this excited after a single day's achievement, how we will feel when we arrive in Brighton. I have tried to imagine it so many times, but my imagination fails me. Only time will tell.

After unloading TT and checking into yet another identikit Chinese hotel, the three of us pottered down to the night market to have some tiffin. The further west we go, the less Chinese the food and culture becomes. The market last night was redolent of an Arabian souk rather than a Chinese street. Vendors sweated over shish kebabs and nearly all the men sported Muslim skullcaps. Sheep's heads grinned in a macabre fashion from tables, and soon-to-be-barbecued fish took final laps of their tanks. While Jack and Jo feasted on various parts of a sheep's anatomy, I ate veggie kebabs and garlic, omnipresent here. At every table is a bowl of peeled, raw garlic, and Jo and I have taken to munching through fistfuls of cloves every day, enough to kill a herd of vampires stone dead. I ate 15 yesterday, but only about six today. Crikey, we must smell.

Today has been such a treat. In 36°C heat, we've explored the market, bought the sweetest melons and apricots, drunk ginger beer in the sunshine, read, washed TT and done about every sand-based activity you can imagine. I'm sitting here now, smelling quite garlicky, with sand glued to my eyelashes and a 15-year-old hacking and phlegming enthusiastically on my right. Every Internet café in China is the same, rammed with sweaty teenagers avidly playing computer games, smoking and spitting on the floor. Nice.

One thing about China that constantly disappoints is the 'scenic spots'. We've been to waterfalls, caves and now sand dunes, and none of them really excites. The Chinese have a special talent for taking a natural wonder and turning it into a plasticised (is that a word?) theme park. Today was a prime example. To see the sand dunes, which surround the city, you have to pay 80 yuan – about £6. Then to climb the sand dune on the back of a moody camel you have to pay another £5. At the top of that dune, you fork out another few pounds to toboggan down 150 feet of sand. Then if you want to go on a quad bike – which we did – you whip out another 100 yuan each. It's a rip-off by UK standards, let alone Chinese ones. And every 'scenic spot' is exactly the same. By far the most beautiful places we've seen in China are the untouched mountains, paddies and deserts that have flanked our route, uninvaded by vendors and tourists and untarnished by the government's extortionate entrance fees. However, grumble aside, the dunes were a laugh, and riding a camel down into Dunhuang at sunset was a memorable experience.

Tomorrow we reach Xinjiang, Jack's province, one of China's five autonomous provinces and home of the Uighur people. It's a fascinating place bordered by Russia, Afghanistan, Pakistan, Mongolia, Tajikistan, Kyrgyzstan, Kazakhstan, India, Tibet and Gansu. A true cultural melting pot.

Sand dunes and beautiful tarmac

The past few days have been good. It's hard to tell why we are both feeling more perky and positive, but it could be a number of reasons. Although we are still driving long hours (11 yesterday), we are having a lot of fun and not just crashing out, exhausted, after our two hours in the driving seat. Our new guide Jack could also be partly responsible for our happiness. He is great fun and together we have a real laugh during our long days. With Sam, you could tell he wasn't happy if we stopped to take photos or have a coffee break. Jack has his own camera (old-school SLR) and is as happy as we are when good photo opportunities arise, such as when we drove next to the Great Wall the other day. Yesterday we had a short strawberry, cucumber, tomato and coffee break, which was very pleasant but ended in a messy food fight.

Another reason for feeling good is that we feel we have cracked China. During the first two weeks it was a real mental and physical struggle having to deal with the long hours, heavy traffic and terrible roads. Now we are heading west, driving longer distances and coping with it well. We will be leaving China in another week but would happily stay for longer to explore the remote north western provinces. Once we arrive in Kazakhstan, the pressure will reduce as we are no longer confined to a strict itinerary and can take a rest day if we need it.

Today was our first real day off in China, and at 11.30 a.m. I finally peeled myself from my bed. The climate here is very hot and dry – very good for sunbathing but not so good for charging around sightseeing – and so we relaxed under a tree and had a light lunch and some tea. I am now so used to Chinese tea that I think it will be strange to go back to English tea. I never thought I would say that – in England I drink about ten cups a day, with lots of milk and two sugars.

After lunch we went back to the hotel and planned to have a short rest before giving TT a bath. She is absolutely covered in mud and muck, in some places nearly an inch thick. We felt like we ought to go and see the Mogao caves today – the mind was willing but the body less so.

As this was our first real break for nearly a month, we both felt like we should be taking it easy. We know that one day we will return to North West China and will then have the time and the energy to spend a full day exploring the caves and their Buddhist art.

This evening we headed to the 9 feet-high sand dunes four miles south of town. I have never seen such huge sand dunes, and they were really fantastic. They would have been even better if they had not been quite so touristy. We had to pay an entrance fee, money for our camel ride (too hard to walk up a steep sand dune, as Ants later discovered), money to go sand-tobogganing, money to go quad-biking, and then more money when the quad-bike dudes asked for a tip (cheeky monkeys). Still, we had a great time, got covered in sand and enjoyed having the spirit and energy to just be tourists and unwind.

Our camels were the two-humped Bactrian variety, but they had lost their shaggy brown winter coats and looked more like their one-humped cousins. Did you know that Bactrian camels have been domesticated for over 3000 years and that their wild brothers number only about 1500? I have just finished a brilliant book in which a British explorer tracked the migration route of the wild Bactrians right into this part of China. I could bore you with more Bactrian facts but I won't... for now. I named my camel Pot Noodle and Ants called hers Clark Gable. We named Jack's Sam!

Now a brief explanation about the title of this blog. The sand dunes have already been explained. The tarmac part occurred yesterday, as I drove TT the final 75 miles to Dunhuang on the most beautiful black, smooth, wide and deserted tarmac. It was an absolute pleasure for us all, and TT enjoyed flexing her three cylinders. Yesterday we drove 275 miles, a new Tuk to the Road record.

As we drove through some sand dunes yesterday, Ants commented that she had never seen a sand dune before. Ants lives in North Norfolk and goes walking on Holkham beach regularly, which is flanked by many sand dunes.

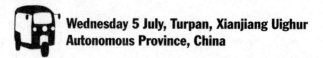 **Wednesday 5 July, Turpan, Xianjiang Uighur Autonomous Province, China**

 Scorchio

It's 42°C outside and after a morning of exploring in the scorching heat Jo and I have retreated indoors to blog and sort out Kazakhstan issues. We arrive at the border in six days and still have a few things to do in order to ensure the crossing goes smoothly and we have the correct documents and insurance. Kazakhstan has the potential to be our most difficult country: corruption is endemic, and even if we have everything in order there is nothing to say that we won't be held up at the border by guards wanting to make a quick dollar. So we are going to be armed with letters from our embassy, our press release in Russian, newspaper clippings and a big smile... and pray that we don't run into any problems. Olov, a Swedish guy we have been in touch with, recently crossed the same border point on a 1938 bike and sidecar he bought in Beijing. For no valid reason, the Kazakh border guards confiscated his bike and fined him a hefty $500 (£260). He has now hired a lawyer to sort out his problems and has advised us to go back to Beijing, cross into Mongolia and avoid Kazakhstan at all costs. Too late. So all we can do is cover everything and hope the guards are feeling charitable when we arrive.

Last night we arrived in Turpan, one of the old Silk Road cities, a manmade oasis inhabiting the second lowest point on the planet, at 250 feet below sea level. Only the Dead Sea lies at a lower depression. Such unusual topography means that the area has baking-hot summers and viciously cold winters: in July the average temperature is 39°C, but in winter this plummets to -20°C. Add to this the fact that there is *no* rainfall, and you wonder why people ever settled here at all. Water is provided by the ingenious *Karez* irrigation system, conceived over 2000 years ago, whereby water from the mountains and glaciers is channelled to the area via 3000 miles of underground pathways. The system provides five billion cubic feet of water per year and means

Turpan has flourished as one of Xinjiang's key cities for over 2000 years despite such an inhospitable climate.

Jack was so worried about driving here in the blistering heat yesterday that for the second time in a week we were up at 6 a.m., with TT loaded and raring to go by 6.30 a.m. Unfortunately, there was no sign of Jack. Half an hour later he appeared, rubbing the sleep from his eyes and apologising profusely for the fact that he had slept in. After getting lost leaving Hami for another half an hour, we eventually got on to the road for Turpan and started our 250-mile tuk through the Gobi. Except for a freak rainstorm at 9.30 a.m., which had us scrambling for the rain covers and getting soaked, our desert drive was uneventful. Jo and I just thanked our guardian angels that the roads here are a million miles better than in the south – straight and pothole-free. Amazingly, we arrived in Turpan by 3 p.m. Never could we have dreamed of covering such mileage in so little time a few weeks ago.

As I mentioned before, Xinjiang is an extraordinary place, bordered by eight countries and home to the Uighur (pronounced wee-ger) people. Thirteen million people live in Xinjiang, eight million of whom are Uighurs. In the 1950s, 90 per cent of the population here was Uighur but, thanks to the region's huge reserves of oil and gas underneath the Taklamakan and Gobi deserts, the Chinese are slowly but surely tightening their cultural and economic grip on the area. As we drove across the Gobi yesterday, this presence was immediately apparent, with nodding oil derricks spotting the desert as far as the eye could see.

The Uighurs are so different from the Chinese that it seems strange they should even come under the Dragon's flag. Being a Turkic people, they look nothing like the Chinese – more Turkish or European than Asian. Their culture was once lauded by ancient Arabic historians, and the Uighur language was used for all edicts from the court of the mighty Genghis Khan. One contemporary commentator even stated: 'He who knows the Uighur language will never experience poverty.' The Uighurs were Buddhists until the fourteenth century, but today they are Muslim – of the 24000 places of worship in Xinjiang, over 23000 are Islamic. Unfortunately, the Arab historian's aphorism hasn't held for today's Uighurs. Few speak Chinese or receive a proper education, and hence they are left with little hope for advancement in Chinese society. Furthermore, since 9/11, the Chinese have been busy arresting any Uighurs they suspect of Islamic fundamentalism, despite their constantly harping on about religious and cultural equality for China's minority peoples.

Jo, Jack and I have had another day off today, so with hats, sunscreen and buckets of water we headed off to the ancient city of Jiaohe this morning. We did have a plan to cycle, but after seeing the decrepitude of the bikes on offer we decided a taxi was a far better option. Any movement in this heat is unadvisable. I went for a run the other evening and felt in danger of entirely melting.

Jiaohe is far and away our favourite Chinese 'scenic spot'. In short, it's the ruins of a 3000-year-old city, built of clay, and destroyed in Buddhist vs Islamic wars in the fourteenth century. It is the first 'scenic spot' we've visited that hasn't been ruined, plasticised and plagued with tacky vendors and recalcitrant camels. Yet another point scored for North West China. For two hours we wandered around, took pictures, groaned about the heat and tried to imagine what it would have been like 1000 years ago, with 7000 inhabitants and a river 90 feet deep. Then it was time for wine-tasting, lunch and air-conditioning. Later this evening we've requisitioned a donkey cart to take us on a wee trip into the countryside, in the company of a few cool Pineapple Beers (a bit sweet but good for the thirst). Tomorrow it's 115 miles west to Urumqui, capital of Xinjiang, for another day off and a swim in a salt lake. That's it from me, but Jo is tapping away next to me so it's a double whammy today.

 Roast arm of Ants with garlic and rosemary

A strange title for a blog one might think, but this was an actual conversation in the back of TT as we tukked through the Gobi Desert yesterday. It is very, very hot here and the heat is dry. When we are driving it is like being in a fan-assisted oven. The advantage of this is being able to develop our lopsided tans (due to only the left-hand side of TT being open). When we return to England we may be classified as a rare hybrid version of the brown-and-white zebra.

We are currently having a rest day in magical North West China in a city called Turpan, which is located on the ancient Silk Road. It is an oasis in the remote Gobi Desert, watered by cleverly constructed irrigation channels and a paradise for growing 600 varieties of grape and the most delicious melons.

During the day here, it is too hot to do anything other than seek shelter from the heat. Today, at 42 °C, is a typical example. In the past – and still in outlying villages – people retreat to underground rooms in their houses, only to resurface in the evening. People also sleep outside, and last night there were beds pulled out into the street and around the main square. We opted to sleep in our air-conditioned bedroom.

We have spent the past two days covering over 550 miles in TT. The roads have been good and we cover 280 miles in between seven and eight hours. I never thought this would be possible after our painful journeys in Yunnan, where it took us the best part of ten hours to cover less than 125 miles. TT is amazing as always, and her oil temperature has yet to go over halfway. She is definitely a hot-weather tuk tuk, and I think the English winter will be a real shock to her system – in the same way I think most English cars would find the desert heat difficult to deal with.

From Dunhuang we drove 280 miles to Hami, famous throughout China for its melons. Most of the traffic on the roads was trucks filled with yellow Hami melons, being driven thousands of miles to other parts of China by the long-suffering lorry drivers. They drive almost continuously and work in shift patterns – one sleeps while the other drives – definitely not a job that I envy. A truck driver was kind enough to give us a large Hami melon, which we are storing in our fridge to enjoy later this evening. The truck drivers in this part of China seem more relaxed and actually have given way to us on a couple of occasions. The roads are less busy, blissfully straight and flat, and the tarmac is far superior to anything we experienced in south and central China.

Yesterday morning was very strange. After being delayed by Jack oversleeping and getting us hopelessly lost, we were caught in a violent storm. It blew up out of nowhere about two hours beyond Hami and started to pour with rain and blow a gale. It must have been about 10 °C, and we sat shivering in TT with all of the rain covers down. Jack said that never before had he experienced a rain storm like that in the desert – we felt truly honoured. Later in the day the sky became clear blue and we were blessed with a 30 °C increase in temperature.

Driving through the desert is a real pleasure as the landscapes are so raw and remote. It makes you so happy to be alive. Yesterday we tukked past the Flaming Mountains, a range over 50 miles long that glow various shades of red and orange during daylight hours.

Tomorrow we head 125 miles west to the capital city of Xinjiang Province, Urumqui. This is Jack's home city and he is going to show us around and take us to a Uighur performance. Ants has filled you in on the Uighurs. She attracted a potential Uighur suitor last night, who was very large and smelt of sheep. He was also very drunk and kept saying 'yes, no, yes, no'. Eventually he left us in peace to enjoy our lamb kebabs cooked in a Uighur restaurant by a Uighur family. We love the Uighurs.

Lots of love from North West China. Everyone should visit this area: it is amazing.

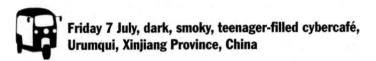

Friday 7 July, dark, smoky, teenager-filled cybercafé, Urumqui, Xinjiang Province, China

Borat be with us

After 4000 miles and 28 days we have nearly made it through China. I can't quite believe it. During those long days struggling along rutted dirt tracks in Yunnan and Guizhou, there were moments when I wondered whether we would ever make it this far, let alone get back to England. So it's quite a feeling to actually be within sight of the Kazakh border – and at the halfway point of Tuk to the Road. Even stranger is the thought that seven weeks ago tomorrow, Jo and I packed our rucksacks and flew out of Heathrow, reaching Thailand in a mere 11 hours. That's roughly one hour in a plane for one week in a tuk tuk.

The next major hurdle is Kazakhstan. Today we have had a day off in Urumqui, capital of Xinjiang. However, we have spent the majority of it in a darkened Internet café, finalising arrangements for the border crossing and for our stay in Almaty. Our contacts in Kazakhstan have been the recipient of a barrage of emails from me recently: should I use my Russian at the border or pretend I know none? How do we get our visas extended when it is technically illegal? How can we get vehicle insurance? Can they recommend a good hotel in Almaty? You may think it's strange that we are two days from Kazakhstan and we still haven't arranged our vehicle insurance, but in every other country it's been a simple case of buying it at the border. With Kazakhstan, however, it's not that straightforward and we have heard that if the border guards are in the mood for a shakedown, they could fine us for not having bought our policy in advance. One of our tasks today, therefore, has been to find a car insurance company based in Almaty that will cover us for our two weeks in Kazakhstan. Having found two companies, the next obstacle is getting through to them and trying to explain in my very average Russian that we need insurance for a tuk tuk. What a tukking palaver.

Kazakh issue number two is the technically impossible matter of extending our two-week tourist visas. Due to being held up in China, our visas are going to be invalid by the time we exit Kazakhstan and we could be in big trouble if we don't manage to extend them. It seems the only option is to take a few days out and go to Bishkek, in Kyrgyzstan, to get new visas. I'm sure Bishkek is a wonderful place, but it's a bit of a pain to have to go to such lengths for such a simple requirement. Moreover, we've already got a stack of things to do in Almaty. It's the halfway point of our tukathon and TT needs a service, Jo and I need to chill out and check out some of Almaty's clubs, the British embassy has organised a press conference, and we've got an appointment with Reuters (who want to film us tukking off into the steppes) and interviews with several Russian magazines and newspapers. When we'll have time to make a visa dash to Bishkek I'm not quite sure.

I could write a whole lot more as we've had a really interesting few days, and a great night in Urumqui last night, but I've got to sort out more Kazakhstan stuff and my eyes are going square.

 ## It was only a bad dream

Urumqui is the cosmopolitan and ethnically diverse capital of Xinjiang. It was very hot when we arrived yesterday, but last night a heavy wind drew in the storm clouds. It rained during the night and again this morning, and the temperature feels more English than we have experienced in the past two months.

We have another day off here – are we starting to take it easy, you might ask? Unfortunately, this is a day-in-the-office day off rather than a touristy day off. We have already put in a two-hour Internet session this morning and have just started our afternoon session. Internet cafés have become our third home, after the inside of TT and the inside of hotel rooms. We are both becoming confirmed technogeeks.

The other evening we got a donkey cart in Turpan and headed into the surrounding countryside and Uighur villages. It was like being transported to another country. The writing was all in Uighur and the houses and smells were very different, as were the smiley faces that shouted 'Hello!' The Uighurs mostly have 'exotic Asian eyes', although not as pronounced as in the rest of South East Asia. Some of them have blue or green eyes and brown hair, and their skin tone goes from dark brown to pure white. They do not look like a homogeneous race, and over the centuries I think they have mixed with other ethnic groups, although our guide says this is quite rare. I suppose it is like every country – some people look different from others. I am English, but only a quarter of my blood actually comes from England: another quarter comes from New Zealand and the remaining half is Swiss Italian.

Yesterday morning we left Turpan and were allowed to drive on the expressway. We couldn't believe our luck. The reason for this privilege was that the old road was under construction and hence all vehicles were mixed together on the super-speedy highway that we have spent the best part of last month fantasising about. TT loved it and used her 550-cc engine to enjoy her new speed limit of 62 mph. The main advantages were that the tarmac (Oh God! Not going on about tarmac again, Jo?) was free of irregularities – i.e. potholes and bumps – and that vehicles driving in the opposite direction were on the other side of the central reservation. This enabled the driving to be considerably less stressful.

We sped along and then visited the 'Dead Sea of China', spending about an hour floating in extremely salty, slightly chilly water, while Chinese techno blasted out from a nearby building. The lake was surrounded by rugged brown mountains on one side and the snow-capped peaks of the Tien Shan range on the other. It wasn't as beautiful and romantic as it sounds though, because as well as the water being brown lots of Dong Feng lorries were driving up and down to the lake to harvest the salt.

After that we carried on towards Urumqui and were met by the side of the expressway by a Xinjiang TV crew. They carried out a brief interview in Chinese while Jack translated for us – the first bit of media work we have done in the whole of our China visit. Then they followed us down the expressway filming with their meaty Sony camera. They had their hazard lights on and didn't pay much attention to the Dong Fengs beeping. They nearly caused a TT sandwich, which I am sure would have provided some excellent TV footage at our expense. Our arrival in Urumqui was slowed on the outskirts by a large truck that was perpendicular to the road, blocking both lanes. Quite how it came to be in that position I do not understand, because it did not appear to have been in an accident. Another mystery from Chinese roads.

When we arrived at our hotel we had to unload the spares from TT's roof-rack because she needed to sleep in an underground carpark with low headroom. We discovered that our radiator fluid had leaked everywhere, soaking most of the spares and ruining the boxes they were in. I am not sure how much spark plugs like radiator fluid, but I hope they will be OK after drying. Anyway, it wasn't the end of the world and I needed access to the spares to change an indicator and headlight bulb anyway.

In the evening Jack had organised for us to go to a night of Uighur entertainment. There was a huge buffet and then we were entertained by tightrope artists (suspended 90 feet up, with no safety net or harnesses), traditional Uighur songs and dance performances. Our spirits were lifted and it was a brilliant evening – thanks Jack for organising it!

We will be leaving China in three days, and I will be so sad to go. It is such a great country and I shed a few tears at the thought this afternoon. I am sure there will be real waterworks at the border. We are both apprehensive about Kazakhstan, after hearing from another traveller who had some problems at the border.

I have been having some horrible dreams recently, hence the title of this blog. The first was being told by medical school that I wasn't suitable for them and therefore my place was taken away and my dreams of becoming a doctor ruined. My second dream was that we went to Kazakhstan and drug-crazed people were trying to kill us with knives. I was having a panic attack and we couldn't find a hotel or escape. The

 ABOVE: Jo and Ants celebrate their eighteenth birthday together. **BELOW:** Jo and Ants aged 17, on the caravanning holiday that inspired them to one day go travelling together.

ABOVE: Our departure graces the front page of a Thai newspaper on 29 May 2006.
BELOW: Traditional Hmong houses beside Route 13 in Laos.

 ABOVE: Some of the breathtaking scenery in Yunnan we got to appreciate at about 15 mph.
BELOW: Torture by (lack of) tarmac. A typical example of the roads we were forced to use in south China.

 ABOVE: A beautiful mountain road in Guizhou, south China.
BELOW: Ting Tong takes on the Dong Feng army.

 ABOVE: The landslide at Linjian. How on earth were we going to get through this one?
BELOW: A crowd of curious Chinese.

 ABOVE: The Union Flag flies high over Gansu Province.
BELOW: Tukking the Great Wall by storm.

 ABOVE: Ants, Jack and Jo on a rare day off, enjoying the sand dunes at Dunhuang.
BELOW: Salty ferrets after a swim in Xinjiang's salt lake.

 ABOVE: Saryam Lake in China, our last stop before Kazakhstan and the perfect goodbye to China.
BELOW: Ants capturing the action in the Kazakh steppe.

ABOVE: Doing a press conference at SATR in Almaty. On the left is Yulia Kaufman, press officer and translator from the British embassy.

RIGHT: 'Kazakhstan 2030' and a typical apartment block in Balkash, Kazakhstan.

ABOVE: A crowd of Kazakhs ask us all the usual questions at a petrol station. (Photo courtesy of Fiona Bolingbroke-Kent.)
BELOW: Jo takes Rudy (left) and Oleg (right) for a spin around Yekaterinburg in Ting Tong.

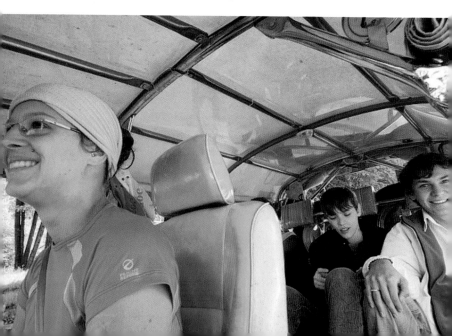

 ABOVE: Ting Tong on the road in Russia, closely followed by one of her Russian boyfriends, a Kamaz truck.
BELOW: Ting Tong straddles the Europe–Asia border seven miles outside Yekaterinburg, Russia. A moment to contemplate all we had achieved and what lay ahead.

ABOVE: Somewhere in Russia...
LEFT: Mamaev Kurgan, a fitting memorial to the millions killed during the battle of Stalingrad.

 ABOVE: Ting Tong waits patiently to cross the border between Russia and Ukraine.
BELOW: Cop Stop in Ukraine – they're far more interested in Jo's leopard-print bikini top than our *dokumenti*.

ABOVE: A traffic-jam in Bavaria. (Photo courtesy of Daniel Snaider.)
BELOW: Jo and her father Bob in Prague, where we were treated to some last-minute luxury.

 ABOVE: Showing our allegiance to Mind in Prague... just in case anyone was wondering what charity we were supporting. (Photo courtesy of Bob Huxster.)

 ABOVE: We made it! Two girls, three wheels, 12 500 miles. (Photo courtesy of *The Argus*.)
BELOW: Jo and Ants with Trisha Goddard, winning *Cosmopolitan*'s Fun Fearless Female Award. (Photo courtesy of *Cosmopolitan*.)

place I dreamt about wasn't really Kazakhstan but a fiction produced by my slightly anxious imagination.

 Sunday 9 July, Saryam Lake, Xinjiang Province, China

 A perfect goodbye to China

Today is our last day in China. How strange. At last, after 30 days driving across this massive country, the Kazakh border is within spitting distance, a mere 40 miles or so west from here.

The past month has been an intense experience – exhausting, exhilarating, stressful, hilariously funny, mind-blowingly beautiful, frustrating and immensely rewarding. After all the trials and tukulations that China has put us through, I never thought I would feel sad to leave it behind. But I am. We couldn't be spending our last day here in a more idyllic setting, and yet today is tinged with a sadness that has really surprised me. More than anything, I can't believe that we have been on the road for six weeks and that we are halfway home. It's as if the gears of time have gone into fast-forward and are catapulting us towards our final destination in turbo mode. And although we are both appreciating every moment, there's nothing we can do to slow it down. It's like trying to grasp a handful of sand; the more you clutch at it, the faster it disappears. Before we know it, Jo, Ting Tong and I will be back in England, and all the weird and wonderful experiences we are having will be locked in the catacombs of our minds. But that's life, just chapters of memories to be cherished and learnt from.

Yesterday was a Tuk to the Road personal best. We left Urumqui at 9 a.m., the streets still deserted due to the city living on Xinjiang time (although the clocks here are officially set to Beijing time, the people live two hours behind, the same as Kazakhstan and the rest of Central Asia), and arrived at this magic lake at 8.30 p.m. last night. In the 11.5 hours and 400 miles since we left Urumqui, we had crossed desert, steppe, fields of sunflowers, empty scrubland and wheat fields, guided all the way by the aptly named Tien Shan – 'heavenly' – mountains. It was hard to believe we had covered such a distance and seen so many sights in a single day.

We set off in the morning, unsure of our destination, our fate to be decided by whether we were allowed on the expressway. Our first attempt failed and the irate lady at the toll told us to tuk off in no uncertain fashion. Undeterred, we tried the tollgate about 12 miles further west. Again, the guards shook their heads and told us to be off to the old road, where other three-wheeled beasts dwelt. But he also added that a few miles further on there was a slip-road where we could surreptitiously tuk on to the expressway, which of course we did. The next 280 miles were spent speeding along on glorious tarmac, slipping through tolls before they could change their mind and waving merrily at policeman who we were convinced would stop us. Although Jo and I feel that not being allowed on the expressways has in fact turned out for the best, there are times when it's a joy to be on them. Without yesterday's luck, we would never have made it to Saryam Lake last night and been able to spend our last day in China riding, walking and enjoying the unspoilt wilderness of China's final frontier.

A bit about the lake. Pronounced 'salim', it's the largest mountain lake in China, covering a vast 200 square miles and being up to 300 feet deep in parts. For me, this is how Heaven, if it existed, would look – cobalt-blue water, brilliant green pastures, perfect velveteen mountains, eagles drifting lazily on the wind, an effusion of wild flowers of every colour, yurts dotting the grassland and Kazakh and Wi nomads herding their animals on horses. I'd like to set up a yurt and spend a long time here, with a large pile of books and lots of tea. Jo has been taking the piss out of me as she says my new obsession is yurts, which I think it is. First it was the Hmong, then the Hexi Corridor, then the Uighurs and now yurts. But yurts really are awesome, and I might have to live in one when I get back to England. Mine might have to have central heating though, as it was pretty chilly last night, even with most of the contents of my rucksack and three duvets on.

Apart from feeling sad about leaving China, today has been perfect. Jo, Jack and I went riding this morning, up into the mountains and across some very gallop-able grassland. Last time Jo and I rode together was when we were bolted on our horses at home, aged 14, laughing too much to do anything about stopping. Today was a bit more genteel, and apart from the odd canter we mostly just lazed along at a walk or trot and enjoyed the view. Everyone here has horses; they're their livelihood. They spend their whole lives on their four-legged friends, herding their flocks and then eating them when they get too old to work. Being a vegetarian, I was delighted to read in our Central Asian Lonely Planet this morning that horsemeat is a national speciality in Kazakhstan. Horse sausage, horse intestine, horse liver... horse everything. I'll just stick to the veggies thanks.

So tomorrow morning, early, we pack up TT for the last time in China and head west to the border at Khorgos. We should reach the checkpoint by 9 a.m. and then, with a bit of luck, be on the way to Almaty a few hours later. It's 200 miles to Almaty, and the roads are allegedly good, so we should be there by early evening, to meet up with my mother who is flying in from the UK tonight. Fingers crossed that this time tomorrow we will be speeding across the Kazakh countryside and all our border worries will have been for nothing.

Beautiful China

I am lost for words by the beauty of this place. The lake is the most perfect bright blue – for those that remember their chemistry lessons, it is the colour of copper sulphate – and is surrounded by mountains, some rugged and some covered in grass. Traditional yurts are dotted on the grassy hills on one side of the lake, and there are herds of sheep and horses. Last night we climbed to the top of the nearest hill and enjoyed the sun setting; I nearly ruined the moment by trying to yodel. I was also wearing my Yi apron on top of my normal clothes, with an army hat and headband to complete the rather strange look. If it had been daylight I would have been deemed an eyesore.

We opted to stay in a pseudo-yurt. Apparently the real ones have a certain sheepy odour to them, are very cold and are not very comfortable. We hope to stay in a proper yurt in Kazakhstan, when it is not so important that we sleep well. Our yurt looks out over the lake and at night is blessed with electricity, but no central heating. We have a carpet on the floor and some basic wooden furniture, and we sleep on and in blankets, fully clothed, with half of our rucksacks emptied on top of us to add to the warmth. Ants also wears her earplugs and eye-mask – apparently my snoring still penetrates the earplugs though.

Last night we did not sleep very well, but to compensate I was woken by the most beautiful sunrise across the lake. Until the sun rises fully here, it is the temperature of England on an early spring morning, i.e. chilly. In the morning we went riding for two hours. I didn't have any long trousers and so the inside of my calves are now suffering, having been rubbed red raw from cantering across the fields. I had forgotten how much I love riding, and it was a magic experience.

So, tomorrow we leave China and cross into Kazakhstan. We are both still nervous about what to expect. I feel like I am being sent back to school at the beginning of term and I don't want to go. I have cried quite a few tears today and will keep the experiences of the past two weeks in my heart forever. I will miss China so much. Jack has been amazing and is now a good friend.

chapter 4
ladaland

 **Tuesday 11 July, Apartment on Samal 2, Almaty, Kazakhstan**

 Kazakhstan, we love you

Yesterday was without doubt one of the most surreal and extraordinary days of my life. After all the sleepless nights, the worry, the 'will we ever make it?' fears, Jo, TT and I made it safe and sound to Kazakhstan, the land of milk and honey we have been dreaming of throughout our Chinese tukathon. And now here I am, sitting in our rented apartment, looking out on the Tien Shan Mountains, with China already slipping into the confines of my memory.

The day started early, before sunrise. As we hauled our luggage out of the yurt and into Ting Tong, the sun was just beginning to stain the horizon orange and cast her golden cloak over the lake and mountains. The odd herdsman cantered past and a group of Chinese tourists looked on curiously as we pulled off TT's cover to reveal the pink lady herself. But Ting Tong dug in her heels. She didn't want to leave China, either. Or, more likely, she didn't like the cold dawn air. For half an hour we tried to start her, but she stubbornly refused. A couple of times the engine wheezed into life for a few seconds and then died again. The next option was to push her on to the road, where there was a slight incline, and give her a rolling start. The Chinese tourists quickly came to our help, and TT was pushed about 90 feet into the starting gates. What a funny sight, TT being pushed by a selection of Chinese, English and Uighurs against a background of yurts and grazing animals. Then, thank goodness, our luck changed. A Chinese man – who assured us he was 'velly good driver' – climbed into the cockpit and got a tune out of her. We were off! Of all the mornings Tingers could have chosen to have a tantrum.

Our last 40 miles of China were beautiful. The road wound through the mountains, past beekeepers, herdsmen, brightly decorated yurts and herds of horses and foals. Rarely has England felt so far away.

Then we hit the maelstrom of the border. We did our usual and weaved TT in and out of the queues of coaches to the front of the fray. At once a crush of people closed in on us, waving wads of tenge – Kazakh currency – for black-market exchange. Gold teeth flashed and questions were fired at us in Russian. Luckily, Jack and TT worked their combined magic and a guard ushered us through the gates in front into the Chinese border compound. TT squeezed in among more coaches, a Chihuahua amongst greyhounds, and Jack and Jo went inside to investigate. In no time several Kazakh bus drivers came up to me and starting asking questions, their smiles revealing more mouthfuls of gold teeth. To my dismay I learnt that it was 230 miles to Almaty on only OK roads. My hopes of our making it that night clouded.

The prognosis wasn't good when Jack and Jo returned. Hundreds of people were inside and there seemed to be little order to the proceedings. Then once again Lady Luck came to our aid and without really understanding what was going on we were in and out after little more than an hour. A quick, sad goodbye to Jack and we were on our own and crossing the divide into Kazakhstan, full of trepidation as to what lay ahead. Our first impression was good. A tall, handsome, camo-clad soldier with a large rifle slung over his shoulder stopped us and told us where to go, in Russian of course. Upon seeing our confusion, he hopped on to the side of TT and hitched a ride 300 feet to the next point, truck drivers whistling as we tukked past. More soldiers then pointed us towards the main area and we were let through some gates to where the action was. Since Kazakhstan has been my organisational baby, along with Russia and Ukraine, I left Jo with TT and, with an armful of documents, went to investigate the situation.

Inside, chaos abounded. A sea of baggage-laden Kazakh and Uighur families, interspersed with the odd Russian, jostled to get to the front. It looked like we were going to have to unload all our luggage again (we'd already had to do it on the Chinese side) to get it scanned and use a lot of elbows in the process. I went to tell Jo the bad news, and we began the laborious process of putting all our things on a huge trolley. By this time, a group of intimidating-looking guards, all with guns, had gathered round. I answered their questions, told them about the trip and showed them our Russian press release. Laughter and smiles ensued. Phew! Then a very tall official with a large badge and Terminator-style shades appeared – clearly the boss. What happened next was quite extraordinary. After verbally confirming we had no contraband, our luggage was loaded back on to TT. We were led inside and taken to the front of the heaving throng, and our passports were stamped while the guards talked about 'Beckham' and 'Rooney' with us. The people who had been fighting for hours to get to the front of the mêlée justifiably glowered in our direction. Then we were told to drive TT round the side, where, accompanied by the big boss in the big shades, we had all our vehicle documentation stamped and verified. The boss queried whether we had husbands, told us about his several wives and children, and asked us about the trip. He then disappeared for a few minutes and returned with a bagful of chocolates, cold drinks, a Russian doll and a carved wooden box. Most amazing of all was the fact that he pushed a fistful of tenge into my hand and refused to accept any dollars in return. Here was one of the apparently notoriously corrupt Kazakh officials giving us presents and money – about £20. To top it all, he climbed in the back seat with me and led us the half-mile out of the border area, soldiers saluting him all the way and gates swinging open in haste. We thanked him effusively and he was gone, another guardian angel sent to help us home. What a feeling of relief and happiness swept over us. I felt like crying, I was so happy. A few miles later we came to the final border checkpoint, where a group of young soldiers creased into laughter and asked a barrage of questions about Ting Tong before we were off. What an incredible few hours. Something we had been so fearful of had turned out to be a highlight of the trip. We couldn't believe our luck. Twenty minutes later, we pulled over beside the quiet country road and just took it all in for a few moments.

I've gone on long enough, so I won't write an essay about the eight-hour tuk to Almaty. But we made it. At 8.30 p.m. we found our apartment, I rang the doorbell and there was my mother. It was so lovely to see her and know she made it here safe as well. The drive here was beautiful, lots of donkey carts, huge wide open spaces, mountains, very strong winds and lots of waving and gold-toothed smiles from the Kazakhs. VW Santanas have been replaced by Audis, Ladas and Mercs, and Dong Fengs by the indomitable Kamaz. Although I was sad to leave China, rarely have I been so pleased to arrive anywhere than here last night, and what a great thought that we've got four or five days to recuperate before we hit the road again.

 Welcome to Kazakhstan

We woke up at 6.45 a.m. yesterday morning and packed up TT before leaving Saryam Lake and heading to the border. Well, that was the plan anyway. It was about 5 °C and bloody freezing. Our fingers went numb and we had problems undoing TT's dressing gown. Once everything was loaded, Ants turned the key in the ignition. Can you guess what happened next? *Nothing!* As I have said before, TT is a tropical tuk tuk and doesn't like the cold. We tried to start her on and off for about 20 minutes, pausing so we didn't flood the engine. She did start three times, but cut out straight away. Jack, Ants and myself tried to push her backwards up a slope, but she was too heavy. Thankfully, some locals came to the rescue and we pushed her up the slope and on to the road, before bump-starting her successfully. Drama over and it was only about 8 a.m. Ants found the whole experience quite stressful, while I chose to laugh and use the opportunity to kick-start my nicotine fix. I would have got stressed if the bump-start hadn't worked, but in these situations you either laugh or cry – and I chose the former.

Finally we set off towards the border, all of us shivering violently against temperatures we were not dressed for and hadn't experienced in a few months. We stopped briefly for breakfast and then tukked the last 20 miles to the border. It was heaving with Kazakh families who, since it was Monday morning, I assume had been visiting China for the weekend. Unlike the other border crossings, this one was packed with people and vehicles, and all of our luggage had to go through an airport scanner. The whole process of scurrying around to sort out passports, check vehicle documents, etc. took the best part of two hours, but thanks to Jack we were processed more quickly than many others. We were fretting about getting to the Kazakh side before their lunch break because we still had nearly 250 miles of driving before reaching Almaty.

We hugged Jack and said goodbye. I burst into tears and felt incredibly sad to be leaving both him and China. Then the moment of truth arrived and we entered the Kazakh side, where we were greeted by a soldier dressed in khaki and spitting sunflower husks on to the floor. He hopped into TT to show us the way. So far, so good. We drove past all of the other vehicles and went straight into the compound, where it seemed that we needed to get all of our luggage scanned again – what a pain.

A group of guards surrounded us and began to ask questions, so Ants handed them our Russian press release, which they read. Then our guardian angel arrived – a man we think was an important border official. After asking whether we had any contraband (the answer was of course '*Nyet*'), he told us not to bother getting our luggage scanned. We were then pushed to the front of the queue with our passports, which were quickly stamped. Then we drove a few feet to get TT processed. The paperwork was all organised within quarter of an hour and we were told to get vehicle insurance in Almaty. Then the kind officer (who was quite handsome and early middle aged) gave me a plastic bag filled with litres of cold drink, a box of chocolates and two Russian dolls. We asked about changing money, but they did not know what to do with our travellers' cheques, and so the border official gave us £20 of local money. We were both speechless at the generosity of this man we had never met before.

I offered him a packet of Chinese cigarettes, which he accepted. He climbed into TT and then we drove out of the border area with all of the guards, officials and soldiers saluting him and opening all of the gates for us. Ants later said that she wondered whether he wanted a lift all of the way to Almaty. He didn't and hopped out after less than one mile. We screamed with delight and relief and were absolutely thrilled to be safely through the border. A couple of miles later we were stopped at an army checkpoint, but all they wanted was to see our passports and to take photos of TT.

The drive to Almaty was over 200 miles and we had heard mixed reports about the state of the tarmac. Some people had said the drive would take us six hours, others eight; one even posited twelve hours. The road had a few potholes, but we could still travel at a good 35 mph. The scenery was stunning, alternating between mountains and grass-covered sand dunes. At one point it was so windy that we were reduced to about 25 mph, with Ants gripping the handle bars with all her might so we didn't get blown back to China. We pulled over by the side of the road and unloaded the roof-rack of TT's spares to try to reduce the wind resistance a little.

We stopped to fill up with petrol and I was pleased that I could fill up TT myself. However, the nozzle lever got jammed and I squirted petrol all over the petrol station and myself at a great velocity. A man then came and did the job for me, but he wouldn't listen to me about putting the nozzle into TT too far. I smugly watched as the petrol squirted out back at him. Why will nobody listen to us about TT's anatomy? I guess they just like to learn the hard way.

We drove into Almaty at just after 8 p.m. and got a tiny bit lost trying to find the apartment we were renting. We finally located Ants' mum, Fiona, and the apartment and unloaded TT. Fiona and I put our stuff in the lift to take to the eighth floor, while Ants went to park TT in a secure compound, which a kind man had offered us. After nearly an hour, Ants still wasn't back. Fiona and I had gone through rational reasons for Ants' delay, before worrying that she had been raped and murdered. Just as we were considering calling the police, Ants returned. Apparently, someone had taken the parking space and the kind man, Aziz, a Pakistani diplomat, had tried to clear the space for TT. Ants knew we would be worried but had no way of contacting us to explain why she hadn't come back sooner. After some anxious minutes, everything was fine, Fiona made a salad, we all had a nice catch-up and then we hit the hay, absolutely exhausted.

The fears have been banished and Kazakhstan looks to be a whole new and wonderful experience, although I desperately miss China still.

 Thursday 13 July, Almaty, Kazakhstan

 A quickie from Almaty

We've been in Almaty for almost three days now and it's been crazy. Almaty is so expensive, statistically more so than Washington, DC, and Boston and with more Porsche Cayennes per capita than anywhere else in the world. Jo and I are both finding it very odd being in the Western world again and being bereft of chopsticks and Jack (not in that order) and are looking forward to hitting the road again.

We'll write more soon as it's been a very funny few days. I got attacked by a Bride of Frankenstein dentist with facial hair and inch-thick kohl, we've been hanging out with the Kazakhstan Feminist League (long story), I found a huge maggot in my salad at a 'snazzy' restaurant, we've drunk fermented mare's and camel's milk, and today we had a press conference organised by the British embassy, with a scary amount of TV crews and newspapers.

 Saturday 15 July, Almaty, Kazakhstan

 Who wants to live forever?

The title of this blog is also the title of a Queen song that I was listening to on Ants' iPod during our last week in China, scaring away the local wildlife by singing along. I find the song very emotive and it makes me want to disagree and say that I do want to live forever. I certainly haven't always wanted to be immortal, and there were a number of years when I wished that I could just fall asleep and never wake up.

This trip just makes me so happy to be alive. Even the difficult and stressful days make me appreciate the gift of life. I am also very grateful to have the opportunity to see so many different environments and cultures. There is too much to see and do in this world that it is not possible to fit it into one lifetime. I would like to live many lives, on the one condition that all the people and animals that I love could share my experiences with me.

I have just finished a brilliant book called *A Fine Balance* by Rohinton Mistry. At the end of the book one of the main characters commits suicide and you are left with so many unanswered questions, in particular why did he do it? This is probably the main question that loved ones ask when someone close to them chooses to take their own life. Suicide may seem like a selfish choice, but suicidal people are not cowards and to judge someone's actions when you don't know their feelings is wrong. I have suffered from depression and I know the feeling when life seems so helpless that there are no apparent reasons to carry on living. I acutely remember feeling like a living corpse, unable to experience any emotions. I knew that I should love my family but I could not connect in any way with any positive emotions.

So, we have been in Almaty for a few days and leave tomorrow for Lake Balkash, a short 450-mile drive away. I am not really sure what I think of Almaty. Everything is very expensive here – £4 for a glass of freshly squeezed orange juice and £2 per hour to use the Internet – and Ants and I are suffering a reverse culture shock after having been in Asia for so long. We intended to relax and rest a little, but instead our days have been filled with chores that need to be done – press conference, registering passports, organising third-party vehicle insurance, getting TT serviced... However, the people here are very friendly and we have met some really interesting characters this week.

On Tuesday evening, we went out to supper with Mike Steen (Reuters Central Asia correspondent) and his wife Gemma, who have provided us with lots of useful information about Kazakhstan. We went to an

Italian restaurant and Mr Ant was lucky enough to have a gleaming white healthy maggot in her cauliflower salad. Well, I am always trying to tell her that she needs more protein in her diet. Thursday was the most serious day of the trip to date. We took TT along to a press conference that had been organised by the British embassy in Almaty. It took place at the headquarters of the organisation SATR, which works with children and young people with mental and physical disabilities. We had no idea what to expect and were thoroughly shocked to be filmed driving through the streets and then to be met by well over 20 journalists and a handful of TV crews. Microphones were thrust towards us as we gave short speeches about our trip (Ants) and about Mind and mental health in England (me). We had to speak in very short sentences so that what we'd said could be translated into Russian. It was a pretty nerve-wracking experience, and I am so glad that Ants and I could share the load of public speaking, one of my least favourite hobbies. Still, it is good to think that we are getting the opportunity to speak about the problems associated with mental health.

Yesterday I took TT to be serviced, and now she has fresh oil (for high-performance cars), a new oil filter, a new fuel filter and new front brake pads. The mechanic was a real character who spoke very little English, and so we communicated mainly through hand signals for three hours. He noticed that part of TT's rear suspension was missing from one side, and after a few minutes with a blowtorch he had fixed the part and reinserted it. I was shocked that the oil cost £20, but I think it is oil designed for very high-performance cars like Porsches. I gave him a packet of Chinese cigarettes to say thank you and asked how much I owed him. He refused to take any money from me and demonstrated yet again the generosity of the people we have met throughout our journey.

We're back on the road tomorrow and I am looking forward to it. We have been in one place for five days and I am getting itchy feet. It is time to hit that tarmac, and I hope it is smooth and beautiful and black.

Monday 17 July, Lake Balkash, Kazakhstan

A lucky escape

I thought the driving in China was bad, but Almaty takes the prize for reckless motoring. As we drove out of Almaty yesterday morning, I was praying that we would manage to leave the city without having an accident. It was the first time that I have really felt nervous driving TT. As we were nearing the city limits, a car ahead of us braked suddenly at a pedestrian crossing and the Lada beside us smashed into a large Mercedes at about 30 mph. We were very lucky that the Lada driver decided to rear-end the Merc rather than swerve straight into us. My heart started pounding and I uttered a few expletives, as did Ants. We drove around the crash to see three rather butch men get out of the Merc and walk back towards the Lada driver... God, I hope he had insurance. Guess which car came off worse? The Merc lost 1–0 to the Lada, which suffered only a small dent to its front bumper.

After leaving Almaty safely, we started on the very long drive north to Balkash across hundreds of miles of endless scrubby grassland to the east, west, north and south. I loved driving through barren landscapes in China, but the steppe did not stir up so many positive emotions. I didn't dislike the drive, but it did feel a bit like driving in a computer game, the monotony broken only by eagles flying overhead and small herds of grazing horses and camels. Petrol stations were few and far between, and a couple of times I was worried we might run out of fuel, which we would have done had it not been for a passing Kazakh family who gave us five litres of petrol from their jerry can – another example of the Kazakh hospitality that has been bestowed upon us and TT.

At one of the petrol stations the petrol was pumped by hand. This involved two men turning a handle very fast to get the petrol from its underground tank into the vehicle. As usual, the petrol attendants wouldn't listen to us asking them not to insert the nozzle fully into

TT, and this resulted in 17 litres for TT and three litres for the petrol forecourt. At least this time it wasn't me that ended up covered in petrol.

Balkash is not a particularly attractive town. It is towered over by large industrial chimneys, which constantly belch out acidic smoke. Ants used her Russian skills to find us a hotel and, after an uninspiring supper, we went to bed, exhausted.

For once I slept like a baby and was woken up by Ants just before midday. We had planned to explore the nicer parts of Lake Balkash today, but instead we spent the afternoon tending to TT as for the last couple of hundred of miles yesterday she was making a grinding noise in her front end. She had also started veering to the right when we braked. As I opened up the toolbox and wondered what to do, a handsome young man came and introduced himself as Maxat and offered to help. We jacked up TT, refitted the brake pads and went for a short drive. The veering to the right was better but the grinding was still there.

Maxat then introduced us to a couple of mechanics, who spent the next couple of hours trying to work out where the grinding noise was coming from. We changed the front calliper and brake pad and had another test drive – the grinding noise continued. They then tried to balance the wheel by removing a washer next to the tyre. This reduced the grinding but did not stop it completely. They concluded that the noise wasn't causing any damage and would probably disappear. We just have to hope that they are right, because apparently there aren't many (if any) motorcycle mechanics in Kazakhstan. We offered them payment but they refused any. God, the Kazakh people are generous and kind.

So far, the best thing about Kazakhstan is the people. They are mostly incredibly friendly, and many have gone out of their way to help us. Many Kazakh people have told us that they are famed for their hospitality and I would have to agree. Tonight TT is tucked up in the guarded forecourt of Balkash police station. The police would like us to take them for a two-hour drive tomorrow morning, but 20 minutes is more likely. As Ants has said, a great photo opportunity. Anyway, bedtime now as it's after 12.30 a.m. and I need to sleep well in my rather small bed in order to be full of beans for another long drive through the steppe tomorrow.

 Tuesday 18 July, Hotel Balkash, Balkash, Kazakhstan

 The kindness of strangers

Kazakhstan has been a revelation. Even more than China, it was a void in our imaginations, filled only with Borat, oil and the steppe. We had no idea what the reality of travel here would be like, and we were convinced that we'd be forking out bribes every few miles. How wrong we were. Every day strangers have shown us astonishing kindness and hospitality, and every day we are left thinking how cold and inhospitable we Brits are.

Anyway, I shall start at the beginning. As I mentioned briefly last week, Almaty is an expensive, westernised city. Having driven from Khorgos through rural villages, where donkey carts far outnumbered cars, it was a surprise to suddenly be in Almaty, with its plethora of German metal. Every second car there is a Mercedes, Audi, BMW, VW or Porsche. Every other second car is a creaky old Lada. We learnt that a great proportion of these cars are driven in huge trucks from Europe, where crashes have rendered them undriveable under EU regulations. Here, however, no one cares – status before safety, it seems.

Such a surfeit of speed makes the driving in Almaty *lethal*. Speed is at a maximum and spatial respect at a minimum. No journey through the city was completed without seeing at least two prangs, and most of the cars carried some sort of battle scars. As Jo has said, on the last day there we were lucky to escape one of these when a Lada careered straight into the back of a black Mercedes less than a yard away from us. The Mercedes came off much worse, and as we tukked off, thanking our lucky stars that the Lada driver hadn't taken evasive action into Tingers, we saw three large Russians emerge from the Merc and stride menacingly towards the quivering Lada driver. I didn't fancy his chances.

The other notable thing about driving in Almaty is the 'taxis'. On day one we noticed that everyone seemed to be hitchhiking, sticking their arms out by the side of the road and immediately being picked up by any passing car. We decided to try it out. Sure enough, 30 seconds later, a wheezing old Lada pulled up, we negotiated a price, and off we went. Having been ripped off by several taxi drivers on our first day, this became our preferred method of transport, and in our week there we got picked up more than once by people claiming to own the 'oldest Lada in Almaty'. It's such a good idea: people do it to make a bit of petrol money as they scoot around town. I might start trying it at home.

So many people in Almaty were so kind to us that I don't know where to start. First up are Michael Steen and his wife Gemma. While talking to my friend Adam about the trip back in February, he said 'Oh, my friend Mike lives in Almaty. You should get in touch with him.' Since then, Mike has been the recipient of a number of emails from me and has obliged us with a wealth of information about travelling here. So it was great to eventually meet him and Gemma, who works for the EU, and thank him for all his help. Mike has been Reuters' senior correspondent here for three years and is a mine of information on 'the Stans'. As Jo has already mentioned, our supper with them at Mamma Mia was spiced up by the presence of a juicy maggot in my salad, which luckily I spied before it was too late.

Next in our line of Almaty angels is Catherine Inglehearn, the deputy ambassador here for the past three years. Catherine, like Mike, has dispensed a great deal of advice and support to us over the past few months, when I am sure she has had far more important matters to deal with. With the help of her press officer, Yulia Kaufman, she arranged a press conference for us at SATR on Thursday. The idea to combine with SATR was inspired, since it made people realise that we are not just two dippy girls driving round the world in a toy car but are trying to raise money and awareness for an important cause. The ensuing articles in *Komsomolskaya Pravda*, *Liter* and the *Kazakhstan Express* all talked about Mind and why mental health is a global problem of which we all need to be aware. As for SATR – what a fantastic place. Its founder and matriarch Dr Gulnur Khakimzhanova deserves global acclaim for her work. It was a privilege to meet her and her team.

Then there was Evgenia Salagdinova and the members of the Kazakhstan Feminist League. Before I left, my Russian teacher Vanda had suggested I email a few of her contacts in Kazakhstan. I subsequently got several emails from various members of Feminist Leagues here, most notably Evgenia, asking how they could help us 'dear ladies'. So, on Wednesday afternoon, Jo and I found ourselves in a smoky basement, eating olives and being interviewed by these lovely people. Evgenia is a delight and, like me, shares a passion for fairies and all things pointy-eared. When she and her husband Alexander came to supper a few days later, she told us how Tolkien is very popular here and that every weekend members of the Tolkien Fan Club dress up in medieval armour and run around in the Tien Shan Mountains acting out scenes from *The Lord of the Rings*. Even better, I now know the Russian words for hobbit, elf, orc, fairy and pixie.

Our last day in Almaty was spent going into these very same mountains, where Shamil Zhumatov, the Reuters photographer, took some photos of us and TT. Shamil, a handsome, black-eyed Tartar, has covered the conflicts in Iraq and Afghanistan and was with the 4th US Marine Division when they captured Saddam. He was one of the few journalists to see inside Saddam's hole. And here he was spending his Saturday photographing TT. Shymbulak, where we went, is the playground of Almaty, where they ski in winter and get married in summer. Judging by the 27 wedding processions we saw on the way down, *no* expense is spared. We wondered where they find enough white Mercedes to feed such extravagant taste.

Betwixt our chores in Almaty we squeezed in a few touristic endeavours – the Zelyony (Green) Bazaar and the Arasan Baths. Apart from being a total rip-off, the bazaar was interesting for its bizarre offerings of *shubat* and *kumys*, fermented camel and horse milk, respectively. Both are Kazakh favourites and while we wrinkled up our noses at the alien taste, Kazakhs queued up for pints of the stuff. As for the baths... for some peculiar reason they induced a panic attack the like of which I haven't had since I used to suffer from them regularly a few years ago. While large, naked babushkas watched in perplexity, Jo had to tell me to breathe and lead me off to recover. Most odd.

So, yesterday, after five days in leafy Almaty, we set off for Balkash, 450 miles north up the M36. Since our notions of camping had been destroyed after hearing of the wolves that roam these grasslands, and with nothing but steppe wilderness between the two cities, we had no choice but to drive this far. The novelty of nothingness wore off after a while and the drive went on and on and on and on and on... Just a straight road, the flat steppe and the unbounded blue vault above. Even more so than the Gobi, this felt like a corner of the earth that civilisation had forgotten about. Every 60 miles or so we passed a crumbling village, where rusting hulls of cars languished and half-destroyed houses stood. Occasionally a herd of camels or horses punctuated the horizon. And that was it.

At last, at 8.30 p.m. last night, we arrived in Balkash, which sits to the north of its eponymous lake. The aquamarine lake stood in violent contrast to the filthy industrial town that greeted us. Balkash is just as you would imagine a ramshackle Soviet-era town to be: depressing apartment blocks, factories belching out toxic fumes, and long-abandoned parks. But having asked two gold-toothed Kazakh men where the nearest *gostiniza* (hotel) was, we found ourselves at the Hotel Balkash, a pleasant anomaly amidst such depressing surrounds. Since TT has got a mysterious mechanical issue, which we've spent all day investigating, we have found ourselves here for a second night. Tomorrow we head north again to Karaghanda, famous for coal and gulags.

A final point, which we have found again and again in our short time here: never have I come across such kind people. Whether it was the passers-by who gave us free petrol from their jerry can yesterday, the taxi driver turned mechanic who refused to accept any money for tinkering with TT today, or Maxat who has asked us to supper with his family tonight, the Kazakhs' kindness is unbounded. It puts us to shame. As I mentioned today in an article I am writing for the *Mail on Sunday*, this trip has shown me that human beings are essentially kind and that the world is a much safer place than we all imagine. I recommend that everyone should do a long-distance trip in a pink tuk tuk. It really does reaffirm your faith in human nature.

 Thursday 20 July, Kurghalzhino Nature Reserve, 90 miles south west of Astana, Kazakhstan

 A country of anomalies

I had every intention of writing a blog last night, until we got collared by a gaggle of vodka-swilling Kazakhs. Since Jo doesn't drink and my mother doesn't like swigging back glassfuls of vodka, it was left to me to do the toasts and keep the Union Jack flying high with our new friends, Valeri, Morgea and Dalod. Unfortunately, that meant no blog, no video diary, a rather pie-eyed attempt at badminton and no intended run.

Back to Balkash, where I last put pen to paper, as it were. In a perverse way, Balkash was one of the most interesting places I have ever been. A few months ago I read A.A. Gill's excellent account of his visit to Moynaq, on the shores of what was once the Aral Sea in west Kazakhstan. He describes it as the 'worst place in the world', with the rusting ghosts of fishing boats languishing in the middle of the desert, 100 miles from the edge of the sea they once fished. Lake Balkash, Central Asia's fourth largest lake, is going the same way and a UN report in 2004 stated that over 700 square miles had already been lost, thanks largely to overuse of the Ili River in China. For the visitor, this is not yet apparent, but the pollution and poverty are. In the 1930s the Russians set up copper smelting works in the town, on the north shore of the lake, and these grim chimneys still pump out poison into the atmosphere daily. Chromosomal diseases are on the rise here, and many of the residents of Balkash complain of constant headaches. I noticed the acid smoke getting in the back of my throat and making me choke. Our new friend Maxat told us that the factory is one of the biggest in the world, employing people of 17 different nationalities, and that British and Canadian pollution experts are currently working to reduce its impact on the environment. Until then, it remains yet another example of the Russian legacy to Kazakhstan, along with the shrinking Aral Sea and the nuclear testing ground at Semey.

Despite the pollution, the filth, the dereliction and the disintegrating apartment blocks, Balkash had its good points. As Jo has already written, we were saved by Maxat, who found us a mechanic and filled the holes that my elementary Russian couldn't cover. Neither of us can get over how kind and generous the Kazakhs are – they will go to any lengths to help you and make you feel welcome in their country. At times, however, this can go a little far. While navigating our way through Karaghanda two nights ago, a white Mercedes drew up beside us. The blacked-out window wound down to reveal a gleaming set of gold teeth owned by a handsome young Kazakh. 'Where are you going?' he shouted in Russian. For the next ten minutes we drove in precarious tandem to our hotel, me attempting to dodge the oncoming traffic while simultaneously conducting a conversation with Goldie next door. Later that night the same man, dressed head to toe in pinstripes and moc-croc, burst into our hotel room brandishing beer and insisting he showed us round the local hotspots. After much polite negotiation, we declined and he was off as rapidly as he had appeared. How he found his way to our hotel room remains a mystery.

The Kazakhs also have a nerve-wracking habit of pulling up beside you at 60 mph, so close you could tweak their moustaches, and firing a barrage of questions at you: 'Where are you from?' 'How much was your car?' 'Where are you going?' 'Do you want to come and stay with me?'

The more persistent people force you to pull over and have impromptu photo shoots, the encounter ending with them handing out phone numbers and insisting you pay them a visit. Yesterday it was two cars full of *poliziya*, all apparently called Eric, and the day before a BMW crammed with well-fed men, whom I felt sure were up to no good.

We have spent the past 36 hours in the Kurgalzhino Nature Reserve, famed for its pink flamingos, of which we have seen not a whisker. It's a strange place, a cursory attempt at eco-tourism that doesn't quite work. We are the only people staying here; the rest of the inhabitants are builders and random, slightly drunk men. Our arrival here the other night was even odder. Having driven along the longest, straightest road from Astana (where I had completely lost my rag after getting lost for ages), we came to the town of Kurgalzhino, which we assumed must be where the reserve was. It was 8 p.m. and the sun was sinking rapidly in the sky. After a brief diversion from the village drunk, we ascertained that in fact the reserve was another 30 miles up a dirt track. So off we sped. At last, out of the gloom, appeared the gateway to the 'famous' reserve, which we had been assured was well signed. As we pulled up, a ruddy-faced, inebriated-looking Russian limped out of a wooden hut, clearly wondering whether he was hallucinating. We discovered that the reserve was closed for the night and we would have to wait until the morning to get in. We looked around despondently – nothing for miles, just the lonely steppes. Eventually, after much pleading and gesturing that my mother was far too old and delicate to camp (which she isn't), and a series of phone calls to 'the director', our luck changed. Nikolai, the limping Russian, who smelt exceptionally sheepy, gave us our tickets and relieved us of $60 (£30) and off we went, assured that five miles beyond was a *gostiniza*, with soft towels and moonshine. As we tukked off down the track into the darkness (it was now 10 p.m.) I found it hard to believe that there was any civilisation in such a place, let alone hot water and a place to lay our heads for the night. What we found was a strange collection of wooden huts, a single yurt and a lot of drunk Kazakhs. After haggling for another half an hour over the costs of our simple hut, we hit the sack, exhausted.

It's eight weeks on Sunday since we left Bangkok. Amazing! Neither Jo nor I can believe it. Even stranger is the fact that we've been in Kazakhstan for ten days and yet it seems like only yesterday that we were sitting by Saryam Lake mourning the end of our passage through China. In two days we will be in Russia, leaving Asia firmly behind us. Kazakhstan has been a curious experience. It's a country of anomalies, where nothing quite adds up – neither Asia nor Europe, but betwixt and between; the ninth largest country in the world and yet with a falling population of only 15 million. Its (benevolent) dictator Nursultan Nazarbayev has a grandiose economic plan for the country – 'Kazakhstan 2030' – and yet everywhere we go poverty stares us in the face. I saw a perfect example of this in Balkash: in front of a decrepit tower block stood a huge 'Kazakhstan 2030' sign, the golden snow-leopard peeling off the blue paintwork. It seemed a microcosm of Kazakhstan, trying so hard to escape the shackles of poverty and the Soviet era but not yet able to shed its old skin.

Kazakhstan is also full of anomalies in other, minor ways. In Karaghanda two nights ago, a steppe town famed for coal and gulags, we found ourselves in a Belgian restaurant serving Hoegarden and waffles. And in Almaty last week, we had a pint of Guinness in an Irish pub called Mad Murphy's, where a trio of maudlin Russians sang bizarre renditions of Beatles songs.

That's it for now. We're off to Astana today, from where my ma flies home, to leave us to Russia and its rhinoceros-sized mosquitoes.

 Our mission to Lake Tenghiz

We left Balkash on Tuesday morning and drove north to Karaghanda. The steppe became less monotonous and was replaced by lush grass and rugged hills to our east and west. Ants and I both thought the scenery looked like Tellytubby land and I expected Tinkywinky to pop up and say 'Eh-oh'. TT cruised happily at about 60 mph, and we enjoyed the drive much more than we had the drive to Balkash from Almaty.

We stayed the night in Karaghanda, where we were led to a hotel by a kind Kazakh guy in his van whom we had asked for directions. He also helped us to check in and managed to haggle down the price a bit. Kazakh people rock. As we drove through the town, people were beeping and waving at us. Most of the time this is good fun, but sometimes people pull up within a couple of feet of us and try to chat or take photos, often when a big Kamaz truck is bearing down on them in the opposite direction. It gives us flashbacks of China and trucks trying to make a TT sandwich.

We ended up at an expensive Belgian restaurant for supper, where the menu was a curious mix of Belgian, Greek and Kazakh food. I had a Belgian waffle with chocolate sauce for pudding, and it was the best waffle I have ever eaten. The plate ended up being licked, much to Ants' amusement, and I ended up looking like a toddler after her first birthday party. My parents would have been ashamed of my behaviour.

Yesterday morning we left about midday for the Khurgalzhino Nature Reserve. Everything was going smoothly until we got totally lost in Astana. There were absolutely no signs and everyone gave us different directions. In the end we found the right road and drove in a straight line for 80 miles until we reached the village of Kurghalzhino. Thinking we must be nearly there, we asked a man for directions, who unfortunately happened to be extremely drunk and clambered into TT before we could do anything. A family in a green Lada then pointed us in the right direction, and we removed the drunk from TT and set off for the reserve, which the family had told us was 30 miles away. Eventually we came to the entrance of the nature reserve and were told it was too late for us to enter. We were in the middle of nowhere, 30 miles from the nearest form of civilisation, the sun had set and it was 9.30 p.m. The man on duty at the gate said that we could sleep in his hut, but we didn't really want to because it smelt of sheep. We were desperate to get to the lake and after a few walkie-talkie calls with the director we were allowed to enter. A short five miles to the guesthouse was all we had to manage before finding a bed for the night. However, a Kazakh five miles is like a Chinese five miles and this means double it and add five.

Just as we were giving up, we saw lights in the distance. Our bed for the night was a small log cabin by the lake, crammed with four beds, a fridge and a TV. We eventually got to sleep after a very tiring evening, relieved to have arrived at all.

Today we woke up to a beautiful hot day – a pleasant change. Everyone in England is having the hottest summer on record, and the weather in Kazakhstan has been mostly cloudy and not that hot. We had heard that there was a beach five miles away, and so after a lunch of stale bread and salad we headed off in TT across the steppe. I was driving and within a couple of hundred feet had successfully got TT stuck in a muddy ditch. I didn't think the puddle was so muddy, but TT had her rear right wheel totally stuck and no amount of pushing or pulling could extract her. We saw a Lada driving over and out got a Russian with a moustache and large belly. He attached TT to his Lada with her dressing gown cord, and after him revving and me revving TT shot out of the ditch and on to dry land.

That evening we were invited to join three men enjoying a feast of vegetables, pasta, rice, horsemeat and of course vodka. We opted to just have drinks and out came the vodka. I pretended to drink mine but didn't really, Ants had three large glasses and Fiona had one. One of the men, Valeri, was a Kazakh Korean who was a doctor in St Petersburg (random), and he pulled out a magnifying glass and looked into Ants' and Fiona's eyes. He then walked around the table and squeezed Fiona's tummy, intimating she was pregnant. He looked at my scars and proclaimed that he could rid me of them in three days. After our brief meeting with our new friends, Ants felt quite tipsy and decided that she would crash out after I refused her challenge to a game of badminton. When it was a bit cooler we had a short game and squeaked and grunted our way around a makeshift volleyball court, watched by all the local men. Tomorrow we are heading to Astana, where we leave Fiona and then head to the Russian border. I hope the food improves, otherwise I will turn into a piece of stale bread.

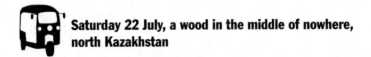

Saturday 22 July, a wood in the middle of nowhere, north Kazakhstan

The rocky road to Russia

The campfire is burning, an orchestra of insects is keeping us company, and Jo and I are camping in a wood in the middle of not quite sure (no)where. Since there are only about three trees in the steppe, this is quite an achievement in itself.

This trip has been a series of 'I can't believe it's. It has progressed from 'I can't believe we are actually doing it' to 'I can't believe we are in Thailand', 'I can't believe we are leaving today', 'I can't believe we are in China', 'through China', 'in Kazakhstan' and now, finally, 'I can't believe we are about to hit Russia'. As I have said before, time has never passed so quickly.

This time tomorrow evening, we will (I hope) be in Russia, in Chelyabinsk to be precise. It seems like yesterday that we were celebrating our passage into Kazakhstan, and the minute we get used to it we are speeding out the other side, in the flash of a gold tooth. Each day Jo and I are so engaged in driving, navigating, blogging, filming, etc. that sometimes the future springs upon us before we are aware it has arrived. Russia is a perfect example. The day before yesterday saw us frantically extracting the Russia Lonely Planet from TT's lock box and investigating what lay ahead. Lots of vodka it seems. When I was writing the route page for our website on a cold winter's afternoon in February, it felt like we would never actually be driving along the far-off roads that I was describing. I remember eulogising about the 'fabled Urals' and wondering what it would be like when one day we arrived there. That day is now only three away.

Our approach to a new border is always accompanied by a certain amount of trepidation and wonderment. Have we got all the correct documentation? Is everything in order? What is in store for us? We have got used to every day being a mystery, but borders are a different kettle of fish. I hope Russia will be as easy as all the rest and tomorrow night we will be happily ensconced in Chelyabinsk, eating borscht and (me) swigging vodka. Before you get the wrong idea by the way, I'm not descending into alcoholism – I'm just partial to the odd cockle-warming voddy.

The past few days, like all our time in Kazakhstan, have been a surprise. Our last night with my mother was spent in the capital, Astana (originally meaning 'capital' in Kazakh). We dined at a hilarious Russian joint called Egorkino, where the waitresses were garbed in seventeenth-century Russian peasant gear and the music provided by a motley crew of gold-toothed Indians. This morning it was time for Jo and I to strike off solo and leave my ma for Russia and home. Tears were shed and we sped off west towards Kostanai, with little idea of how far we would get today but just a desire to get as far as we could. Thanks to terrible roads and TT-swallowing potholes, we now find ourselves in the only wood in North West Kazakhstan. Having felt rather unsure about camping, it has turned out to be an absolute delight. As the sun set and burnt the steppe gold and orange, we tukked into the wood, erected the tent in a masterly fashion, whipped up a fire and settled down for the night. Now, as I type, Jo is gathering firewood and a kestrel is crying overhead. Camping isn't so bad after all.

Back to the campfire, over to Jo and onwards to Russia.

 We left peaceful Lake Tenghiz on Friday morning and headed back towards Astana. As we were leaving we bumped into Nikolai, the sheepy Russian who allowed us into the park at 10 p.m. the other night. He met us with huge smiles and asked to come back to England with us in TT – this is quite a frequent request. He also wanted me to get together with his 18-year-old son. When I told him I was engaged, he suggested throwing away the ring and marrying him instead. Next was the petrol station, my least favourite hangout in Kazakhstan. The petrol was 50 per cent more expensive than anywhere else and there was a crowd of very drunk locals, who decided it would be funny to steal our keys. They finally gave them back and we tukked off quickly, because the men were all drunk and quite creepy.

During the drive it started to rain and strong gusts of wind reduced our speed to 35 mph. After about four hours we got to Astana and ferreted out a hotel that seemed like a ripoffski for what it was. Apparently the hotel prices in Astana have skyrocketed over the past couple of years, and so we were reluctant to search around to save a few dollars.

As it was Fiona's last night, she kindly took us out for supper. We picked a local Russian restaurant and enjoyed a mixture of salads, chicken (not for Mr Ant as she is vegetarianski) and mushrooms with cheese. During supper we were serenaded by a group of men who looked decidedly un-Russian or Kazakh. It turned out they were Indian. They sung beautiful Russian folk music while flashing us their gleaming gold gnashers – I think they have been in Kazakhstan a while and picked up the local fashion.

This morning we said goodbye to Fiona and headed for Russia. When we stopped for lunch at a roadside café, a wedding party pulled up and insisted on the bride and groom having a photo shoot with TT. The bride was wearing a flowing white gown and TT made her look even more stunning. Lunch was the usual exciting stuff: tomato salad, fried eggs, macaroni and bread. I bet you're jealous when you guys in the UK are probably enjoying Pimms and BBQs. Bastards (only joking).

After lunch the wind picked up and the roads began to deteriorate. We both started having flashbacks of Yunnan in China. Still, straight perfect tarmac can get a bit boring after a while. We soon realised that we didn't have a hope of getting to our intended destination. So right now we are in a wood sitting around a roaring campfire. We have had some samphire (sea asparagus picked at Lake Tenghiz by Ants and Fiona), tomatoes and bread. I have managed to burn myself on a hot brick and our tent is erected and ready for us to crawl into. I hope we won't be disturbed by drunk locals or wild animals. Any sleep would be a bonus. Tomorrow we continue towards the border. This time tomorrow,

I hope, we will be in Russia. I cannot think of a more perfect way to spend our last night in Kazakhstan.

I nearly forgot a couple of things so I will add them now. Three is the magic number and to prove it I was stung today three times by small bees. Kazakhstan is a multicultural country: we started our campfire using a Chinese sanitary towel and a Swedish FireSteel, we are drinking Russian vodka, TT is a Thai tuk tuk and our tent is from Korea. We have witnessed some amazing sunsets here – particularly over Lake Tenghiz – and we have been privileged to see birds of prey hunting in their natural environment. That's all folks.

 Sunday 23 July, Kostanai, Kazakhstan

 The end of the earth

Well, we didn't make it to Russia today. Tonight, Jo, Ting Tong and I find ourselves in Kostanai, a big town in North West Kazakhstan, a hop, skip and a jump away from the Russian border. As we sat round the campfire last night, we didn't think for a minute that we would be spending another night in this country. We were sure that today would see us crossing the border at Troitsk and tukking on to Chelyabinsk.

On Friday night, in Astana, we got talking to Nurzhan, a handsome, expensively dressed Kazakh. Jo and I had been sitting in the bar of our hotel poring over the map and deliberating our best route to Russia. Since we were racing against time to beat the expiration dates of our Kazakh visas, we were after the fastest route possible. It was either north to Petropavlosk or north west to Kostanai. Nurzhan strolled into the bar and, as is customary here, immediately struck up a conversation with us. Being a native, we felt sure he could advise us of the best route. After a short period of careful consideration, he pointed towards Kostanai: 'Zees one ees best I think. Zis is ze main route to Europe, ze. route all ze big trucks take from Russia and Germany.' Since the road was encouragingly called the M36 and cut an impressive red line across North West Kazakhstan, our decision was made. The M36 it was.

Cut to 18 hours later, where Jo and I are driving along this Central Asia–Europe superhighway. It's a single-lane track across cornfields and we haven't seen a car for two hours. Kostanai is another 210 miles. At 8 p.m. we decide we haven't a hope in hell or heaven of reaching civilisation by nightfall, and we set up camp in our little copse.

I'm not the best of campers. I love the romantic notion of being in some beautiful spot, at one with nature, the stars twinkling overhead, and waking up to the sun rising over a meadow of flowers. But the reality is somewhat different – a cold, sleepless night spent terrified that the local axe-murderer will come and finish me off. Last night, however, was excellent. Yes, it was a little cold, and no, we didn't get much sleep, but it was so much fun camping in the middle of our wild wood at the end of the earth and warming our mitts round a blazing campfire that I'm willing to gloss over the minor discomfort. So it was with high spirits that Jo and I tukked out of our sylvan shelter at 8.30 a.m. today. Having been freezing all night, we were both attired a little strangely. Jo in her Yi apron of course and me at the wheel in two rugs and my sleeping bag. Just as we emerged from the trees, with Jo running beside TT to guide us out, a truck drove past and we were met by an 'Am I seeing things?' look from the quizzical driver. What a funny sight we must have been: a pink tuk tuk and two very odd-looking girls emerging from the undergrowth early on a Sunday morning.

Our high spirits soon evaporated when the reality of the road became apparent. For two hours we saw not a single car. The road, dotted with sporadic signs to Yekaterinburg in Russia, was cratered with *huge* holes. Moreover, the sky was an angry mass of low black clouds and an ill wind was buffeting Ting Tong in an alarming manner. All we saw were flocks of black crows taking off in fright as we tukked past, and the occasional herd of horses. No houses, no cars and no people. Just as we were becoming concerned about our petrol situation and I was wondering whether this road really went anywhere, a town appeared in the distance.

As we drew closer, I could see that the houses were dilapidated, the windows mainly smashed and the roofs full of holes. It must be derelict, I thought, and began to get the feeling that this whole area had been abandoned with the collapse of the USSR, hence the hideous disrepair of the road and the antiquated signs to Yekaterinburg.

I was wrong. As we drove through the edge of the town, I saw an old babushka hobbling along the street and a bashed-up Lada creaking along a track. More surprising, we were able to find petrol, where the prices on the rusted pumps were still in roubles. The whole place was eerie. Neither of us could believe that people actually lived here in this desolate, windswept corner of the steppe. It felt like a ghost town, with people clinging on to the shreds of civilisation. I wonder what life must be like for the inhabitants. Judging by the shelves full of vodka in the local store, escapism is a popular choice. (The average life expectancy for men here is 58, thanks mainly to alcohol abuse.) My, oh my! Seeing that place made me appreciate how lucky we are in our cosy little Western lives.

Lunch was a classic. Jo and I stopped at the only café we'd seen for hours and extricated ourselves from Ting Tong, both still wearing our ridiculous outfits. For some reason, Jo's Yi apron never ceases to make me cry with laughter. It must look even funnier to a bunch of Russian truckers in a roadside café. Our hair was standing on end from all the wind, and we tripped into the café in a flurry of ponchos, rugs, aprons and sleeping bags. Whether it was the apron, Ting Tong or our English charm, we quickly befriended two truckers, who'd seen us on TV in Almaty. When we asked for the bill, they very kindly insisted on paying and off we went.

After eight freezing windy hours, we arrived in Kostanai. Neither of us expected to experience such bitter weather in Kazakhstan, even though we are just south of Siberia. Today was a chilly reminder that TT sure ain't a cold-weather car. Tomorrow we are going to equip ourselves with some hardcore cold-weather gear in case of further inhospitable climes in Russia.

Enough from me for now. I'm off to have a sauna to warm up and then tip into bed for an early night. Tomorrow we hope we really will be in Russia.

 Wednesday 26 July, Yekaterinburg, Sverdlovskaya oblast, Russia

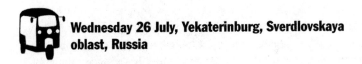 From Russia with love

I know, the title is a terrible cliché, but sometimes clichés are hard to resist – and Jo and I were so relieved to make it into Russia late on Monday night it was love at first sight.

On Monday morning, after a rocky 125-mile drive from Kostanai, we tukked up to the Russian border at Troitsk, 125 miles south of Chelyabinsk on the edge of the West Siberian Plain. We had every reason to be a little nervous, since our Kazakh visa had expired four days previously. Earthquakes, mechanical problems and bad roads meant that we'd been unable to keep to the tight two-week visa issued to us three months ago in the UK, and it's basically impossible to extend tourist visas in Kazakhstan. So we were just going to have to smile angelically and hope the guards were in a good mood.

In the shadow of three colossal factory chimneys belching black smoke across the plains, we pulled up at the back of a small queue of (mainly) Ladas at the border. Jo insisted we behaved well and didn't do our usual habit of queue-barging since, as she said, we didn't 'want to draw any attention to ourselves'. Considering the nature of our vehicle, I thought this was fairly impossible, but I complied anyway. Fistful of documents in hand, I walked into the small wooden hut by the barrier, where a woman with scarily dyed red hair was officiously stamping documents and a man was snoring noisily in the corner. A faint whiff of vodka hung in the air. Ten minutes later I was gone, clutching more documents and feeling very relieved that Red Hair hadn't noticed the little problem of our invalid visa. It seemed that all we had to do now was wait until, car by car, we were let through the barrier to passport control.

Three hours later we were through to the next stage, and Jo and TT waited while I went to meet our fate at passport control. A surly-looking man said '*Zdrastvuyte*' through the small window and took our passports, while I gave him my most winning smile. It didn't work. Within a nanosecond, the window was abruptly slammed shut and the man disappeared into another building across the road. Two minutes later he and another guard reappeared and summoned me into a small dreary room where a number of officials came in and questioned me about why we were late exiting the country. I gulped as one of them told me glumly that we had a '*bolshoi problem*' and would have to go back to Astana to validate our visas. Considering it had taken us over two days of hellish driving to get from the capital, this was a most unappealing option.

Yet once again the gods were on our side. No one it seems can resist the charms of Ting Tong, and I was soon told that we could go... not even a fine. Unbelievable. Here we were in Kazakhstan, a country notorious for corrupt officials dying to extract dollars from all and sundry, we had every reason to be fined and beaten, and we were about to sail through to Russia without even a slap on the wrist.

As we were leaving the hut, we saw the other side of the coin. Three Turkish men were engaged in heated conversation with the same group of officials who had been so lenient with us. The youngest of the Turks came and spoke to us, furious that they were being forced to pay money for no reason. They'd driven from Ankara to here, and nowhere else had they experienced problems. I guess we were very, very lucky indeed.

It was 5.30 p.m. by the time we tukked across the border, waving goodbye to Kazakhstan and hello to Russia. Only Ladas, barriers and wooden huts stood between us and the biggest country in the world. Once again I took our documents and headed for the barrier hut, where I was greeted by Anatoly Konstanteenovich Lookanov, the lone guard on duty. His green eyes twinkled with mirth as he looked through the documents, asked about the journey and tried to decipher TT's Thai registration documents. So fascinated was he by the sight of this rare Thai species that he left the confines of his hut and came for a closer inspection, joining the gold-toothed crowd that had gathered in my absence, and creasing with laughter at TT's three wheels and hot-pink paintwork.

More waiting... For another three hours we sat in the queue, making friends with everyone, letting all the children have a TT experience, playing badminton, letting people take pictures... until finally the barriers opened and the whole queue of cars was ushered through to passport control. The end was in sight – and within ten minutes we had all the right stamps and were heading for the door. Then we remembered the small matters of insurance for Ting Tong and the dreaded *deklaratzia* (customs declaration form). Insurance was easy enough, once the bleached-blonde assistant had got over the shock of the Thai registration papers, but the *deklaratzia* took us an agonising extra two hours to finalise. In short, a *deklaratzia* is a vital piece of paper for anyone coming into Russia. If you don't fill it in correctly and get all the right stamps, you are liable to get all your money and equipment confiscated when you leave. This would have meant losing cameras, laptops, the BGAN, etc., etc. – not an option. As Dimi, the 26-year-old guard, was filling out our *deklaratzia* for the eighth time, I asked him whether many English people came through this border. He screwed up his face and thought hard. 'In May we have a Holland, and in February we have two Australians. I can't remember Eenglish here.' No wonder it was all taking so long.

At last, at 10.30 p.m., in the dwindling light, we walked out to TT and into Russia. Five or six guards came over to ask casually whether we had any drugs on us and to send us on our way. After drawing us a map to a hotel in Troitsk, the nearest town, we waved goodbye and tukked off into the darkness. What relief! What a day!

But it wasn't over yet.

In Troitsk, 20 miles from the border, we drew up outside the aforementioned hotel, a grandiose mansion in the early stages of decrepitude. The receptionist shook her head. They were full. Yeah, right, I thought – a huge hotel like this full on a Monday night. We'd heard that some Russian hotels can be unwilling to take foreigners, a hangover from the Soviet era, and I am sure it was this unwillingness rather than a genuine lack of rooms that was the reason we were turned away. The same thing happened at the second hotel, and Jo and I started to wonder whether we might have to pitch our tent on the pavement. But thank goodness – hotel number three, the Gostiniza Kaspi, said yes, they had one room left. Phew!

At 11.45 p.m., tired, grubby and much in need of tipple and tiffin, we sat down for supper in the hotel restaurant. Our only fellow diners were three very drunk men in one corner, and a pair of heavily made-up, fairly drunk 30-something women in another corner. It wasn't long before we were spotted by the former, and subsequently accosted, while a DJ appeared out of nowhere and put on hideous, ear-splittingly loud eurotechno. Having successfully used eating supper as an excuse not to join them, our prospective paramours – Mikhail, Dimitri and Alexei – retreated to the dance floor and began throwing some serious shapes and blowing kisses in our direction. Very funny. They soon returned, however, to propose that they be our boyfriends in Russia – despite the fact they were all wearing wedding rings and Jo and I said we were married. We'd been warned this might happen a bit here...

At 2 a.m. we crashed into bed, elated to be in Russia and looking forward to the next stage of the adventure.

The next morning I awoke early and left Jo snoring in bed to go and investigate the local market. We'd been so paralysingly cold in the past few days that I wanted to find us some warm clothes so we wouldn't have to drive in our sleeping bags.

Two hours later I returned, not with any warm clothes but with a baby hedgehog called Henry. I'd found Henry in the market, being sold by two mischievous little boys who'd caught the unfortunate beast the day before. Henry looked very unhappy in his little box, being prodded by passers-by, so the only solution was to rescue him and think about what to do with him later. He was *so* sweet, with beetly black eyes and a long twitchy nose. It was tempting to secrete him in TT, give him some goggles and bring him back to England with us. But of course this wasn't possible, and two hours later we released him in a silver birch copse in the middle of some farmland, where he scuttled off into the undergrowth without even a wave goodbye.

Our destination that day was Yekaterinburg, about 250 miles north west of Troitsk. We hadn't intended to go there, but we decided it sounded more interesting than Chelyabinsk, plus it would add a few extra miles to our world record bid. At 3 p.m. the heavens opened. Anuwat warned us to be careful in the rain and that Ting Tong's spark plugs wouldn't be happy if they got wet, but we'd always been OK before. We carried on driving through the rain at a sedate 25 mph. Anuwat's wise words soon became reality and TT began to splutter in an unseemly manner. It wasn't until 11 p.m. that we finally made it here, to Yekaterinburg, having crawled along in the rain at 25 mph for the last 100 miles, with TT choking and backfiring.

We've only been in Yekaterinburg for 36 hours and once again Jo and I have been overwhelmed by the kindness of strangers. While fruitlessly searching for our hotel late on Tuesday night, we met Ivan, a local radio presenter, who speaks very good English. Without him we would never have found the Gostiniza Academia Geologia, tucked away on a dark side street behind Prospekta Lenina. Nor would we have found a safe place to park our three-wheeled friend. Ivan, a philosophical, highly intelligent 31-year-old, was fascinated with our trip and went home and posted all about it on a local website. Among those who read the site were two 21-year-old boys, Oleg and Rudy, who, with nothing better to do, decided to go and search for the 'tuk tuk girls'. So there we were, in a random little Internet café yesterday evening, when two (very handsome indeed) boys came over and said 'Are you the two driving the pink car to England?' They had come to this café to use the Internet and track us down – and walked straight into us. Extraordinary – Yekaterinburg is a big city with 1.4 million inhabitants and they had stumbled upon us by total chance. Even funnier was when they showed us the website on which Ivan had posted, with a long thread all about the funny pink car that had been spotted last night coming into the city. Oleg and Rudy knew exactly where we had been, where we had got lost, where we had parked to ask directions... all from the replies to Ivan's posting.

This morning Jo has gone off with Ivan, Oleg and Rudy to get TT seen by a mechanic found by Ivan through his posting, and I've gone off to take our DV camera to the Sony service centre and do Internet chores. The little bugger has an audio problem that might not be fixable. I don't even want to think about it, and I begged the engineer at the centre to do his very best to sort it out.

Having spent four years attempting to learn Russian at school, it's wonderful to finally make it here. My Russian teacher, Mrs Ainsworth (she'd married an Englishman, hence the surname), appeared determined to paint as bad a picture as possible about her homeland to her three pupils, and she delighted in showing us videos about the Aral Sea, Chernobyl and glue-sniffing street urchins in Moscow. But then it was the early 1990s, when Russia was emerging painfully from the mantle of Sovietism, and the fistfuls of roubles Mrs Ainsworth would show us in class wouldn't even buy a loaf of stale bread. She didn't manage to dampen my desire to come here one day though, and I feel sure it will be one of the highlights of the trip. The driving is a bit hairy, but it has been everywhere. By the time we get back to England we'll be tailgating, overtaking on the inside verge and beeping like the best of them.

 Thursday 27 July, Yekaterinburg, Russia

 Ting Tong, the people magnet

We left Troitsk two days ago with a special gift from the local market, where Ants had gone to get some food and drinks and also to try and find us some warmer clothes. When she returned to our room she instructed me to put out my cigarette and close my eyes. I opened them to see a box with a pink towel in it, which on closer inspection I found to contain a baby hedgehog that Ants had bought at the market. We named him Henry and gave him a saucer of milk to drink. Then we had to smuggle him out of the hotel without the babushkas catching on to our little animal-rescue mission. As we drove through town, Ants popped to the local market again to get Henry some meat – a chicken wing, some sausages (which I ate) and some local pâté, which looked similar to what we feed our cat in England. We hit the main road and turned off on to a farmer's track and headed for some woods. Henry, Ants and I waded through a waist-high wheatfield and found a shady collection of trees far from the road and civilisation. We gave him some more milk and put the pâté in his box. Henry wasn't interested in hanging around to eat his lunch and scuttled off into the undergrowth, to a free and happy life I hope.

Then began our nightmare drive. The weather was cold and windy and it soon started to piss down with rain. Big trucks and cars were flying past TT, sending torrents of water all over us and her. Anuwat had warned me that in very heavy rain the spark plugs might get wet and cause problems. Sure enough, TT started to misfire, struggle and lose momentum. We pulled over and I had a real 'Oh, shit!' moment. We were in the middle of two cities, with nothing really in between, it was pouring with rain and TT had semi-broken down. Some locals we had met earlier had warned us that there were mafia and banditos on this road – great. Furthermore, our phone had decided not to let us make outgoing calls, and so we had to just hope that the rain would ease off and TT's sparks would dry out, if indeed that was the problem. I pulled out my faithful *Auto Repair For Dummies* and read all the info relating to spark plugs. I knew that we had about ten spare sparks, but I wasn't too keen to start trying to change them by the side of the road in the pouring rain. Luckily, my dad phoned at that moment and provided much-needed moral support. He told us to wait for about 30 minutes and then to try driving again.

It continued to rain, although with less intensity. We had no choice but to keep driving, and I prayed that TT would be able to safely take us to our intended destination. She was still having some issues and could drive at only about 30 mph, but at least she was moving. We finally arrived in the outskirts of Yekaterinburg at 10 p.m. but were initially delayed by a police stop, where our documents were checked and we were kept waiting for a good 20 minutes. This was the second time we had been stopped by the police that day, and we were cold, stressed, tired and not really in the mood to make small talk.

Then came the next challenge – trying to find our hotel. With TT farting, i.e. backfiring, around the streets of Yekaterinburg, we searched unsuccessfully for the right street. At 10.30 p.m., feeling cold, tired and pissed off, we pulled over and Ants went into a shop to ask for directions. While I waited, a guy came over to me and started asking about our trip – luckily for me, he spoke English. His name was Ivan and he was a presenter for a local radio station. In desperation, Ants asked him if he would hop into TT and join our search for the elusive hotel, which to our surprise he did. Twenty minutes later we finally located it, well and truly hidden down a back street. We unloaded our bags and set off with Ivan to find a secure place to park. After a couple of tries, we managed to persuade a security guard to let us park TT outside his hut for 60 roubles a night. Relieved, hungry and tired we then ended up in a Belgian restaurant with Ivan, eating Greek salad and drinking beer at gone midnight. We then returned to our hotel and hit the hay.

After a lie-in the next morning, we headed into town to register our visas, which tourists in Russia are obliged to do within three working days of arrival. When we tried to register our visas, we were informed that it would not be possible because first we had to go to the state bank and pay a rouble for each of the days that we planned to be in Yekaterinburg. As the office was closing soon, we would have to wait until Friday to register our visas. This meant that we would be a day late registering and may end up having to pay a £26 fine each – I hope we can work some TT magic and escape unpunished. Ants and I had no idea that these complicated rules for registering existed, and we didn't know where the state bank was. Luckily for us we got chatting to a lovely couple who offered to take us to the bank and help us. Christina was a local and she was with her Turkish boyfriend, Elich, who needed to get his visa registered. They had been dating for two years and met through an Internet chat site. Christina showed us to the bank and helped us to fill out our forms in Russian, before we paid the cashier six roubles each. I will let you be the judge of whether this makes sense or is economically profitable for the Russians. We then went out for a drink and had a long and interesting chat with our new friends about Turkey, Russia and life.

The following morning Ants went off to try and fix the video camera and I went off to get TT fixed. Ivan said he knew a mechanic but the guy didn't have a phone number. About 30 minutes later, Rudy and Oleg arrived with their friend Alexei, a keen photographer who also knew a good BMW garage. Alexei led the way in his BMW, and we arrived at a very professional garage full of smart Beamers. TT could hardly contain her excitement at being in the company of such attractive, powerful and sleek cars. I explained about the problems with the accelerator, spark plugs and windscreen wiper (which was misbehaving and had developed a mind of its own) and Rudy translated into Russian. I got out three new spark plugs and the mechanics set to work, promising that they would let me know when it was time to change the spark plugs. Meanwhile I relaxed upstairs on a leather sofa watching National Geographic and playing with a black kitten, which the guys informed me couldn't understand English.

I was fetched to see the old spark plugs and watch the new ones being inserted. The old ones were coated in black muck, probably due to the poor fuel quality we have had during our 7500-mile drive from Thailand. They showed me how to insert new ones and I watched carefully, in case the need arises for some DIY mechanics on the road relating to spark plugs. TT started first time with her new plugs and revved happily. Then it was time for a quick photo with all the mechanics, who then refused any payment for their services. What total dudes.

We headed back into town and stopped to get some petrol. Oleg phoned up a local news station and they agreed to come and film us when we arrived back in town. I tried to track down Mr Ant, but she was still ferreting around town. After a quick pizza we met the TV crew and they interviewed me, Rudy and Oleg, before filming TT driving around town. They found Ants' bottle of vodka and I had to hold it up to the camera, as well as my mechanics book and a Russian map that I can't read.

Tuk to the Road PR over, and we went back to the hotel and met up with Ants, who had been for a jog. After a quick shower we headed out for supper and some drinks and a bit of sightseeing. Apparently we were on the news at 8.30 p.m., but we were out and I didn't have to worry about seeing myself on camera. Now we are back in the hotel and I am sitting in the shower room writing this blog. I need to get to bed as it is 1.30 a.m. and we have an early start. We are splitting up again, with Ants off to the British Council and me to get our visas registered. Then around midday we are meeting Ivan for a radio interview.

I am very pleasantly surprised by Russia, although I didn't really know what to expect. It is an interesting place, the food is good, the cities are attractive and, most importantly, the people are great. Goodnight.

 Saturday 29 July, Yekaterinburg, Sverdlovskaya oblast, Russia

 Raving with the Romanovs

A glaring anachronistic impossibility I know, but read on and all will make sense.

Jo and I are still in Yekaterinburg, where we've been for four days. We didn't quite mean to stay this long, but since Russia is the first country we haven't had to pelt through in a dash to make our visa and permit deadlines, we thought we needed to wind down for a day or two. TT is now happily fixed and purring like a pink pussy cat, and we've got ourselves registered with OVIR (Office of Visas and Registration) – two essential chores we had to do here. Unfortunately, the problem of the DV camera hasn't been resolved and we've either got to wait here for three weeks while it is sent off to Moscow for a spare part or see whether I can get another one sent out from England. The latter option is far more likely.

Yekaterinburg is an interesting city, somewhere rarely frequented by foreigners and famous predominately for three things: the Romanovs were murdered here, Yeltsin was born here, and there was a spate of violent mafia killings in the early 1990s. Furthermore, the Second World War turned the city into a major producer of arms and hence it was closed to foreigners until 1990 because of its plethora of defence plants. Today the surrounding countryside still hides a number of these plants – the father of someone we met the other day is the boss of one such place, which produces ground-to-air missiles from a factory deep beneath the woods outside the city.

With Jo engaged with her bevy of BMW mechanics on Thursday, and my camera-fixing errands over, I set off for a walk round the city to explore some of this history. The highlight was the grandiose Church of the Blood, built in 2003 on the spot where Tsar Nicholas II, his family and servants were horribly murdered by the Bolsheviks. The house where they died, Dom Ipateva, was destroyed by the then governor Boris Yeltsin in 1977, and today the exact spot is marked by a simple cross in the shadow of the new gold-domed church.

The tale of the Romanovs' demise doesn't make for pleasant reading. On 16 July 1918, the tsar and his family were murdered by their Bolshevik guards, having been imprisoned for months in the wake of the Bolshevik revolution. For decades the question of what happened to the family after their deaths remained unanswered. Then, in 1976, a group of local scientists discovered their remains near Ganina Yama, ten miles outside the city. So politically sensitive was this issue during the Soviet era that the discovery was kept quiet, and the remains were not excavated fully until 1991, when the bones of the nine people found were tentatively identified as those of the tsar, his wife Alexandra, three of their four daughters, the royal doctor and three servants. Absent were the bones of the fourth daughter, Anastasia, and the only son, Alexey.

In 1992, with the help of the DNA of Prince Philip (a grandson of the tsarina's sister) and the pioneering work of a British forensic team, it was established with 98.5 per cent accuracy that these were indeed the Romanov remains. The full story of their ignominious end was then unfurled by a Russian inquiry.

According to this inquiry, the bodies of the five children and their parents were dumped in an abandoned mine shaft near Ganina Yama. Grenades and acid were used to destroy the remains, but the job was done so badly and the operation so bungled that the bodies were still almost fully intact when unearthed 73 years later. What a gruesome end for Russia's last tsar and his family, who today have been sainted and buried at St Peter and Paul Cathedral in St Petersburg.

It seems strange to me that a short walk from the Church of the Blood is Prospekt Lenina, where an austere statue of Lenin dominates the main square. Yet it was his party, his revolution, that killed the Romanovs, whom the city has recently gone to great lengths to commemorate. I went to see Kevin Lynch, the British consul general here, yesterday and put this question to him. He replied that of course the Russians are aware of the contradiction, but Lenin is an integral part of their history and what happened in 1917–18 cannot simply be wiped from the history books. A fair and valid point of course, and I would be intrigued to find out more about how Russians today view Lenin and the Bolshevik Revolution.

Right, history lesson over... on to the raving bit.

Last night Jo and I hit the tiles for the first time in our nine-week tukathon. After a few drinks with Kevin Lynch and a gang of British and American diplomats, we tripped off to Yekaterinburg's number-one nightclub, the Snow Project, with Oleg and Rudy.

Jo and I obviously met the right boys in Oleg and Rudy, for we strolled into the uber-hip Snow Project at midnight waving the free VIP passes they had procured for us all – it normally costs 500 roubles to get in. I'd expected to go to a few clubs in Russia and had heard that there were some decent ones, but I never expected to find anywhere like this. After going though the obligatory metal detectors – everywhere here – and getting our UV stamps, we entered the most incredible main room, far more glamorous and better decked-out than any British club I've ever been to. Girls with the most ridiculous pairs of legs danced on podiums and sashayed past in absurdly high heels, skirts they might as well not have bothered wearing, and make-up several inches thick. Enormous sunglasses and blingtastic jewels completed the look. And there were Jo and I, in our jeans and trainers.

With Graeme Lloyd, from Turnmills in London, on the ones and twos, we all danced until 5 a.m., leaving as the sunrise was flooding the horizon red. Graeme spun some great tracks and we were introduced to him after his set. We had a quick chat, before leaving him to two keen blondes. All in all it was a fantastic night out – Jo and I think we should make it the first of many on the European leg of the trip.

Which takes me on to my next subject... Russian women. When on earth do they make the transition from tottering dolly-bird to doddering babushka? It must be overnight, for there doesn't seem to be any in-between stage. Jo and I stick out like sore thumbs here, for the simple fact we lack three-inch heels, heavily dyed hair and a hefty helping of make-up.

After five days here we're finally leaving in the morning, for Ufa, via the Urals. After six miles we'll cross the divide into Europe. What a strange thought – home is almost in sight.

 Monday 31 July, Hotel Tourist, Ufa, Bashkortostan Autonomous Republic, Russia

 TT does it five times in one day!

We left Yekaterinburg yesterday morning, driving in convoy with Rudy and Oleg to the Asia/Europe border, where we parked TT with her front end in Europe and her back end in Asia. It gave us a brief moment to reflect on how long we've been tukking and how far we've travelled. We left Bangkok nine weeks ago and have travelled 8000 miles. Being back in Europe has made us think about our arrival back in Brighton. We need to start planning for a big homecoming and work out quite how we are going to raise another £29000 for Mind.

Saying goodbye to Rudy and Oleg was really sad, and I cried. Even though we'd known them for only four days, we'd spent nearly every waking moment with them and become really close. If it wasn't for meeting them, TT would never had got to flirt with those sexy Beamers; nor would we have been on the local news and got to speak about our trip and mental health. It was also sad saying goodbye to Ivan, the first friend we made in Yekaterinburg, after we kidnapped him to show us where our hotel was.

On Friday night Ants and I hit the tiles for the first time on this trip, with Rudy and Oleg. Ants and I had both been quite tired earlier in the day and had returned to the hotel for a siesta before even contemplating going clubbing. We surprised ourselves by managing to stay up until 6 a.m., hanging out in the VIP area all night and hitting the dance floor a couple of times to throw some shapes. Some of the people in the club looked (and acted) like they were high on more than just the music. The music was house, not garage and not uplifting garden shed. Why the stupid names for dance-music genres? There was an English DJ playing, and Ants and I were introduced to him once his set had finished. He asked what we were doing in Yekaterinburg and I explained, before thrusting a business card into his hand and telling him to read our website.

Russia has definitely exceeded my expectations and I would suggest that people come and check out areas outside St Petersburg and Moscow. My only complaints are the Baltic weather and the overly efficient traffic cops, who have stopped us seven times in the past two days, including five times today. Mostly they just want to see our documents and ask questions about TT. Even though Ants speaks very good Russian, when we get pulled over with that irritating white baton she speaks as much Russian as I do – *none*! Given that the weather has been incredibly English, i.e. cold, wet and grey, we are starting to find these all too frequent police stops in the cold a little trying.

 ## Crossing the divide

After five days off the road, the travelling trio once again hit the tarmac yesterday morning to head for Ufa... and Europe. Under a leaden sky we loaded up a sodden Ting Tong and headed out of Yekaterinburg, Jo driving, with Oleg in the back, and me with Rudy, filming our soggy exit from the city. We never even meant to go to Yekaterinburg, let alone stay there for four days, but as Ivan, quoting Voltaire, said: 'Everything happens for a reason.' I don't go for the full Celestine Prophecy version of everything being some part of a predestined design, but I do subscribe to the attitude that many occurrences in our lives are more than simply an accident, and Yekaterinburg was a classic example. Jo and I went on a whim, deciding it sounded interesting and worth the 200-mile northern diversion, and thanks to that whim we ended up meeting Ivan, Rudy and Oleg, all extremely lovely people, who did everything they could to help us and show us round their city. As we said goodbye to Ivan, he said it was his dream to come to England: 'To see Stratford-upon-Avon, and to perform *The Tempest*. But first I must be wise – for a man to perform thees play, I think he must be wise.' Ivan, with his passion for Shakespeare, Voltaire and Irish folk music, is already wise, and it was a joy to meet such an unusual, intelligent person in the midst of a city we never intended to visit.

Just six miles outside of Yekaterinburg we came to the Europe/Asia border, where we parked up, took some snaps and contemplated what had been before and what lies ahead. As I stood with one leg in each continent, I thought of all the places and faces we have seen, and all the extraordinary experiences we've had, and wondered what the next leg of Tuk to the Road had in store for us. I wondered how you can just draw a line and say that right there one world ends and another begins. Moreover, the Russia we have experienced has rarely felt even faintly Asian. The last time I felt we were truly in Asia was at Saryam Lake in China, among the nomads and yurts. Since then, that Asian sense of otherness has faded, each day seeming more and more familiar, more European. But then again, Russia doesn't feel quite like the Europe most of us know – there's an edge to it you don't get in the Bois de Boulogne, plus a hell of a lot more hookers and hummers. But it feels a very long way from North West China, where only a month ago we were sweltering at 40°C.

After our first lunch in Europe, we said a sad goodbye to Rudy and Oleg and set off in the general direction of Ufa, not really sure of where we would end up that night. There was no direct road, and so after studying the Russian atlas we decided to go the scenic route, dropping down through the Middle Urals into the Bashkortostan Republic. Aside from the incessant rain, which we all have a strong aversion to, and the almost as incessant police checks, we had an uneventful drive through beautiful country. Not since China have we driven through such natural beauty. The road plunged, weaved and climbed through rolling green countryside, populated by silver birch copses, herds of grazing animals and an abundance of wild flowers. Freshly cut piles of hay dotted the fields and farm workers laboured with scythes, looking up in astonishment as we drove past. Occasionally we passed through a village of wooden houses, all with ornate, brightly coloured windows. Beautiful.

Five police stops later, at 8 p.m., we came across a roadside hotel and decided to call it a day, where I left Jo with TT and dived in to check it out. After the corpulent receptionist had finished getting her oversize knickers in a twist about the fact that, first, we were *inostranka* (foreigners) and, second, we had a curious vehicle that was *nyet motocikla i nyet mashina* (not a motorbike, not a car), we were allowed in. Twenty minutes and one beer later, Jo and I had acquired our next pair of Russian boyfriends, Roma and Zanil, both from Tyumen in Siberia. As we have both said before, Russians are wonderfully friendly people, sometimes the men a little over so, and it's hard to sit anywhere for five minutes without being accosted by a potential suitor. Before long, a third, slightly inebriated, gentleman had come over to our table and was declaring undying love for Jo. It was 1 a.m. before we finally got to bed.

This morning we set off, again in the rain, for the last 100 miles to Ufa, capital of the autonomous Bashkortostan Republic, home to the Muslim Turkic Bashkir people. We met our first Bashkir, Zoofar, last night, who very kindly asked us to his sanatorium – a kind of Russian Champneys – *bezplatno* (free of charge). Although the idea of being pampered in the mountains for a day was very appealing, we opted to hit the road and head south west in search of the sunshine. Having spent the last week getting cold and wet every day, we're craving some heat and have decided to reroute south along the Black Sea coast via Odessa for a few days of sun, sea and surf.

This afternoon was spent tukking along a spectacular road across the heart of the Urals. Trucks loaded with German cars bound for Kazakhstan clanked past us, and a constant line of bored-looking babushkas hawked honey by the roadside. Although honey isn't the most practical thing to travel with, we couldn't resist and pulled over by the neediest-looking babushka we could find to make a purchase. A Kazakh lorry was parked 60 feet away and I had a quick chat with the driver, who told me he drives back and forth between Germany and Kazakhstan covering 4500 miles in ten days. Poor man – I don't envy his job.

As we turned Ting Tong on to the road, a lady selling berries next door ran after us and pushed a large jar of raspberries into my hands, wishing us a good journey – a small gesture that is typical of the kindness of the Russians.

It's midnight now and so time to go to bed... but one last anecdote before lights out. As we arrived at our hotel this evening, a stumbling, red-faced group of army officers lurched out of the adjacent bar. One of them, toad-faced, middle-aged and more than a little tipsy, locked his eyes lasciviously on Jo and planted a lingering, sloppy kiss on her cheek. By the time I had got us a room five minutes later, Jo had been fully groped, kissed repeatedly and proposed to. Evoking our imaginary husbands was no use at all, and Jo and I had to dash into the hotel under the cover of our baggage to avoid further gropage. At this rate we could have multiple husbands by the time we leave Russia, should we wish. What a thought.

Wednesday 2 August, Samara, Volga oblast, Russia

 Rain, rain, go away

It is 11 a.m. and I am sitting in bed listening to the deluge of rain falling on the windowsill outside. Neither of us expected weather like this, and TT hates it even more than we do. After the episode when her spark plugs got wet on the way to Yekaterinburg, we are now very wary of driving in wet conditions. Therefore, we will be staying a second night at the Hotel Ripoffski.

We left Ufa yesterday morning and it was my turn to drive first. Ufa is a very strangely designed city, being over 12 miles long and shaped like a dumbbell – it must be a total pain if you are a teenager and your best mates live the other end of the dumbbell. Having got a little lost leaving Ufa, we then followed the M5 all the way to Samara – but don't think it is anything like the lovely motorway connecting the West Country to the Midlands. Actually, it wasn't a particularly bad road; for the most part it was in good condition and we could drive at up to 60 mph.

We beat our record yesterday of police stops and managed eight. Strangely, most of the police that stopped us knew we were travelling from Thailand to England. I can only assume they are somehow communicating and warning the next patrol unit to watch out for a strange pink vehicle. Only once were we asked for our documents. Ants and I have had a bet as to how many times we think we will be stopped in Russia in total. I estimated under 30 and Ants over 30. At the rate we were going yesterday, Ants is likely to win the bet.

After what felt like a really long day on the road, we arrived in Samara in the dark and set about finding a hotel. The first place was full, the second place didn't accept foreigners, and the third was thoroughly overpriced and we were told that all of the hot water in the city had stopped working, i.e. they had problems with their plumbing. As it was dark and raining we were left with no choice but to stay at the last Hotel Ripoffski.

We were told that if we wanted a shower we would have to go down to the second floor. I felt quite tempted to go down to reception and drop my towel, in protest at the fact that our bathroom is useless for washing and they are not offering any kind of discount for the inconvenience. Unfortunately for them, I decided not to bless them with my naked flesh.

Last night we encountered a strange sight. As we walked along the banks of the mighty Volga, Europe's longest river, we both stopped in our tracks to stare at a large python wrapped around a young woman. She offered us 'photo with the snake', which we declined and instead opted to stroke the cold scaly skin of this impressive reptile. Thank God I wasn't walking my ferrets at the time.

Ants and I both feel a little strange at the moment. Personally, I feel pretty flat, uninspired and uninspiring. I am hoping it is just a phase and that I will come out the other side. Even though we are doing this amazing trip, it is not possible, I don't think, to always feel happy and be having an amazing time. Emotions are something that wash over you continuously, even though you may not want to feel a certain emotion at a certain time, i.e. feeling below par even though there is nothing in particular to cause the feeling. I have said it before, but I think the weather is having a huge effect on my mood. I hate the rain, and when it is cold, grey and miserable in England I hibernate indoors. We cannot do that on this trip and have to carry on tukking, regardless of the weather. I am not complaining, because I love this adventure. It's just that sometimes my heart doesn't love it as much as I want it to.

 Not the Samara we had envisaged

The Lonely Planet says of Samara, where we now find ourselves, that 'in summer the Volga's riverbanks are packed with bathing beauties, rollerbladers and beer drinkers'. With this idyllic image at the forefront of our minds, Jo and I left rainy Ufa yesterday, feeling very excited about a day or two sunbathing by the banks of Europe's longest river. Such was not to be; as has now become the norm in Russia, I awoke this morning to the symphony of mosquitoes dive-bombing my head and rain hammering on the windows. Visions of spending a sybaritic day lounging by the river evaporated in an instant. And since Ting Tong has made it very clear that driving in the rain is not her favourite pastime (or ours) we opted to don our very fetching tropical ponchos and hang out in soggy Samara for the day instead. What a riot.

Yesterday was our longest day on the road for a while, and it seemed to go on and on and on and on... The countryside was beautiful and the roads passable, but nothing spectacular. The oddest thing was the endless police stops – eight yesterday. But although all our previous stops have included a demand for our *dokumenti*, all but one of yesterday's cop stops were simply to have a nose at Ting Tong and ask all the usual 'Where are you going?', 'Where are you from?', 'Aren't you cold?' (yes!) and 'Where are the men?' type of questions. Furthermore, most of the police stopping us seemed to know the basic details of our journey, i.e. that we were travelling from Thailand to England. We suspect that this is thanks to the two policemen who bought us cake and chatted to us in a truckers' café at lunch, who then must have warned their cohorts further down the line of the pink oddity heading their way. We can now pretty much guarantee that at every police checkpoint, that irritating black-and-white baton will wave us down as we try and tuk past inconspicuously.

I've discovered in the past 24 hours a peculiar paradox that exists in Russia – one of many I am sure. Our blog during the past week has been full of praise for the incredible hospitality and friendliness we have encountered here. But our infuriating, exhausting quest for a hotel room late last night, after ten hours on the road, in the rain, was hindered by what I can only call xenophobia. The hatchet-faced receptionist at hotel number one, the disgusting-looking Hotel Rossiya, informed me very frostily that they had no rooms. At hotel number two, I didn't even get past the door, being physically blocked from entering by a bad-tempered old goat who curled his lips in disgust at the sound of my foreign accent and told me that this was a hotel for Russians only. I tried to duck past him to verify this with the receptionist, but he barred my way and sent us packing. Hotel number three was the same, and hotel number four, the wildly overpriced Zhiguli, let us in. Jo and I objected to paying 3300 roubles (over £60) for a room with no hot water, but it was either that or the pavement.

Finally, I want to add an appendage to my blog about the Romanovs from the other day. My father, the Biggest Boffin in the Business, who has been to St Petersburg twice, wrote the following in an email a few days ago: 'I have in front of me a four-page article from the *St Petersburg Times* dated 17 July 1998, which casts a huge amount of doubt on the whole business. The most significant piece of evidence is that Tsar Nicholas was attacked by a madman during his 1891 visit to Japan and that his skull was permanently scarred. No sign of such a scar was found by the investigators of the Commission of the Identification of the Remains established in 1993. At the time of the reburial in St Petersburg, nearly every leading Russian newspaper published articles doubting the authenticity of the bones.' Maybe my next foreign sojourn will be a hunt for the real Romanov remains...

That's all for today. I wish the rain would stop because it's getting boring. With luck, this time next week we'll be soaking up some rays in the Crimea, where we have decided to reroute to in search of sun and extra mileage.

 Saturday 5 August, Volgograd, Volga oblast, Russia

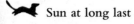 Sun at long last

We have arrived at our last city in Russia before crossing into Ukraine early next week. We are staying in the originally named Volgograd Hotel, which is a huge characterful building that has been restored to its original splendour after being destroyed in the Second World War.

We left Samara two days ago in the sunshine. The rain had decided to stop, and Ants and I were thrilled to cast aside our ponchos and jackets to wear T-shirts again. Ants went off to get TT while I packed up and finished checking out. Ants returned after about 30 minutes with the bad news that TT had stubbornly refused to start. So I stopped emptying our room and we both returned to TT, determined to get her running. Of course I took my faithful *Auto Repair For Dummies* with me.

We nearly got TT started, but in the end we had to accept the kind offer of a pull-start from a Lada. Drama over, we drove TT back to the hotel. However, the drama was only 50 per cent over as TT was misfiring like a trooper again, as the old spark issues seemed to have returned with a vengeance. We decided to leave her in the sunshine to see whether this would cheer her up enough to drive smoothly. In the meantime, Ants contacted a local TV crew with whom she had been in touch and they came over to interview us. We gave an interview and farted up and down the street in TT, before parking her up again and heading off for lunch.

After lunch we went back to the hotel and loaded up TT. As we emerged from the hotel, we were surprised to find a British hearse parked outside – a team from the Mongol Rally called The Hearse Flies. The aim of the rally is to drive a cheap car from England to Mongolia as fast as possible and auction the car for charity on reaching Ulan Bator. We would have loved to chat to the brave hearse drivers for longer, but we were being shown out of the city by our new pals from the TV station and couldn't keep them waiting.

We started the long drive towards Volgograd, planning to stop somewhere around Saratov to camp. In the early evening we pulled off the main road and drove about one mile into a field of newly harvested hay. I was a bit worried that we were trespassing and might get into trouble, but our spot seemed pretty remote and we couldn't see any signs of civilisation, so we parked TT behind a haystack and set up our tent.

We had a typical camping meal of pasta and tomato sauce from a jar, checked our emails and had a game of badminton, before retiring to our tent, covered in 100 per cent DEET to try to ward off the large persistent mozzies that had been attacking us all evening. If a local farmer had come across us he probably wouldn't have believed his eyes – two foreign girls playing badminton in the middle of his field next to a bright-pink tuk tuk.

We awoke the next morning to sunshine and another day of good weather. After a quick breakfast of porridge, we packed up TT and tried to start her. Can you guess what happened? She wouldn't start. So, we pushed her further across the field into a patch of sunshine and let her sunbathe. After about half an hour she did start and we tukked off towards Saratov, with the intention of reaching Volgograd that night, some 350-plus miles away.

TT flew along for the first couple of hours but then started to misfire again. I checked that the boots covering her sparks were attached securely and found that one of them was not secure enough. She seemed a bit better but was still not driving brilliantly, so when we stopped for lunch we drove TT over to a neighbouring garage, where the mechanics discovered that one of her three new sparks had already gone. We replaced all three and set off for Volgograd, arriving late last night, exhausted but relieved to have arrived for a weekend of relaxation and, we hope, some sunshine.

 A geek's tour of Volgograd

After 400 miles on the road, Jo and I chased the setting sun into Volgograd last night, very tired but happy to have got through another momentous day of Tuk to the Road. TT's recurrent troubles and a night of being besieged by monster mosquitoes hadn't helped our cause over the previous 36 hours, and we were both looking forward to a weekend off in the sunshine.

Arriving in a big city on a Friday night was a novel experience for both of us. Having thrown off the shackles of the working week and no doubt having already imbibed the odd tipple, the inhabitants seemed particularly glad to see Ting Tong. Girls tottering across zebra crossings screeched drunkenly as we tukked past and a red sports car crammed with overexcitable Russian boys escorted us most of the way into the centre. 'Russian boys... Eenglish girls... gooooood!' they shouted hopefully, begging us to pull over 'just for two minutes to have a chat'. On the other side of us a minibus driver shouted questions at Jo, and hence we drove into Volgograd blocking the three-lane carriageway, cars glued to either side of Ting Tong.

For me, Volgograd means one thing, the battle of Stalingrad. Fought between July 1942 and February 1943, this was one of the vilest and most vital battles of the Second World War. Had the Red Army not fought so doggedly against the Germans, the war, and subsequent European history, could have been played out very differently. But victory came at a terrible cost, with at least 600 000 German troops and a million Russians lost in the fighting. Russian casualties here roughly equalled the number of Americans lost in the entire war, and by February 1943 the ancient city of Tsaritsyn (renamed Stalingrad in honour of the Great Leader) lay in ruins, not a building remaining intact. Walking around the city today, with its leafy boulevards, cosmopolitan cafés and swanky shops, it's hard to believe that only 63 years ago it was razed to the ground.

In delicious blazing sunshine this morning, after Jo and I had watched a load of wedding antics by the Volga, I set off to find out a bit more about the battle, while Jo, suffering from a nasty Russian cold, retired to our room to recuperate. The only evidence that such a struggle occurred here is the ruin of a flour mill, left as a memorial to the battle. Otherwise, the city has been entirely reconstructed. There is, however, an awe-inspiring memorial to the battle, Mamaev Kurgan, crowning what was known as Hill 102 during the struggle, the scene of particularly vicious fighting. Mamaev towers over the city, 210 feet high, a magnificent memorial to the dead. As I stood and craned my neck up at the gigantic statue, I felt a pang of sadness about the hideous loss of lives that took place here. It is said that even the Germans were shocked by the Soviet army's tactic of sending massed ranks of men towards the German machine guns, so their bodies would shield the troops behind.

I know that I have harped on about history quite a lot in my recent blogs, but Russia, more than anywhere else we've been, visibly bears the scars of its tumultuous twentieth-century history. Whether it is cities that were closed to foreigners until 1991 (Yekaterinburg, Samara), tanks and fighter planes on display in city centres, the Romanov remains or stern Communist statues glaring down at you in every main street, you are never allowed to forget for long what has happened here since 1917.

Back to Samara...

The further we go on this journey, the more we believe that everything happens for a reason. Two days ago, as Jo has mentioned, TT threw a tantrum and wouldn't start in Samara. It was those pesky spark plugs again, revolting against the cold and rain. All we could do was wait until they dried out. In the meantime, Irina, a journalist I'd been in touch with for a while, rang me. She was keen to do a TV interview and, after playing phone tag for the past 24 hours, TT's misdemeanours allowed us to finally hook up. The interview went well and we had a chance to talk about Mind, mental health and the reasons behind our trip. Interestingly, she was the first journalist to ask about Jo's scars, which I find odd. Aren't journalists supposed to ask pertinent questions?

After the interview, the three of us had a quick lunch and a really interesting chat about Russian literature, mental health here, and how the Russians feel about their Communist past. Irina seemed hesitant to talk about the issue of mental health, saying that even though the Soviet era is long gone, journalists still need to watch what they say, particularly to foreigners. I've asked quite a few people here the same questions about mental health, and the answer is always unclear. Suicide rates are very high, self-harm is common and alcoholism and domestic abuse are notoriously rife, and yet the provisions to care for those with mental illness are barely in place. Aside from that, no one seems able to tell us any more.

At 2 p.m., after we'd had lunch and our spark plugs had pulled themselves together, we set off down the P226 in the general direction of Volgograd. Six hours later we called it a day and pulled into our home for the night, a freshly harvested hayfield near Saratov. Lovely as it was, the night was spoilt slightly by the mosquitoes, which seemed unperturbed by the fact we were both coated in 100 per cent DEET. We snuggled down for a night of typically unsatisfactory tent sleep. I've yet to master the art of proper sleep when in such close proximity with Mother Earth and, since I burnt a hole in my inflatable sleeping mat the first time I used it, it offers little respite from whatever lurks beneath the groundsheet.

As I lay in my sleeping bag, my mind strayed to the puzzle of the Romanov remains and the big question: if they weren't the bones of the tsar et al., then whose were they? I concluded that the 'identification' of the bones in 1991 smacks of political spin and is suggestive of an attempt to discredit the Communist past and bolster patriotism at a time when the new Russia was throwing off the mantle of 73 years of Soviet rule.

Jo and I are very relieved that the sun has at last got his hat on and come out to give some respite from the rain. Ting Tong says she's very happy too, and I hope those darn spark plugs won't give us any more gyp from now on.

Monday 7 August, Volgograd, Volga oblast, Russia

 Success and sunbathing

We have spent the past two days enjoying the sunshine in Volgograd, soaking up the sun on the local sandy beach with our uneven zebra tans. Actually, most of our tan had disappeared after the rubbish weather we have experienced during the previous three weeks.

To reach the beach we had to get a boat to the other side of the Volga. The beach was absolutely packed, not only with people but also with rubbish – a real shame, because it could have been a nice beach. We settled down for the afternoon and quickly forgot about the miserable rain and cold weather we had thought would never end. It seems that the weather here can be as changeable as that back home.

In the evening we went to see Mamaev Kurgan, a huge striking statue that Ants has already mentioned. It was a beautifully clear evening and we enjoyed a spectacular sunset, while Ants explained to me the significance of the spot where we sat and the blood that had been shed during horrific battles in the Second World War. I do not understand why people still feel the need to go to war, including our embarrassing present government. Violence breeds violence, and there can be no such thing as a just war.

Today we had expected to hit the road and head west towards Ukraine. However, we were waiting for a parcel from England, which did not arrive. We were told that we may have to wait for another couple of days, and so we decided to hit the beach again. As it was Monday the beach was emptier, but that didn't stop us attracting attention from the local drunk. His name was Valeri and Ants suddenly forgot (intentionally) all of her Russian. Valeri indicated to me that I needed a manicure and he proceeded to try and clean under my fingernails with a biro, which actually just made them go blue. He also then took a grasp of my love handles and didn't let go until Ants and I both let out a yelp. We decided we'd had enough sun and headed back across the Volga.

When we got back to the hotel we were thrilled to find that our parcel had arrived. Now we can hit the road tomorrow and should be in Ukraine on Wednesday. After a relaxing and sun-filled weekend we are ready for another tukking week.

Tuesday 8 August, Hotel Volgograd, Volgograd, Volga oblast, Russia

Our escape from Volgograd

After an unintended four-day sojourn in sunny Volgograd, it looks like Jo and I will actually be heading south again tomorrow. Here we come, Ukraine, referred to by a post on this blog as our 'last doggy spot'. I think the doggiest thing there will be the *poliziya*. We just hope they fall for TT's charms as all their international counterparts have.

When we arrived here on Friday night we intended to stay only for the weekend, hoping that a new DV camera being couriered from England would arrive on Monday morning and off we could go. Monday morning arrived but the camera didn't. After tracking it down to a depot in Moscow and pestering the staff at our hotel on an hourly basis, we decided there was nothing to be done except head for the beach, again, and wait. If it had got as far as Moscow, it couldn't be too far away. Our patience and sun-worshipping were rewarded by the arrival of our package when we got back. Phew! We could hit the road again this morning.

But the courier company had obviously been a bit rough with the camera and, having excitedly reset it and headed into town to do some filming last night, I quickly ascertained that its focus was gone. I despaired. We'd already hung around in Volgograd for longer than necessary, and although Dan at ITV very generously said he'd send out *another* camera, that would have meant risking wasting more time and potentially having the same happen again. I lay awake for most of last night puzzling over what to do. Should we buy another camera here, risk another one getting sent out, or find someone here who could fix one of our two cameras... today?

The last option seemed the only viable one, so first thing this morning I was on the phone to Rudy in Yekaterinburg. Could he try to find us a Sony centre here? Of course he could – ten minutes later, he emailed three options and in a flash I was in a taxi to Planet Service.

A bevy of techies gathered round the two cameras. Heads shook and the word '*nyet*' was repeated far too many times for my liking. But I wasn't taking no for an answer. Somehow they had to fix either the sound on camera number one or the focus on camera number two. Today. After much cajoling, Sergei, one of the overworked engineers, gave me his mobile and said to ring at 3.30 p.m. He'd see what he could do.

And do what he could he did. At 4.30 p.m. I was walking out of the centre, having thanked Sergei, my new best friend, profusely, with camera number one intact. The relief! The gratitude! So now Jo and I are back on track, with all our equipment intact, and ready to head home. I'm so happy, albeit a little tired from my sleepless night.

 Thursday 10 August, the Russia–Ukraine border

 Camping it up

I am sitting here on the road next to TT while we wait in a queue of 40 cars to cross the border from Russia to Ukraine. The sun is shining and we know from previous experiences with border crossings that we could be in for a long old day. Oh well, at least we can work on our tans.

Last night we camped just outside Rostov-on-Don, which I think is a very funny name for a Russian city. We were stopped by the police five times yesterday, which means I have lost my bet. I estimated we would be stopped fewer than 30 times in Russia, and Ants correctly guessed over 30. I think the total now is 34. My prize as the loser is to pose for a photo naked in the Yi apron with TT in a public place. Ants, as chief photographer, will try to keep the photo as decent as possible.

Camping was fun, as it has been all three times we have camped on this trip. Although we never end up getting much sleep, being outside in the middle of nowhere with just the birds and bees to keep you company is quite a special experience. Last night there certainly were bees around, because we camped near some beehives in the woods. Poor Ants was stung on her bottom and has just been stung again this morning. Up until last night Ants had managed to avoid being stung, whereas I have already been stung four times, including three times in one day. The bee that stung Ants last night was already dead and so it managed to get its own back from the grave. I tried to be sympathetic, but when someone is stung on their bottom it is quite amusing – even Ants saw the funny side.

The drive out of Volgograd was well signposted, for once, and we were soon on our way to Rostov. One of our first police stops of the day made me laugh: the policeman collected coins from China and Mongolia and, after we explained about our trip, he asked if we had any Chinese coins. We searched through our bum-bags and were able to add a one-yuan coin to his collection.

Ants has just returned from an office at the border with some bad news. Apparently they don't accept credit cards for our Ukrainian insurance, and we don't seem to have enough money. That could mean a 30-mile trek to the nearest town. Bugger!

Problem over – after ferreting around in our bum-bags we have enough money, with only 25p to spare. Ants also just informed me that she has been stung on the bottom again and walked off rubbing her left cheek (that's the second time today!).

Next time we write a blog, I hope we will be in the Crimea, where Ants will be exploring the history of the area and I will be looking at rock formations. I am also on a mission to find a naturist beach so that TT can get an all-over tan.

One more thing: TT's spark plugs seem fine now and she is driving like a dream. I am hugely relieved, because as chief pseudo-mechanic I would have had to start checking inside her carburettor and distributor, and these jobs are best left to the pros. Changing the accelerator cable is about as skilled as I get. For those who are interested, we have now covered 9600 miles from Bangkok. Only about 3000 miles left before England, and then I hope TT will fly into the record books for having completed the longest-ever journey by an auto-rickshaw.

 Borderland

Another border, another pair of underpants, as Jo would say. After 16 days in Mother Russia, we have eaten our last eggy breakfast, been stopped by our last Russki *poliziya* and drunk our last Russian Baltika beer. Now for country number six, Ukraine, which lies merely a field from whence I now write. So near but yet so far. With 35 cars between us and the barrier, we could be in for a long wait. But at least the sun is shining and we know that on the other side lies the Crimea, with its beaches, Silk Road fortresses, cave cities... and naturist beaches.

Jo, being a devout naturist, is very excited about the latter. She's been trying to drag me to one since we were 13. The last time I was naked in public was at the Arasan Baths in Almaty, where the experience induced a panic attack and Jo had to lead me to safety while a gaggle of portly, unclad babuskhas looked on. Whether I'll be able to get over my fear of getting my kit off is yet to be seen. I may have to hide behind a large rock while Jo struts her stuff.

Our last night in Russia was spent in a field, watching a harvest moon rise over the trees and listening to a cacophony of insect life, several of which stung and bit us. Once again the tent experience led to little sleep but was most enjoyable, although unfortunately I left our cutlery in Volgograd so we ate our pasta with toothpicks. There are few things more pleasurable than sitting outside on a warm summer's evening under a full moon. It seemed an appropriate way to be ending Russia, and Jo and I sat and chatted about the past two weeks and the three and a half weeks we have left on the road. Time is slipping by so fast, and Brighton is looming out of the future at an alarming rate.

This trip has been like scaling a huge mountain. Our four-month preparation was akin to galloping across the plains towards the peak ahead, leaving Bangkok the first step towards the clouds. At Almaty we reached the summit and prepared for the descent. Now I feel as if we are scrambling down the other side, with home just visible through the clouds below. I know that we still have 3000 miles to go and anything could happen at any moment, but I feel as if we are on the home stretch now, and it's a funny feeling. My friend Al wrote me an email yesterday in which he reminded me of Gandhi's philosophy that life is one long journey, the only destination being death. As I lay in the back of TT yesterday, I thought about it a lot, how doing this journey and getting home are all a microcosm of that 'Journey'. When we cross the finish line in Brighton, this journey may end, this chapter close, but then another chapter will open and the next part of the 'Journey' will begin. What that next chapter will be neither Jo nor I knows. As for Ting Tong, her next chapter will be cohabiting a garage in Brighton with 11 smelly ferrets. I don't envy her.

Thanks to another five police stops yesterday and two today, I have won our bet as to how many cop stops we racked up in Russia. Our final tally is 35.

Police were one of the things we were most worried about in Russia, but on the whole the stops have been no more than an excuse to have a closer inspection of Ting Tong. A cursory glance at our *dokumenti* is always accompanied by the usual tukking questions and disbelief that we have no *moosh* (husbands) with us, are in a three-wheeled car and are going all the way to England. One policeman yesterday was a keen collector of coins so we added to his collection with some yuan and tenge. So far that is the only money we have had to hand over to men in uniform. At the next stop the policeman, half-joking, asked us whether we had any 'heroin, cocaine, *narkotiki*'. Yeah, right. If a smuggler were to dream up the worst accoutrement to smuggling they could imagine, Ting Tong would be it. Today, however, we met our first bad egg. It was quickly apparent that he was determined to extract roubles from us. He examined our documents, asked to see the engine number, bombarded us with tiresome questions and then marched off to the police station with our passports. But since our documents are perfectly in order and he could find nothing wrong, we headed off in the direction of Ukraine with our wallets and tempers intact.

All in all, Russia has been a great experience. Rain, spark-plug issues and technological hiccups have not dampened my enthusiasm for this country or its people. More than anywhere else, the Russians have loved Ting Tong. Barely five minutes have passed on a Russian road without people laughing, shouting questions out at us, begging us to stop and chat, asking to swap cars and whipping out video cameras. Some classic comments have included 'What is this apparition I see before me?' and 'Is it a car, is it a motorbike, is it a tractor?' Some Russians have also been just as surprised to see *Anglichankas* (English girls). In Yekaterinburg one man lurched up to us, beer can in hand, and said 'Eenglish... never before have I seen an Eenglish' and then just stood and stared. Most bizarre. Apart from the odd Communist fossil and sulky waitress, I have found the Russians to be fun, positive, kind and welcoming – a far cry from the cold, hard stereotype we feared. I hope the Ukrainians will be the same.

P.S. Jo just told a queue-barger to fuck off in Russian. Then the babushkas joined in, and now he's reversed in a fury to the back of the queue. I hope he doesn't hunt us down on the other side. Eek.

 Saturday 12 August, The Crimea, between Sudak and Yalta, Ukraine

 Love at first sight

We've been in Ukraine for a mere 48 hours and already I am under its spell. The countryside is beautiful, the people wonderful and the nightclubs highly entertaining. I think Jo and I have got a great ten days ahead of us, and as we tukked round the Crimean coast in the blazing sunshine today I felt the holiday mood set in. Although this journey has been unbelievable it's also been fairly exhausting at times, and for the next few days we are going to kick back, slap on the sunscreen and pretend we are just a normal pair of Brits abroad. Bliss.

Last time I put finger to keyboard was at the border two days ago, sitting in the back of Ting Tong. I was a little nervous at what lay ahead as we had a little problem with our *dokumenti*. Unbeknown to us, the customs at Troitsk had only given Ting Tong a Russian passport until 7 August. We were exiting Russia on 10 August. Their mistake lay buried in the small print of one of the many vital documents we carry around, and had a policeman not pointed it out to us on a routine check the night before we would have had no idea. Now we could be facing serious trouble, through no fault of our own.

The problem was spotted quickly and, at the Kazakh–Russian border, Jo and I were frogmarched into a small stark room by an enormous, cross-looking official. I didn't fancy our chances. For ten minutes we were at an impasse, with me trying to explain that we had no idea why Troitsk had made the mistake and him shaking his head and repeating that we had a problem. Then Jo whipped out a copy of *Komsomolskaya Pravda*, featuring an article about us written by our friend Evgenia in Almaty, and in an instant the issue of our faulty documents was dropped. He read and reread the article, went and copied it, then came back and opened a large safe in the corner of the room, from which he produced a handful of Ukrainian hryvnia and some euros. As he handed them across the table, he said that he understood about mental health problems and we both got the feeling he had either experienced them himself or knew someone who had. Whatever his motives, it was an extraordinary incident, and with our new friend in tow we skipped out of the office and into Ting Tong. After some photos and lots of thank yous, the barrier rose up and we said goodbye to Russia. We couldn't believe that at a second border crossing, we had actually been given money by people who are notorious for exactly the opposite. What a brilliant end to our two weeks in Russia.

The Ukrainian side of the border passed without major incident, and after six hours in Borderland we sped into country number six. Since we were both dead beat after a night of camping and a series of insomniac nights in Volgograd, we stopped for the night in the first place we came across, which happened to be Maryopol, a fairly large town on the Sea of Azov. When we found a hotel, which I can't begin to remember the name of, I went in to investigate while Jo held the TT fort. The heavily made-up, perfectly dressed receptionist took one look at my filthy T-shirt and grubby Thai fisherman's trousers and snottily said that they had no rooms, only *luxe*, i.e. you can't afford it so piss off. But since Jo and I had camped the night before and were in no mood for hotel hunting, she had to eat her words and *luxe* it was.

When I skipped out to tell Jo the good news, I found her surrounded by a group of handsome young men, all asking the usual questions, with Jo looking perplexed and not understanding a word. Not taking no for an answer, they carried our bags up to our room, bought us beers and supper, and then insisted we come out dancing with them. Both of us could think of nothing worse. We were shattered and pretty grubby and could hardly string a coherent sentence together in English, let alone Russian. But for some reason we found ourselves saying yes...

Half an hour later we were washed and downing our first shots of vodka. An hour later we were at the Santa Barbara nightclub, with two bottles of vodka being planted in front of us and seven excitable Russians toasting England, Russia, three wheels, etc., etc. Sasha, Vittya, Sergei, Alexei et al. told us they lived in Novosibirsk in Siberia – where it regularly hits -40 °C – and were all metalworkers. Vittya, who had multiple tattoos, bullet wounds and shaved hair dyed leopard print, had spent four years fighting in Grozny. From what I could understand, the experience had affected him deeply. He was only our age and for the umpteenth time on this trip I appreciated what tame, easy lives we live in England. Sergei had several gold teeth and a bad case of wandering hands. Sasha was apparently married and had a daughter but spent the evening looking lasciviously at Jo and dragging her off to dance. They also taught us an interesting Russian custom, which I still think they made up just for our/their benefit. Apparently it's customary for two people to link their arms, drink shots of vodka and then kiss each other passionately on the lips. To demonstrate that they weren't having us on, Sergei and Sasha shared a very unmanly kiss on the lips and then told us it was our turn...

At 2 a.m. we staggered home, *locked* the door of our bedroom and passed out. But not before Sasha and Vittya had begged to come in for a 'nightcap' and Sasha had been on his knees begging for 'Diana' (Joanna after too much vodka). What a funny and totally unexpected night.

Yesterday we awoke, feeling a little bleary eyed but full of the joys of Ukraine, and set off west for the Crimea. At about 6 p.m., with a storm brewing in the distance, we pulled over at a *rinok* (market) to get some veggies in case we had to camp. The vendors were all Crimean Tartars – more about them another time – and they loaded us up with every vegetable imaginable and then refused to take any money. As we were leaving, Jo asked one man whether he had email, so we could send him pictures. He let out a throaty laugh and said 'Internet? We have no money, only potatoes. How could we have Internet?' They had nothing and yet had just given us so much. It was another one of those incidents that leaves you feeling humbled, incredibly grateful and wishing you could give something back.

I've written enough now and need to go to bed, so more tomorrow. We're in a village in the Crimea, somewhere between Sudak and Yalta. No idea what it's called but it has a beach and we're sharing a house with some Russian punks from St Petersburg who we met in a café this afternoon.

 Monday 14 August, Vecolny, The Crimea, Ukraine

 Ting Tong's summer holiday

Those of you who speak Russian might have noticed something funny about the name of the village we are staying in. It means 'merry', which is fitting, since the three of us are indeed having a very merry time here. The sun is shining – almost too hard – the sea is on our doorstep and we have spent the past few days being deliciously idle on the beach. Apart from my rather hot three-mile run this morning, our time has been spent horizontally, reading and simply soaking up the rays.

It's not that interesting reading about people lying on the beach doing nothing, so I'll keep it short. One thing I do want to say, though, is that

Jo and I found out this afternoon that out of 16 000 entries, we have made it down to the last ten in *Cosmo's* Fun Fearless Female Award, which is dead exciting. I think the final decision is in September.

 Brown girl in the ring

We managed to locate the local naturist beach yesterday, which involved an energy-sapping scramble over rocks in the midday sun. The naturist beach was less of a beach and actually some rocks where people either decided to wear clothes (pecker checkers and beaver patrol) or chose not to (naturists). Ants and I found a reasonably flat rock and toasted ourselves.

We're still living with the aforementioned punks from St Petersburg. They are not really punks, but they do have a strong penchant for facial piercings, Mohicans and tattoos. The three of them, Nastia, Vova and Anna, are living here for the summer and running a club on the beach. We went down last night and I got far too excited by all of the Boney M tracks they were playing, hence the title of this blog.

Nothing much more to report, other than that TT has decided she likes to steer to the right when we apply the brakes. This same problem happened in Kazakhstan and we solved it by changing the front brake calliper, and so tomorrow we will have to drag ourselves away from the beach and deal with Ting Tong.

 Friday 18 August, Tanya's House, Bakhchysaray, the Crimea, Ukraine

 Another tukking tantrum

After several divine days of chilling by the Black Sea, it was back to reality on Tuesday afternoon, when we limped into Sudak with Ting Tong in a quest to get to the root of her latest troubles. We weren't sure whether the problem was with the calliper, as in Kazakhstan, or whether it was a new ailment. We had no idea where to find a good mechanic with whom we would be able to communicate – my Russian doesn't stretch to mechanical technicalities, and very few people round here speak any English.

A hot traipse around Sudak finally led us to Signal, a tiny shop piled high with every sort of auto part you can imagine, apart from callipers. The nearest place we could buy one, they told us, was Odessa, over 350 miles away. We looked at each other and groaned. As the reality of our problem was sinking in, a heavily accented voice piped up on my right: 'What are you looking for?' I turned to discover the owner of the voice was a smartly dressed, good-looking 20-something man. He introduced himself as Redvan, a mechanic. An hour later he was at our house, stripped down to a pair of fetching satin shorts, and inspecting our sick baby. Despite our misgivings he soon ascertained that the problem was not with the calliper but with our front suspension, which had gone again. Boris, a biker we had met the day before, had said the same but we had dismissed his prognosis, convinced it had to be the same problem as in Balkash. This was bad news – we had already used our spare shocks in China, and the nearest ones were in Bangkok, about 9000 miles away.

We now had three options: wait for up to two weeks while the new shocks were couriered to us, fly to Bangkok to physically pick them up or find someone who could somehow fix them. The only realistic option was the latter, and with Redvan leading the way on his moped we bumped off to the best mechanic in town, Serva, who lived down a dusty track among half-built houses on the outskirts of Sudak. Yes, he said, he thought he could do it... come back in three hours. So Jo, Redvan and I went off to Redvan's uncle's café and drank coffee and smoked hookahs, waiting anxiously for the outcome. If he failed, we were in serious trouble...

As we waited, Redvan, only 26 and married for four years, told us about his people, the Crimean Tartars, and about Stalin's terrible expulsion of them in 1944 – within a space of a few days, Stalin exported every single one of them to Uzbekistan, Kazakhstan and Siberia. Thousands died on the journey and, although given an official apology by Khrushchev in 1967, it was not until 1989 that they were officially allowed back to their homeland. Today, about 12 per cent of the Crimean population is Tartar, but life is hard for them and many struggle against poverty and racial prejudice, all because of the whim of a single megalomaniac.

Full of coffee and Tartar tales we returned after three hours to find Serva putting the finishing touches to Tingers. A test drive would reveal whether he had managed to mend her. And guess what? He had! Jo and I couldn't believe it. He had managed to do in one hour what had taken ten men seven hours in Jinhong. Moreover, he had never seen or attended to a three-wheeler before. We thanked him, thanked him, thanked him, thanked him some more, took photos of him and his wife, and gleefully drove off into the sunset. Problem solved. Our evening was thus spent celebrating over a few beers with Redvan and his friend Rostom. Please, please, let it be the last problem Ting Tong has before we get home in two and a half weeks. If Redvan had not been in Signal at the same time as us, goodness knows what might have happened. Thank you, guardian angels, for coming to our rescue again.

This morning we packed up and said goodbye to Nastia and Vova and our Tartar hosts, Ismail, Aisha, Gulya, Esme and Eleonora, plus their four dogs, Naida, Akbar, Dinai and Puppy. The downside of the trip is saying goodbye to all the wonderful people who cross our paths and become part of our journey, and I felt as sad about leaving them as I have about leaving anyone else. But the road and Brighton beckon, and it was time to move on.

Now we are in Bakhchysaray, the old Tartar capital of the Crimea, staying in a little house in the garden of a lady called Tanya. It's very beautiful here, and our lodging is costing us the grand total of £3. At 7 a.m. Tanya is going to make us breakfast and then we'll head for Odessa. The Crimea is fantastic. We love it. You've all got to come here.

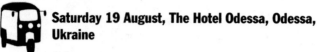 **Saturday 19 August, The Hotel Odessa, Odessa, Ukraine**

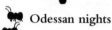 Odessan nights

Odessa, the creation of the indefatigable Catherine the Great, is famous today for several things: neoclassical architecture, Ibizan-style 24-hour nightclubs, lissom girls and a rampant HIV epidemic. The lissom girls have also made it a major destination for lonely cashed-up Western and Turkish men, one of whom has just mistaken me for a Ukrainian hooker in the lift and launched himself upon me.

For the past few hours Jo and I have been luxuriating in the Turkish hammam and pool in our hotel, our first slice of luxury in a long time. As I got into the lift up to our room on the seventeenth floor, a lecherous-looking Turk scurried in after me. I was clad only in a white bath robe. When he said something to me, I replied, in Russian, that I was English and I didn't understand what he had just said. Being Turkish, the same applied to my answer. He looked at me in an undesirable manner and then said 'Sex?', which I did understand. He lunged at me, kissing me on the cheek as I swerved his advance. I ducked several more advances as we sped up through the floors and then bolted for our room. Yuk. And he had bad breath.

Apart from that little episode, which in retrospect is quite funny, Odessa has been great. We left Bakhchysaray at 8 a.m. yesterday, having breakfasted under the fruit trees in our host Tanya's garden, and headed north. We had 350 miles to cover in one day, so knew we were in for a long one.

Unsure of which road to take out of Bakhchysaray, we pulled over and asked a man waiting for a bus. Before we could object he'd hopped into the back of TT and offered to show us the way, which he did for the next 20 miles. Jo was driving, so I chatted to him in the back. He told me that his name was Emil, that he was a Tartar and that he had returned from Uzbekistan only the year before. Life is clearly not easy for him. He's 36, is married, has a child and earns only £200 a month as a mechanic. Considering petrol costs 50p a litre here, that sort of salary doesn't get you far. At Simferopol he hopped out and off we went. It's funny that after three months of nobody except Jo, myself, Jo's dad, my ma, Jack and Sam being in TT, we had four alien passengers in 24 hours, since everyone we stopped and asked for directions in the Crimea insisted on getting in to show us. Not to mention a man leaping out of his car at some traffic lights and kissing us both.

Believe it or not, the Ukrainians appear to love TT more than the Russians did. In the past few days she has been called a helicopter, an ant, a tractor and an apparition. When people ask where we are going and what we are doing, they all say two things – '*Klyass!*' and '*Malatyets!*' – which mean 'Class!' and 'Good girls!' or something similar. They also press packets of cigarettes, fruit, vegetables and jams into our hands as gifts. What lovely people.

The drive here was uneventful, so I won't dwell on it. At 7.30 p.m. we passed the sign announcing our arrival in Odessa. Unsure of where we were going, we tukked towards the centre, past docks, train lines and auto repair shops. Then suddenly we were in the centre, with the famous Potemkin Steps on our right and the towering Hotel Odessa on our left. Jo was instantly under the spell of the latter, a glitzy glass and steel affair occupying what must be the best piece of real estate in town. Although mentioned in the guide book we'd dismissed it as too expensive, but since we were tired and it looked big enough not to be full we opted to give it a try. Half an hour later TT was in her pyjamas in the hotel parking lot and a porter was unloading all our baggage. Yes, the price was far too much, but since we've been roughing it for a while we felt the sudden urge for white bathrobes, swimming pools and panoramic views. Thankfully, the hammam, pool, sauna and gym have made up for the fact that the room is identikit and motel-like and it's basically a revolting rip-off, but that's Odessa in the high season for you.

Jo and I had a late, luxurious breakfast this morning and then set off for a potter around the city. The guidebooks rave about the Potemkin

Steps, the location of a famous scene in Sergei Eisenstein's *Battleship Potemkin* (1925). Not being an expert on black-and-white films I am afraid I have never heard of it, and for me the steps were just a hot climb that necessitated a cold drink at the top. However, Odessa is as beautiful as its lofty reputation states. Crumbling, neoclassical buildings line the streets and well-heeled Odessans sip coffee in Parisian-style cafés. It's a shame we have only a single day here and that today, at 39 °C, it was a little too hot for extensive exploring.

Tonight we're going to hit Arkadia Beach, which is 'Ukraine's Ibiza', crammed with 24-hour clubs pumping out house, drum and bass, et al. No doubt we will feel underdressed, given the Ukrainian proclivity for very short skirts and very high heels. Unfortunately, I haven't got my Guccis stashed away in the bottom of my rucksack, so Birkenstocks it'll have to be.

Two more weeks to go till Brighton, and 13 weeks ago today we left England. It seems so long ago.

Kamaz, Kamaz, Kamaz, Kamaz, Kamaz...

What am I going on about? Well, yesterday on our 350-mile drive from Bakhchysaray to Odessa, we came across a queue of Kamaz – Russian mega-trucks – on the M24. I first spotted a line of about a half a mile of trucks snaking around a dirt track by the side of the road. As we drove along the road the line of trucks went on... and on... and on... for a total of about six miles. I have never seen anything like it in my life. It got to the point where we actually started to find it a bit freaky. We didn't stop to say hi to them, but we waved at a few as we drove past in the opposite direction. I would have loved to know what they were doing in that queue. It must have contained nearly all of the Kamaz trucks in the whole of Ukraine. Ants and I feel that we are almost part of the trucker fraternity, as we have some appreciation of what it is like to drive long distances day in day out. In my early twenties I had considered being a trucker or cabbie, but now I don't think I could deal with driving as a career.

Apart from the Kamazes, the drive yesterday was nothing interesting and we arrived in Odessa as the sun started to set. After six days using squat loos and outdoor showers, I was seduced by the glistening structure where we are now staying, the Hotel 'Ripoffski' Odessa. Ants and I both agreed that despite the identikit rooms, the price was worth it for the comfy beds, cleanliness, hot shower, swimming pool, buffet breakfast, gym and free parking. The frustrating thing about yesterday's drive was that our darling TT has started pulling to the right again. Just when we thought she was sorted, the same problem rears its ugly head again. We both think she has raging PMT at the moment.

After checking in last night and settling into our room, Ants started to read all of the blurb about the hotel that you get in such establishments. She spotted that as we were staying in a 'superior' room, then we ought to have an adjoining room with a balcony. A quick call to reception resulted in housekeeping bringing us a key to get into this extra room. I was in the shower at the time and Ants popped her head around the door in hysterics. She had unlocked the door and walked in on a couple in bed together. She quickly retreated and relocked the door. We then planned all sorts of unpleasant tricks on our neighbours, a few of which I will mention: taking everything from their mini-bar, putting Boovie and Wirral (our snuggle blanket and pet squirrel, respectively) in their beds, climbing into bed with them in the middle of the night... I could go on, but I have told you only the more innocent pranks we hypothesised. I can tell you that, 24 hours on, we have not done anything to our neighbours.

 Tuesday 22 August, Hotel Wien, Lviv, Ukraine

 Into the setting sun

On first impressions, Lviv, a UNESCO World Heritage Site, has got to be one of the most beautiful cities I've ever been to, if not *the* most beautiful. Jo and I have just had a brief meander round its cobbled streets and crooked alleyways, past a cornucopia of renaissance, baroque, rococo and neoclassical buildings, but sadly we are both too exhausted to give the city justice and have had to put ourselves to bed for the afternoon instead. I know that sounds feeble, but the past two days have been a bit of an endurance test and with only 12 days to go until Touch Down we need to preserve our energy. If not, then Jo's nightmares about collapsing with exhaustion on Brighton Pier will be in danger of becoming reality.

After posting our last blogs, we got our best glad rags on and hit the tiles in Odessa's Arkadia Beach. Lauded as Ukraine's answer to Ibiza, this pulsating strip of the Black Sea is a mass of bars, clubs, restaurants, buff boys and tottering girls. We're used to the Russian and Ukrainian girls dressing to kill, but this was something else. The average girl that strutted past was dressed like a hooker and wearing so much make-up you'd have to dig it off with a spade to see what they actually looked like. Skirts were indistinguishable from belts, and heels were at least four inches high. If Jo and I had decided to go out in nothing but G-strings and six-inch gold heels no one would have batted an eyelid. The boys here must love it.

Having fortified ourselves with a vodka and watched open-mouthed at the human traffic parading past us, we bought our tickets for a club called Ibiza, getting there at 12.30 a.m., just as a Levi's fashion show was kicking off and a troupe of anorexic models was parading down a catwalk. The club was even more glamorous than the Snow Project in Yekaterinburg – all open-air, with white troglodyte-style booths cascading down to the dance floor. Champagne-swilling mafia types were everywhere, surrounded by scantily dressed girls clutching Gucci and Chanel handbags. Labels, labels, labels.

The fashion show was followed by the dancers, an array of pornographically (un)dressed boys and girls who were high on a little more than life. Quite a spectacle and very, very different from the sort of clubs we're used to in London, like Fabric and Turnmills. All a laugh though, and at 3 a.m. we crawled into bed not looking forward to our 250-mile schlep the next day.

Just as we were checking out the next morning (Sunday), two English men called Donal and Gavin came up and pressed $30 (£15) into our hands, saying we had to have a 'beer on them on the way home'. We'd met them the day before in the lobby, and I had jokingly asked them whether they were in Odessa looking for wives, like every other older western man, but in fact they were Davis Cup organisers, the tournament this year being held at the Odessa Lawn Tennis Club. They were the first western people we have spoken to in seven weeks.

Jo and I have both been baffled by the reaction of the Ukrainian police to Ting Tong. We'd been warned that the police here could be even trickier than the Russian or Kazakh police – who turned out to be more nosey than tricksome – but so far we have been stopped only a handful of times. On most occasions, they look so flabbergasted as we drive past that by the time they've composed themselves enough to wave their baton and stop us it's too late.

No doubt spurred on by Jo's very short shorts and leopard-print bikini top, one group of bored cops did stop us on Sunday. They were interested not the least bit in our *dokumenti* but in taking pictures, sitting in Ting Tong and groping Jo's boobs. We got a classic photo of one of the policemen sitting in the driver's seat, grinning widely, his hand clasped firmly to Jo's leopard-print breast. Jo and I have come to the conclusion that the average Russian or Ukrainian man has an overdose of testosterone pumping through his veins; they make English men seem incredibly tame in comparison.

Apart from the randy cop stop, our drive on Sunday was uneventful. We cruised up the main road to Kiev, turned west at Uman and set up camp in a wood about 200 miles from Odessa, both desperately in need of a good night's sleep. But, as usual, sleep was not forthcoming in tent land and we awoke early the next morning feeling pretty jaded, but with over 250 miles to cover before Lviv. I'd also managed to pour a saucepan of boiling water over my hand the night before, which was agony. Thankfully, Nurse Jo and our Nomad medical kit saved the day and my hand is now swathed in special burn bandages. If that's the worst injury we sustain on our trip, we'll have done well.

Only 12 days now until we get back to Brighton, and so we've been busy sorting out the Touch Down plans. At the moment, we are going to land in Brighton at around 3.30 p.m. on 3 September and be finished officially by the mayor, Bob Carden. Fingers crossed, we'll be granted special permission to end in Bartholomew's Square, outside the mayoral office. Then it's on to a bar for some tukking serious celebrations.

Poland tomorrow... then Prague at the weekend... followed by Cologne, Brussels and home. I can't believe it's getting so close.

chapter 5
the final furlong

Thursday 24 August, Hotel Alef II, Krakow, Poland

 Welcome to the European Union

Oops! I have been a bit lazy at following up to our night on the tiles in Odessa. Suffice to say, it was quite an eye-opener and most red-blooded males/lesbians would have been in heaven.

The following morning we set off for somewhere between Odessa and Lviv, with the intention of probably camping. As the sun began to set, we pulled off the road and found a quiet wooded clearing to set up camp. Unlike in Russia, there were no killer mozzies, but instead we were bombarded by bugs that liked the look of the head-torch. After supper Ants had a bit of an accident and let out a yelp. I thought she had been stung (again), but it turned out that she had managed to get boiling water all over her right hand. Poor Ants ended up having my dirty T-shirt wrapped around her hand while I ferreted around in our medical kit and found a burn dressing. I then proceeded to bandage her up like a boxer, hoping that her injury would not stop her driving the rest of the trip back to the UK. It is a running joke between us that we don't want the other one to get hurt in any way that will stop them driving. Much as we adore driving TT, we are not too keen to have the sole responsibility of driving her.

The following morning we dragged ourselves from our idiot-proof tent, packed up and hit the road for Lviv. As we arrived in the city it became quite apparent why it is a World Heritage Site. The combination of the attractive buildings and cobbled streets made quite an impression on me. Although our hotel was a bit tricky to find, it turned out to have a great location right on the main square.

The next day we had planned to explore Lviv, but we managed only a half-hearted attempt due to our ongoing problems with fatigue. I can understand why we get tired on this trip, but the fact that Ants and I seem to have spent most of the trip not sleeping soundly is extremely annoying and means we get a double dose of tiredness. When we get home I am going to get into my bed for 24 hours and not move.

That brings me on to yesterday. We left Lviv at 9 a.m. and hoped to be in Krakow in the evening. The border was only about 60 miles from Lviv, but we were delayed by TT suffering from a broken accelerator cable. We changed it, but I made the job a whole lot more challenging by removing the wire from its plastic sheath. At the border we joined a very long queue of 100 or so vehicles and had to wait for about three hours, which wasn't too bad considering how many cars there were. Just as we neared the front of the queue, the heavens opened and TT had a shower. Not only was it raining but also it was cold. Ants and I shivered away, cursing the weather and border crossings.

After we had successfully left Ukraine, we had to wait for half an hour in no-man's land before being processed by the Polish officials. This was the easiest entrance to a country we have encountered. As Poland is part of the EU, we didn't need any stamps, visas, *declaratzia*, import papers, etc. They just entered TT's and our details on the computer and we were free to go.

Poland, like Almaty, was a reverse culture shock. I have never seen so many road signs in my life, and Ants and I dry-retched when we came across a 24-hour Tesco, a Shell garage and a McDonalds, all within a couple of miles. Yuk! Multinationals like these are things that I have not missed about England.

The drive to Krakow was frustrating for a number of reasons. First, the road to Krakow passed through towns and villages with such frequency that it made driving a slow process and we constantly had to slow down to 25 mph. Second, TT started making the most unbelievable hissing sound. It was so loud that initially I thought it must be coming from some nearby roadworks. We pulled into a garage and I got on my back and had a poke around. I thought I had found the problem when I spotted that the hose from the air filter had come loose, so I resealed it and hoped that the hissing would stop. We drove along for a few miles before TT started making a racket again. The weird thing was that she didn't always make a racket and the whistling came and went. By this time it was after 11 p.m and dark. The final challenge was lots and lots of roadworks, which meant more slow speeds. Still, I was driving in true granny style anyway because of TT's hissing and the darkness.

We arrived at our hotel at 12.30 a.m. last night. I felt like it was 7 a.m. and I had been clubbing all night – not pleasant. Time for bed now. I am all blogged out.

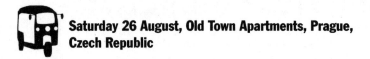 **Saturday 26 August, Old Town Apartments, Prague, Czech Republic**

 It's not over until the fat lady sings

I'm not quite sure who the fat lady is, but this aphorism sprung to mind early yesterday morning as – with Jo at the wheel – a security guard, the local mechanic and I pushed a recalcitrant Ting Tong around a carpark in Oswiecim. As it had been a little chilly the night before, the Pink Lady's spark plugs had once again revolted and said they weren't going anywhere until they had warmed up. It was the fourth time in two days that Her Ladyship had caused us problems, reminding us that we may be nine-tenths of the way through our 14-week tukathon but it isn't over 'til it's over.

To our great relief her engine finally turned over and we turned out of our hotel carpark towards Prague, 320 miles away.

The last time I wrote a blog was in Lviv, when Jo and I had been too tired to appreciate the beauty of the place after two very long days on the road. After another bad night's sleep, feeling far from refreshed, we set off early the next morning for Krakow, 185 miles away in Poland.

At 10.30 a.m., the first of the day's incidents occurred when the accelerator cable suddenly went ping. Jo was asleep in the back and was rudely awoken by some bad language coming from the driver's seat and the news that we were going to have to perform a mechanical procedure. Under a leaden sky, in biting wind, we extracted the toolbox and got to work. An hour and a half later we were on our way again, having had a few issues with pieces of wire not fitting where they were supposed to.

At about 1 p.m. we spotted a very, very long queue of cars, which signalled our arrival at the Ukraine–Poland border. The crossing was lengthy but uneventful, and four hours later we were in Poland, both very sad to be waving goodbye to Ladaland. We've spent six weeks in Russian-speaking countries and have met so many fantastic people and seen so many interesting things. Entering Poland, and the EU, meant saying farewell to all that we had become familiar with: clapped-out cars, outdoor showers, Kamaz trucks, gold teeth, Tartars, *smetana*, vodka and officious police. It also meant that we are well and truly embarking on the final leg of our journey and that our arrival in England is scarily imminent.

Driving into Poland was like entering a new world. Within ten miles we had spotted a Tesco and a McDonalds, those vile totems of westernisation. Gleaming BP and Shell garages were in place of their more dishevelled Ukrainian and Russian counterparts. A surfeit of shiny new road signs marched along the roadside, and everywhere the EU stars reminded you of Poland's new identity. Never before have Jo or I seen so many road signs. It is as if Poland has gone overboard in an attempt to become a paradigmatic EU nation.

To complement our grey moods at having entered the western world, at about 5 p.m. the heavens opened, much to the disdain of TT's temperamental sparks. They didn't force us to a standstill but they did slow us down and the next few hours were accompanied by the sound of their spluttering disapproval. That and non-stop roadworks meant that at 10 p.m. we were still 60 miles short of Krakow... at which point

Ting Tong threw yet another tukking tantrum, suddenly emitting an alarming hissing sound from within the depths of her engine. She'd hissed before, but this was a different matter, and Jo demanded that we stopped and investigated further. I was all for limping on to Krakow and dealing with the problem in the fresh light of morning, but Jo, being the sensible one, decided otherwise. So we pulled into the next petrol station and for the second time that day went through the rigmarole of unscrewing the driver's seat to get into the engine. The chief mechanic, aka Jo, swiftly identified a large hole in the air hose, which, after a bit of fiddling, looked like it was sorted, and we carried on. Ten minutes later TT was hissing again, but this time we decided there was no more we could do, so we ploughed on to Krakow. We pulled up outside our hotel at 12.30 a.m., dizzy with fatigue, and after a glass of wine fell into bed and passed out. God, what a day – certainly our longest yet at fifteen and a half hours, and probably the hardest.

Krakow, like Lviv, is an incredibly beautiful city, with street upon street of architectural delights. And once again, like Lviv, we were far too exhausted to check it out. I didn't actually get out of bed until 2 p.m. the next day, and we spent the afternoon ambling about, chilling in cafés and taking a horse-drawn carriage around the Old Town. What surprised us both was the volume of tourists and the number of American and English voices we heard amidst the crowds. Ukraine and Russia felt a world away and we both hankered for what we had left behind.

There's an interesting legend about Krakow. Many moons ago, Lord Shiva threw seven magic stones towards seven parts of the world, one of which landed in Krakow, in the Wawel Castle. The places that had been hit were instantly imbued with the god's energy and remain so to this day. The seven places, known as the world's chakras, are Delhi, Delphi, Jerusalem, Krakow, Mecca, Rome and Velehrad. You may dismiss this as hippy nonsense, but apparently all sorts of dowsings, tests and divinings have been done here and numerous studies published, and they all seem to confirm there is something a little bit magic about this place.

The next morning we headed straight for the nearest mechanic and then south west out of Krakow, in the general direction of Prague. Our last stop in Poland was Oswiecim, better known by its German name, Auschwitz, synonymous with unfathomable cruelty and suffering. Under gathering rain clouds, we covered up TT and headed into Birkenau, the first of the two museums here. Birkenau, which held up to 100 000 prisoners, is where the Nazis murdered hundreds of thousands of Jews, Poles, Gypsies, homosexuals and anyone else they felt like. Although the SS, sensing defeat, tried to cover up evidence of their atrocities, much of the camp still remains. As you wander amidst the barbed-wire fencing and blown-up gas chambers and crematoriums, you get a sense of the scale of the Nazi operation. It felt suitable that it was such a dank, miserable day. At the far end is a massive monument in memory of those who died here, which states, in every European language, 'Let this place be a cry of despair and a warning to all humanity'. It's shocking to think that what happened here was only 62 years ago and that so many innocents endured such horror.

Next stop was Auschwitz, two miles down the road. Established in 1940 for Polish political prisoners, Auschwitz was expanded in 1941–42 to take in European Jews from as far away as Corfu, Greece and Hungary. No one quite knows how many people died here and at Birkenau, since as the war progressed the Nazis didn't bother registering their victims – they just unloaded them straight off the trains and into the gas chambers. Tragically, many of the Jews who arrived here had been duped by the Nazis into believing they had been transported for 'resettlement'; the Nazis sold them non-existent plots of land and offered them work in fictitious shops and factories.

Of course I knew about the Holocaust before, and how disgustingly bigoted and cruel it was, but it wasn't until we walked around Auschwitz that it truly sunk in, seeing those thousands of photographs and piles of belongings, reading about the tales of heroic resistance movements, and pondering the conditions in which the prisoners were forced to exist. Harrowing is not the word, and not for the first time history made me cry. Perhaps worst of all was a photograph of a woman who had weighed 11 stone when she arrived but a pathetic four stone when the photo was taken. As in Volgograd, I was left horrified at humanity's capacity for cruelty and mass destruction.

Almost everyone knows about the Holocaust, but fewer people are aware of how badly the Poles suffered at the dual hands of Hitler and Stalin in the Second World War. Both men set out to wipe Poland off the map, again, and by 1945 Poland had lost over 20 per cent of its pre-war population. Worst off were its intelligentsia, whom Hitler and Stalin feared the most. A total of 57 per cent of Poland's lawyers, 40 per cent of its doctors and 30 per cent of its university lecturers were murdered by these two megalomaniacs. It is no surprise that the handful of Polish pilots who fought for us in the Battle of Britain were some of the most lethal fighters we had.

After seeing the museum, we spent the night at the unremarkable Hotel Glob. The next morning we had the debacle of TT refusing to start once again. By the time she got her act together it was 9.30 a.m., and off we sped towards the Czech border. I was only just beginning to get used to Polish zloty and having an almost recognisable alphabet, and it was time for another country.

Amazingly, the border crossing took a mere two minutes and was a matter of flashing our passports. Then 280 miles later, having cruised along immaculate Czech tarmac, we hit Prague. My, oh my, we were glad to get here last night and meet up with Jo's pa. And wow, there are a lot of tourists here.

 Tuesday 29 August, Prague, Czech Republic

 No butt-surfing, please – we're British

Our departure from Krakow on Saturday morning was delayed slightly by some TT mechanics as I poked around to try to find the source of the hissing and attempted to rethread the accelerator cable. Both jobs were unsuccessful, and a guy who was working in the hotel had to try and sort out my botched job. Next stop was a local mechanic. He managed to rethread the accelerator cable but didn't really try to find the source of the hissing. Instead, he tightened her drive belt slightly. We didn't feel particularly confident that she would be sorted, but we tukked off anyway and decided that we could stop at another mechanic if the hissing became unbearable.

Our next stop was Auschwitz. It was a suitably grey and drizzly day and the sites were very well designed to educate tourists about the atrocities committed. We left feeling a bit depressed that any human being could cause such suffering to other human beings, i.e. their brothers and sisters. However, it seems that leaders never really learn from the past, and our supposed democratic governments in the western world still think that it is justifiable to kill innocent women, children and men. In the case of the USA they pass it off as that rather vulgar euphemism 'collateral damage'. There can never ever be any justification for killing innocent civilians, whether intentional or unintentional. When will some of the people in this world get it into their thick skulls that they are wrong?

The following morning we were up early for a long drive to Prague. Our darling TT decided that she didn't want to start and so we had to enlist the help of a young mechanic to get her going. Once we were on our way the drive was OK, the highlight being driving TT at just over 70 mph on the Czech motorway, a tukking record. The border crossing was incredibly simple and took a mere two minutes – unbelievable.

I will now explain the title of this blog. Butt-surfing is not something that people do in the privacy of their bedrooms. What I am referring to is the behaviour that we call tailgating in England – basically, stupid drivers who think it is a great idea to get right up another vehicle's ass. We have had to deal with this behaviour during the whole trip, but the faster the vehicles travel the more potentially lethal it becomes, regardless of whether the vehicle has ABS or not. We have seen so many accidents that have occurred as a direct result of butt-surfing, and therefore we drive TT a good two to four seconds behind the vehicle in front. Sometimes, the large gap we leave between ourselves and the vehicle in front is far too tempting for drivers behind us, and they force us to briefly butt-surf as they cut in right in front of us. Do people not realise that when you take control of a motorised vehicle you are in control of a potentially lethal piece of machinery? Dangerous driving also encompasses drink-driving, and anyone that indulges in either is an incredibly selfish idiot. I should have bought the sticker that I have attached to the back of my Vectra in England: 'Unless you're a haemorrhoid, keep off my ass.'

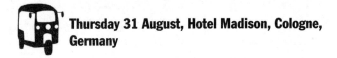

Thursday 31 August, Hotel Madison, Cologne, Germany

Bavarian sausage to eau de cologne

It's 8 a.m., we're in Cologne and very soon we have got to load up TT, hope she starts and tuk off to Brussels. Somewhere en route we are meeting up with a BBC cameraman who has come out to film us for the day, before we do a live feed from Brussels city centre tonight. Help.

Apart from that, I'm writing this in serious haste, so there is not really enough time to fill you in on all the details. I'll just jot down some of the vital stats, as it were.

In the past few days we've tukked, in filthy rain and cold, from Prague to Cologne, via Bavaria, where we visited fellow tuk tuk enthusiasts Daniel and Susi. Last year they drove one of Anuwat's tuk tuks over 23 000 miles from Bangkok to Germany, via Japan, Mongolia and Libya. We'd originally planned to tuk due west from Prague through Bohemia but, having been in touch with Daniel and Susi since February, couldn't resist the minor diversion to Bavaria in order to give Ting Tong a chance to flirt with another tuk tuk and swap tukking tales. They fed us pizza, and Daniel spent the whole evening and next morning helping us with

TT, who is being a Bad Girl. We're having problems with her every day now, and I'm having visions of her falling apart at the finishing line in Brighton in a comedy fashion. The most serious problem is her veering to the right, which we can't get to the bottom of. Daniel and Jo tried everything yesterday – changing the wheel, putting on a new calliper, changing the disc brakes, removing washers... I think she probably needs new front shocks, but there is nothing we can do about that until we get back to England.

With TT patched up as best as we could manage, we hit the autobahn for Cologne, in the north of Germany. The Chinese and Russians may take the biscuit for bad driving, but the sheer speed of the traffic on the *autobahn* was as scary as any crazed Dong Fong driver. While we cruised along at a steady 60 mph the other cars zoooooomed past at well over 120 mph. It must be a funny sight: Porsche, BMW, Audi, Mercedes, BMW, Porsche, VW... Ting Tong.

The police must have thought it was a funny sight too for, as we were about to come off the *autobahn* last night, some blue sirens appeared behind us and we were pulled over. The two policemen were convinced that it was illegal for us to be driving a Ting Tong on their autobahn and held us up for half an hour while they checked all our documents, questioned us and made a number of phone calls. Much to their dismay, they couldn't find any valid reasons to tick us off, and we tukked off smugly towards Cologne, where we got extremely lost and quite cross trying to find our hotel.

Cologne provided us with another reverse culture shock – multiculturalism. It's something we take for granted in England but have barely encountered since Bangkok. Our hotel is owned by Albánians, the cleaner here is Chinese and we ate at an Italian restaurant late last night. Welcome to the western world, or, as our hotel owner on our first night in Germany said, 'Welcome to civilisation'.

We've got just two days left of this journey. I can't get my head around it, but at the moment we are so occupied with the matter of getting

Ting Tong home that there isn't the headspace to worry about what Sunday will be like or what will happen after.

That's all for now, as we've got to hit the road to Brussels.

 Friday 1 September, Brussels, Belgium

 Feeling a bit frazzled

It's the first time I've blogged for a few days, so I'll recap a bit. We had a lovely weekend in Prague with my dad, and it was a chance for Ants and I to chill out, eat some seriously good food, catch up on our sleep and make the final plans for our last week on the road. I have to admit that I don't think Prague quite lives up to its glowing reputation. Yes, it is a lovely city, but it didn't bewitch me like Lviv and Krakow. There were too many tourists and I found the city a little too quaint and sterile. Plus the road system is a real headache, and we ended up getting very lost and nearly driving into the path of a tram. I think I prefer to share the road with donkey carts than trams.

On our final morning in Prague, we went to a press conference at the British embassy, which was a less hectic affair than our experiences in Kazakhstan and Thailand. As always, it was good to be able to talk about mental health and Mind and a pleasure to meet the diplomats, who were so kind and hospitable towards us. It is an honour to be invited to take part in a press conference with the embassy, not only in Prague but also Bangkok and Almaty. It gives our trip a voice that we wouldn't have otherwise.

When we said goodbye to Dad there were no tears, because I knew I would be seeing him in a matter of days at the finishing line – providing we make it. TT has been misbehaving, and her issues of not starting and veering to the right have been causing us a huge amount of anxiety.

As we tukked west through the Czech Republic towards Germany, we raced against some ominous-looking rain clouds, which finally caught up with us as we approached the border with Germany. It was raining so much that I expected the old spark-plug issues to start at any moment. The thought of breaking down on the autobahn in the pouring rain and darkness was not our idea of fun, and so we went straight to the nearest hotel.

The following day the weather was still bad, although cats and dogs had been replaced by drizzle. But since we were on a tight schedule to get back to Brighton on time, we had to push on. Eventually TT started and we set off for our next engagement, with another very special tuk tuk and his parents, Daniel and Susi. I won't repeat Ants, but suffice to say it was a great moment meeting Daniel and Susi, because nobody understands what we have experienced as much as they do. Even though we had only exchanged brief emails and spoken once on the phone, I felt a strong bond with them. Their tuk tuk was good-looking, but not nearly as beautiful as TT. Funnily enough, theirs didn't even have a name or gender, but I think it was definitely a boy. Daniel spent a good couple of hours trying to get TT running better, but she was having none of it and was still being a right little madam. I think she just needs a damn good service, some new front shocks and a holiday.

I don't know what it is about Western Europe, but it's been one of the most stressful parts of our journey. We had both expected this last leg to be the easiest, but I would say that the exact opposite has been the case, due mainly to TT's troubles and the constant bad weather. Also, we were bound to feel slightly strange towards the end of an adventure like this, and I think the combination of many things has contributed to our anxious moods. We are so close to home now and although I am really sad that this adventure is drawing to an end, my mind is racing ahead to the finishing line.

chapter 6
touch down

 Saturday 2 September, East Sussex, UK

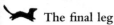 The final leg

To sum up the driving skills in Western Europe, I would say that the French are better than the Germans but definitely worse than the Belgians. After driving around the M25 this afternoon, I am proud to say that we Brits are definitely the best. Yup – can you believe we have made it back to England? I'm not sure I can either, but we're not quite finished yet and the champagne will have to wait for another 24 hours.

We made the Eurotunnel train by the skin of our teeth this afternoon, thanks to the French authorities deciding to carry out extensive road repairs on the main road into Calais. It was such an odd feeling to be so nearly home, and I smiled for the whole journey. I had fully expected to burst into tears once we alighted in England, but instead I felt a strange sense of bewilderment. When we pulled into a petrol station I just gazed around, feeling disoriented. Ants and I both felt like strangers in our own country, but I'm afraid that I cannot articulate that feeling any better.

Tonight we are staying in a hotel about 20 miles north of Brighton. We both hope that tomorrow is a special day and that TT makes her grand entrance into Bartholomew Square at 3.30 p.m. without any breakdowns or dramas. Emotions are whizzing around my head, but I can't really put them into any perspective at the moment. All that is left for us to do is enjoy our last night of this amazing adventure, get a good sleep and look forward to what will probably be the best day of our lives. Goodnight.

 Touch Down

14 weeks and over 12 500 miles later we have made it... as far as England at least. At 3.30 p.m. today the three of us waved goodbye to foreign fields and tukked on to the Eurotunnel, much to the amusement of our fellow passengers. An hour later we were hogging the inside lane of the M20 and heading for Brighton. Now here we are, tukked away in a leafy corner of the south of England, preparing for final Touch Down tomorrow afternoon.

Yesterday was very funny. We'd made some rather fluid plans with a BBC cameraman to meet 'somewhere between Cologne and Brussels'. I know Ting Tong's pretty visible, but I wasn't sure how easy it was going to be to spot each other while travelling at speed down opposite sides of a Belgian motorway. But Peter, the sharp-eyed cameraman, tracked us down and we spent the rest of the drive to Brussels engaged in a number of filming activities, narrowly avoiding mishap as Peter hung out of the window to film us and drove and filmed at the same time.

It was thanks to his work, however, that we avoided what could have been a sticky situation at the Eurotunnel terminal. Jo and I were concerned that our bid for Brighton could be foiled at this very final hurdle, since technically we are not allowed to drive TT on the British roads until she has undergone an MSVA (Motorcycle Single Vehicle Approval) test. But rather than the English customs officials asking us any difficult questions, they all flocked out of their huts and said 'We saw you on the BBC news last night – congratulations for getting this far!' and other such niceties. The power of the press, eh?

Our last night abroad could not have been more perfect. We had the privilege of staying with Sam and Bea Rutherford in Brussels, who spoilt us rotten and fed us amazing Belgian chocolate brownies and champagne. I mentioned them both on a blog months ago: Sam drove from London to Sydney in a pink Land Rover called Pinky in 1998–99 and gave us lots of invaluable advice before we left. It seems like months and months ago that he and Bea, over a glass of wine in Winchester, asked us to come and stay with them as we tukked past Brussels. Thanks, guys, for a wonderful European send-off.

Being in England is *very* strange. Jo and I have both got the sensation of being impostors in our own country. It feels like we have been away for ages and seen so much. It's almost too much to take in that tomorrow it all comes to an end – a sad thought. Last night, after a few too many glasses of white wine and champagne, the thought of coming back to England and finishing this glorious adventure made me cry. I know it will be wonderful to see everyone, but after that it's Monday, and reality, and all those 'What next?' questions.

So many thoughts and feelings are galloping through my head about the last few months, about tomorrow, about next week, next month, next year... but they'll have to wait until next week to be blogged. All I can say is that the past few months have been both the most exhilarating and challenging times of my life. I am so grateful to have had the opportunity to do such a journey, to meet the people I have, and to have travelled with two such wonderful companions. I know there will be more tears tomorrow.

Tuesday 5 September, Brighton, UK

 We've tukking made it!

All three of us are back home safe and sound, having officially driven 12561 miles in a tuk tuk – once Guinness have given this the rubber stamp, it means we are the new world record holders for the longest journey by auto-rickshaw.

It was pretty strange driving the last stretch to Brighton. I couldn't believe that we had actually made it in one piece and was totally paranoid about crashing just before we ended. We pulled up on the outskirts of Brighton to meet the Brighton tuc tucs, which looked so diddy next to TT. Then began the ceremonial two-mile drive to the finishing line. We pulled up just around the corner from Bartholomew Square so that Ants' friend Chaz could get the video camera set up and film our final moments. I had a quick cigarette to calm my nerves and we drove the last 100 yards into the square. We tukked through a pink ribbon and were greeted by the shouts and screams of family and friends – it was such an amazing moment and completely overwhelming. I thought I would burst into tears, but my eyes remained totally dry until one of my ferrets, Shrimp, was placed in my arms and the waterworks started. My mum said she thought it was nice the way I cried over a ferret but not over her – sorry Mum, but if you had whiskers, fur and a pink diamanté collar you would make me cry too.

We had photos and a couple of interviews, and then it was time to say hi to everyone who'd been kind enough to welcome us back. Unfortunately, there was not enough time and too many people to speak to everyone properly. However, I would like to say a really big thank you to everyone who turned up – it was very special and probably one of the best moments of my life. It was a great day and I was so full of every kind of emotion: anxiety, happiness, relief, fear, euphoria, confusion.

It feels a little weird to be back, but not as strange as I felt just after disembarking from the Eurotunnel. I have returned to drinking copious amounts of tea, playing with the ferrets and going to bed too late with great ease. Life is still the same. The only thing is that I now have four months of great memories to dip into whenever I feel like it. I have successfully forgotten how challenging the trip was and am already fantasising about tukking back to Thailand via the southerly route, i.e. Iran, Pakistan and India.

I have now had a couple of days to reflect on our adventure and get my thoughts into perspective. I feel so incredibly grateful to have been given the opportunity to drive a tuk tuk from Bangkok to Brighton. Ting Tong is such a beautiful machine and she made the experience special in so many ways. People just seemed to fall in love with her everywhere we went, and I am convinced that we would have had more problems if we were driving a regular car. Although we initially cursed her three wheels when we were banned from the expressways in China, it actually worked out for the best, because we experienced a China that few tourists are lucky enough to see. We used to refer to TT as a 'people magnet', and through her charms we met some truly amazing people: Anuwat, Dow, David Fall, Jack, Rudy, Oleg, Ivan and Shamil, to name just a few.

It does feel good to be home, but I really miss the fun of the open road. Even when the going got tough, it was still an awesome experience and some of the most difficult times stand out among the memories. It's also weird being separated from Ants, because we have been like a married couple for the past four months. I really miss her. We had an amazing time on the trip and I would like to thank her more than words can say for joining Tuk to the Road. I have had the best time of my life.

I hope that this trip has taught me some lessons. I think that I am slightly calmer and more patient. It will be interesting to see whether I retain these qualities now I am back in the western world. I have also learnt that people all over the world are more similar than different. We may all look slightly different, worship various gods and live diverse existences, but we all share the same fundamental human characteristics: the need for love and acceptance and the desire to help our fellow human beings. Perhaps I am being slightly optimistic on the last point, but the individuals that we were lucky enough to meet on our trip were almost without exception kind and giving. Maybe our overwhelmingly positive experiences have given me a naive view of the world in which we live, but I would like to think that most people are good. I will endeavour to apply what I have learnt to my everyday life: to treat others as I would like to be treated myself and help those in need when the opportunity arises. I feel like I have had a very privileged life so far. I am not talking about the private education or comfortable upbringing, although I am grateful for this. What I am talking about is being brought up surrounded by a loving and caring family and loyal friends. I think it is easy to forget what is really important in life. We are surrounded by the trappings of the material world and, as much as we may enjoy these, without love and our fellow human beings life would feel pretty meaningless.

 Tuesday 5 September, Kelling, Norfolk, UK

 We've only gone and done it!

We've done it... we've done it... we've done it... yeeeeeehhhhhhhaaaaaaaaaaah!

I remember tapping away on this computer a few months ago beside a blazing campfire in northern Kazakhstan, musing how this trip had been a series of can't-believe-it moments. And now here we are, back in England, in three whole pieces, having driven almost exactly halfway round the world. It's by far the biggest can't-believe-it moment of them all. Even odder is that for the first time in 15 weeks I am bereft of Jo and Ting Tong, having said goodbye to them and Brighton last night and come home to Norfolk. I feel like I've lost a limb and have spent a good deal of time today wandering around the house like a lost puppy, unsure what to do with myself. I think the next few weeks will be quite odd, but we've got to hold on to all those amazing things we've seen.

Now back to Sunday and Touch Down.

Sunday can be summed up in one word: surreal. We had spent 14 weeks inching around the Tibetan Plateau, across the Gobi Desert, through the Central Asian steppes, over the Urals, down the Volga, along the autobahn… and here we were in England, poised to cross the finish line. Neither of us could quite get our heads around the reality of finishing, seeing all our friends and family, and kissing goodbye to Tuk to the Road. As we packed up for the final time and did interviews with the BBC World Service, Radio Five Live, the Press Association and the *Eastern Daily Press*, I felt a tangle of emotions welling up inside me. We'd so nearly made it – this was the moment we had driven 12 500 miles to reach – how fantastic. And yet, on the other hand, crossing that line meant diving into the unknown and the life that I had become so accustomed to vanishing in an instant. No more living out of a rucksack, no more shivering in the back of TT, no more smiles and looks of amazement as we flashed past, no more *Auto Repair For Dummies*. I thought back over the weeks since we had left Bangkok, remembered people we had met along the way – Ivan, Oleg, Rudy, Jack, Nastia, Vova, Evgenia. I thought about strangers who'd helped us and the extraordinary sights we'd seen. I remembered that magical day we drove across the Gobi Desert into the sunset at Dunhuang, the crowds of curious Chinese, our night camping under a full moon in Russia. There were so many special memories to hold on to, things I would cherish for my whole life. I didn't want it to end.

Ting Tong didn't want to finish either – no doubt having heard the rumours about the ferrets in her new home – and threw a minor tukking tantrum before finally starting and allowing us to drive the final 30 miles. In perfect English drizzle, with butterflies in our stomachs, we wound our way down the A22 towards Brighton, past Maresfield and Lewes, nervous of having a crash in the very final stages and thinking of that fat lady singing. On the outskirts of Brighton, we were met by two of the new tuc tuc taxis and the three of us tukked in glorious three-wheeled unity into the city centre and along the seafront, beep-beep-beeping as we drove the final stretch with people waving and shouting 'Are you the ones from Asia?' There it was – the sea, the pier, Brighton, the place we had driven across two continents to reach.

The next hour was the most surreal of all: driving through a pink ribbon, saying hello to everyone, being greeted by the mayor of Brighton, Jo's ferrets appearing – cue tears – interviews with the BBC, *The Argus*, the *Eastern Daily Press*, lots of photos. All our families were there – parents, cousins, aunts, uncles, siblings – plus Anna, Lisa, Alexia and Tessa, Daisy and a handful of friends from Norfolk and the wonderful Charlie, who had flown all the way from Scotland to be there. Then it was time for the pub, where much champagne was drunk and lots of hugs and kisses dispensed. The pub was followed by supper at, appropriately, a Thai restaurant, which was followed by a club. By the later stages, the numbers had dwindled to the faithful few: my sister, Charlie, a few of the Norfolk crew and cousin Bert. All I can say is that at 5 a.m. we were all dancing on podiums at the Zap Club and a hell of a lot of champagne had been consumed. Needless to say, our 8 a.m. radio interview with BBC Southern Counties was a little bleary-eyed.

At 1 a.m. last night, after my father had decided to take the scenic route from Brighton to Norfolk, I eventually made it home, to my own bed, which, after nearly 16 weeks away from it, was extremely odd.

I think it is going to take me a long time to fully comprehend and appreciate the experiences of the past few months. Everyone else has been living their normal lives here, and we've driven halfway around the world in a comedy car. Somehow it just doesn't feel real, like it didn't *really* happen. The fact that I'm sitting here in my house in Norfolk, at the same desk I sat at before we left, makes it even harder to believe. Have I just woken up from some weird dream? I think it's going to take a while for me to fully take it all in and move on. Not that I know what I am moving on to or how I'm going to fill the gap that is life after tukking. Jo, Ting Tong and the open road are going to be a hard act to follow.

One thing I do know, however, is that the past 14 weeks have been the best of my life. Very hard at times, exhausting and stressful, but also incredibly exhilarating, mind-blowingly beautiful and hysterically funny. I've laughed, cried, despaired, marvelled and questioned my own sanity. Driving across the world in a pink tuk tuk is something I would recommend to everyone. It's proved to me that humans are essentially kind, that humour is the key to survival and that risks are always worth taking.

two months later...

 Thursday 9 November, Brighton, UK

Fun fearless females

We did it! On Tuesday night, Ants and I won *Cosmopolitan*'s Fun Fearless Female award in the Friends and Family category. It was an amazing night, although I can't quite remember every detail. More of that later...

It seems a very long time ago that we were driving across the Gobi Desert in North West China, when Mind emailed to tell us that they had nominated us for the above award. England, *Cosmopolitan* and awards ceremonies were so far removed from where we were that we didn't really give it much thought. We certainly never believed that four months later we would be presented with a large silver statue by Trisha Goddard and Fearne Cotton.

The award ceremony was held at the Bloomsbury Ballroom, a snazzy venue in central London. *Cosmo* kindly put us up at the very trendy St Martins Lane Hotel for the night. It was the first time that I had worn make-up in a long time, and Ants had to doctor my overly decorated eyes. Basically, when I can't get my silver eyeliner equal on both eyes, I just add more and more until I feel that equilibrium has been reached. The result was that I looked like the Snow Queen from Narnia.

At 6 p.m. we were chauffeured to the event and had to walk across the pink carpet to get to the drinks reception, which involved passing a wall of snaparazzi. We tried to scuttle past but were asked to pose for photos – they were most probably wondering who these two random ferrets were. Neither of us had eaten much during the day, and free alcohol awaited for the next five and a half hours. This is not good news for someone like me, who is normally a non-drinker.

There were some really inspirational women at the event, including Dame Kelly Holmes, Trisha Goddard, Camilla Batmanghelidj (who set up Kids Company, a charity that works with disadvantaged young people in London – see www.kidsco.org.uk) and many more. When we received the award I said a few words of thanks, but honestly I cannot remember whether any of what I said made sense. I blame the bubbles in the champagne. The rest of the evening passed in a bit of a drunken blur, but we had a brilliant time.

Ants and I tossed to see who got the award first. I guessed tails correctly and so the heavy silver statue is now proudly displayed on my mantelpiece. TT will be very jealous and might try and glue it to her dashboard, but after Barry the Buddha – her last dashboard accessory – jumped ship in Ukraine, I won't risk it.

Thanks to Mind for nominating us, *Cosmo* for such a wicked night, Trisha for presenting our award and, most importantly, Ants, my best, fun and fearless friend. Right, now I am off to nurse my small collection of injuries from the party – one grazed knee, one grazed elbow and two blisters on both of my little toes.

frequently asked questions

Did you do any mechanical training before you left?

Jo: I bought a motorbike two years before the trip with the intention of learning some mechanics, but I never got round to it. A couple of months before we left I purchased a book called *Auto Repair For Dummies*, which became one of our best friends on the trip. In Bangkok, Anuwat's mechanics gave us a few hours of mechanical training on TT, e.g. changing the brake pads, oil, filters, spark plugs and tyres.

Ants: No! I didn't even know how to change the spare tyre on my car.

How did you choose your route?

Ants: There were two basic routes we could have taken – the northern one via China and Russia, and the southern route via India, Pakistan and Iran. We always favoured the former and, once we knew this was possible, the finer details of our itinerary were decided on geopolitical grounds, with Jo in charge of South East Asia and China and me in charge of the former USSR. Our small engine meant that high mountains were to be avoided, while having three wheels dictated a need for tarmac wherever possible. We spoke to as many people as we could who had first-hand knowledge of the roads and countries we would be travelling through– the website www.horizonsunlimited. com was invaluable for this. With China, however, our route was set for us by the CSITS, the Chinese agency that arranged our passage through the country. Apart from China, the route we chose wasn't set in stone and there were several points along the way where we deviated from the plan. For example, we went to Yekaterinburg on a whim and our excursion around the Crimea was a last-minute diversion motivated by a desire for sun and sea.

Is Ting Tong just a regular tuk tuk, or was she modified specially for the trip?

Ting Tong was custom-built for us and the trip. Because Anuwat had previously built two tuk tuks that had been driven to Europe, he had a good idea of what modifications were needed. Here's a list of what makes Ting Tong stand out from the crowd:

- Raised suspension, for added clearance over rocks and uneven road surfaces.
- Lights wired in parallel, to make them easier to fix and more reliable.
- Extra lights, to make us more visible if we ever had to drive at night.
- Seatbelts, to conform to EU regulations.
- A special driver's seat – most tuk tuks have a hard, upright front seat. Ours has an extremely comfortable car seat. We might have had very sore bottoms without this.
- A 550-cc engine, so she can cruise comfortably at 60 mph.
- Roof-rack, for all that extra luggage.
- Headrests, for added comfort.
- Sony CD/MP3 player – although the engine was so noisy we could never hear it.
- Ultraseal, our secret weapon in the war against punctures.
- A bigger fuel tank – 50-litre capacity rather than the regular 25-litre tank.
- Steel chassis 10 mm thick rather than the standard 7 mm.
- Alarm and immobiliser, both of which could be controlled remotely.
- Roll-bars, in case we were unfortunate enough to tip over.

What was your favourite country?
We drove through a lot of spectacular scenery on our journey, but North West China really stands out. It was so unlike anywhere else we went and I don't think at any other point on the trip we felt further from home. South China had been very tough, both physically and mentally, but at Lanzhou, after 3500 miles of tukking, we turned west for the first time and encountered a very different China. We were now on the old Silk Road, and we spent exhilarating days speeding through the vast wildernesses of the Gobi Desert and alongside the ruins of the Great Wall. Our route took us through ancient Silk Road oasis towns such as Turpan and Hami, and desert and snow-capped mountains filled our vision as far as the eye could see. These were magical days. The icing on the cake was Jack, our Chinese guide, whose enthusiasm, knowledge and sense of fun made sure North West China remained in pole position. Runner up was Ukraine, for its people, nightclubs and beauty.

Were you ever scared?
Ants: Anxious, stressed and tired, yes. Scared – very rarely. During the months of preparation in England, people would often ask us if we were scared, but, first, we could never believe it was really happening to us and, second, we were far too busy planning the trip to be scared. Having said that, though, there were a few isolated incidents on the trip when I was momentarily scared. The first one was the incident described in the blog titled 'Grubby tukkers', when I was shouted at by an irate Chinese truck driver and spent the next two hours convinced he was going to appear in the rear-view mirror and send us hurtling off the edge of a mountain. That really did make my heart pound. Another time was when we were caught in a violent storm late at night, again in China. Ting Tong was being battered by the wind and the rain as we drove along a precarious stretch of mountain road, and Jo suddenly screamed that the battery was on fire. At that point I not only felt a pang of fear but also wondered whether we would ever make it out of China, let alone back to Brighton.

Jo: I remember feeling most worried when we were driving on mountainous, steep, windy roads, for example in Laos and south China. It is not much fun approaching a hairpin bend with a huge drop off a mountain right next to you. Overall, though, I think I felt more nervous than scared. The times I got most anxious were when we had mechanical issues with TT. I was in charge of all things mechanical and therefore felt a huge responsibility if there were any problems with her. We probably should have felt scared after we were stranded by an earthquake in China, but we ended up partying with the locals instead.

Where did you get petrol from?
Petrol stations! We chose our route carefully to ensure that we never encountered roads that were going to be impossible on three wheels. On the whole, this meant we travelled along fairly main roads and never went more than about 200 miles without seeing a petrol station. Even in the Gobi Desert, Sinopec or PetroChina stations dotted the route at fairly frequent intervals. The only time we were in danger of running out of petrol was in Kazakhstan, between Almaty and Balkash. Thankfully, a Kazakh family that flagged us down to take our photo gave us five litres from their jerry can, typical of the kindness of the Kazakh people.

As for fuel quality, the lowest we had to go was 91 octane. Usually we were able to get 95 octane, although in much of Kazakhstan, Russia and Ukraine this dropped to 93 octane and sometimes 91 octane.

How many litres to the gallon does Ting Tong do?
People always ask us this, but we never worked it out as it was so dependent on the speed, incline and road surface. She wasn't as economical as we expected, though.

Did you both drive?
Yes. We drove in two-hour shifts and took it in turns to drive first in the mornings. After two hours, we'd stop, have a cup of tea or coffee from our flask, swap drivers and carry on.

Where were the worst roads?
Yunnan in south China. They were unbelievable – filthy quagmires with a total absence of road surface and huge potholes. The roads were so bad that our average speed was reduced to around 15 mph, and in ten hours on the road we would cover little more than 125 miles.

What was the hardest part of the trip?
Two stages of the journey were particularly challenging – the first two weeks of China and Western Europe. The roads we were forced to use in Yunnan, Guizhou and Sichuan were appalling and having to drive 10–12 hours a day in such conditions was utterly exhausting. But we had no choice – we were banned from the expressways thanks to being three-wheeled and yet we still had to be out of China by 7 July, when our permits and licences expired. Not only this, but we also had mechanical problems, issues with our satellite modem and Sulky Sam to contend with.

Ironically, Western Europe, the leg of the expedition we had given the least thought to due to its size and close proximity to home, was also very tough. It started to rain near Krakow and continued to do so most of the way back to Brighton. Ting Tong developed a whole host of problems, including not starting in the mornings, misfiring, steering violently to the right when we braked, grinding and emitting loud hissing sounds from the depths of her engine. The closer we got to home, and the more troublesome Ting Tong was, the more anxious we became, haunted by that old adage 'It's not over till the fat lady sings'.

Did you ever break down?
The only times when problems with Ting Tong bought us to a halt were the two occasions when our accelerator cable snapped and once in Russia when we had to stop and wait for the spark plugs to dry out after a rainstorm. Although we had a variety of other mechanical issues, they never caused us to actually break down.

Did you have any punctures?
We didn't have a single puncture on the whole journey and we would

strongly recommend that anyone doing a road trip uses Ultraseal. This is a special formula you squirt inside your tyres that acts as a magic preventive against punctures and blow-outs.

Where did you sleep?
Wherever we found ourselves at the end of the day: hotels, our tent, people's houses, Ting Tong (once), a Chinese pavement (once). Our only prerequisite was that there was somewhere safe to park Ting Tong for the night.

Did either of you have any really bad habits?
Jo: I snore really badly, which is pretty difficult to live with. When we were camping in Kazakhstan, Ants hit me to try and get me to shut up. Ants had a habit of saying 'Are we nearly there yet?', which used to drive Sam absolutely mad after ten hours of driving on terrible roads in south China.
Ants: Yes, far too many to list here... but the 'Are we nearly there?' syndrome was one.

Did you argue?
Considering we were in such close proximity and enduring such an intense experience, we got on amazingly well and had only one major argument. This was in Yekaterinburg, on our fifth day in Russia. We were exhausted and fed up with the rain and Ting Tong's spark-plug issues, and one morning it all kicked off. We stomped off into the streets of Yekaterinburg in opposite directions... but two hours later we bumped into each other in an Internet café and it was all forgotten. We only had each other on the trip, and we knew that we could not afford to fall out. Plus, there isn't much room in a tuk tuk to sulk.

How did it feel getting back?
Ants: The worst thing about doing something like drive 12 561 miles in a tuk tuk is having to step out at the end and return to the real world. Jo and I both knew it would be tough, that after 15 weeks away from home Reality would be a hard concept to grasp... and we were right. Most of us know that post-exam feeling: you've been focusing

on something for weeks, unable to see beyond that final wonderful moment when you walk out of the exam room for the last time. You celebrate wildly, and then The Void appears. What next? you wonder. Arriving in Brighton on 3 September was akin to walking out of that exam room and reaching that point that had always seemed so far away. As we rounded the corner into Bartholomew Square, a crowd of friends, family, supporters and press surged toward us, clapping, waving and shouting. It was a fantastic moment. And yet at the same time it was surreal, and for the rest of that day Jo and I drifted around in a dreamland, unable to grasp that we had actually done it. After 14 weeks on the road, we'd made it home and completed a journey that so many people had doubted we could do. The wild celebrations lasted well into the early hours of the next morning, and the next week was a blur of interviews, phone calls and 'How was the trip?' questions. The surreality continued all that week, neither of us able to get our heads round being back. Already, those long days in China seemed like another world, like they had happened to someone else.

Moreover, everything at home seemed so alien. I remember seeing a familiar-looking man in the paper the day we got back and taking a good 20 seconds to realise it was David Cameron. I didn't know any of the songs on Radio 1, I hadn't heard of the new Almodovar film everyone was raving about or the band that had won the Mercury Music prize, and in my 15 weeks' absence three of my friends had got pregnant.

Worst of all was driving a normal car again. Having spent 14 weeks tukking across the globe in a three-wheeler, I had to rediscover the joys of right-hand drive and a normal gear stick. My first four-wheeled foray was in my mother's Saab. Within one journey I stalled several times and nudged a wall in a multistorey carpark. I felt like a 17-year-old who'd never driven before.

But the hardest thing I found about coming back was not really knowing what to do next. I would recommend anyone considering a trip like this to have a solid plan in place for their return: know where you are going to be living and have a firm idea of what you are going to do to fill the post-expedition void. Many people speak of falling into depression when they return from such epic adventures, and I can understand why. Having a positive idea of what you want to do when you return is a good way of avoiding this. Also, try to take some time out to reflect on what you have done, where you have been and all the incredible experiences you have had. Jo and I saw and learnt so much on our tukathon that I think I will be digesting it for years to come. However hard it was coming back, I kept reminding myself of how lucky I was to have seen the world from three wheels, when so many of the people we met along the way had hardly enough money to feed and clothe themselves. It's easy to forget, in our cosy western world, how lucky we are to have what we have, and doing this trip made me realise that more than ever. Tukking across 12 countries in 14 weeks was the best thing I have ever done; although the post-tukking twilight zone was a little gloomy, I wouldn't have missed it for the world.

Jo: Arriving home felt very odd. After first setting foot on British soil, we both felt like strangers in our own country. As we drove into Bartholomew Square to cross the finishing line, it was so overwhelming. Our family and close friends were there to greet us, and the combination of seeing loved ones and actually arriving home safely was wonderful. It was such a relief to have made it, particularly as the last few days in Europe had been really stressful.

I was really sad to say goodbye to Ants the day after we returned. We had spent the best part of four months in each other's pockets 24/7, and now we were going our separate ways. However, the human ferret had now been replaced by my darling furry ones, and it was great to be able to cuddle and play with them. I had missed them so much while we were away.

After my parents went home, I spoke to my fiancé in India and decided on an impulsive five-day trip to see him. We hadn't seen each other for nearly five months, and if I didn't go before university started I knew I wouldn't get another opportunity until Christmas. One evening we went to the cinema with his family. As we were pulling in there was a crash; when I got out of the car, I realised that we had hit a motorbike carrying a man, his wife and their ten-year-old child. Thank goodness none of them was injured, and it really hit home that we had been so lucky not to have had an accident on our adventure.

The day after I returned from India I started my medical degree in London, and since then it has been non-stop. Initially I didn't feel depressed to be back, because I was so busy. However, since we have been home, three of my ferrets have passed away and that has made me feel really down. I can't say whether it was the ferrets dying or the reality of normal life that has contributed to my low mood, but I felt pretty crap for the four months after we returned.

Are you still speaking?
Of course – most days.

What would be your top tips to anyone planning a trip like this?
- Don't be put off by other people's opinions and experiences. Get out there and find out for yourself.
- Give yourself a realistic amount of time to achieve your goal.
- Never forget your sense of humour.
- Talking to other people who have done similar trips is the best source of advice and information and can save you a lot of trawling on the Internet.
- Savour every moment. It's a once-in-a-lifetime experience and however hard it may seem at times, it's all part of the adventure. Wouldn't you rather be running out of petrol in the Kazakh steppes than stuck on the Tube in the rush-hour?
- Organisation and thorough research are the key to success, so you know what to expect and are aware of any potential problems.

Are you planning another trip?
Ants: My next dream is to drive a pink Lada from St Petersburg to Vladivostok. Long journeys in novel forms of transport are definitely the way forward.

Jo: I would love to drive TT to India to visit my fiancé. If Myanmar (Burma) becomes more stable, then it would be amazing to drive her the whole way back to Thailand.

How much have you raised so far for Mind?

At the time of writing, we have raised just under £40 000, which is £10 000 short of our original target. We are pretty determined to reach that target and we hope to do this by giving talks and selling thousands of copies of this book. If all else fails, Jo is going to take Ting Tong on a naked tour of Britain.

What's happened to Ting Tong?

Jo: When we got back she lived in my garage in Brighton with my pet ferrets and just chilled out. Now she is in my parents' garage in Surrey and goes for the odd gentle drive. She has told me that she can't wait for the summer when the weather will be better. After flirting at a Christmas shopping evening, she is now dating a large red fire engine.

What are you two doing now?

Jo: I am at medical school for the next 5½ years and hope to marry my fiancé this year and start a family.

Ants: Finishing this book and working at a TV production company in Bristol called Icon Films. I'm also about to start work on making the 40 hours of footage we shot into an hour-long documentary.

a tukking quick guide to fundraising

 Fundraising is a competitive business these days. Everywhere we turn, people are trying to make us part with our hard-earned cash in order to support a worthy cause. In the past year I've had friends swimming the Channel, trekking across deserts, climbing mountains and running marathons – every one of them for a good cause and every one of them wanting my support.

As the challenges get wackier and the causes multiply, standing out from the crowd is becoming increasingly hard. If you want to achieve your fundraising goal, you've got to be innovative, passionate about your cause and unerringly determined. However, don't be deterred. If you go about it the right way and give yourself enough time, fundraising can be incredibly rewarding.

First things first. Before you do anything, you need to decide which charity you want to support and what your fundraising target is going to be. You can then start to dream up ways in which you are going to raise this money. With us, these choices were easy, as our idea had always been to drive a tuk tuk back to the UK from Thailand, and both of us had strong personal reasons for supporting Mind. Our original target was £100 000 but we quickly decided to downgrade this to £50 000 – still an ambitious amount, but we felt it was more realistic.

The next thing is to work out a fundraising plan. How are you going to raise this money, and how long have you got to do it? What events can you put on in order to raise extra funds? This could be anything from a curry night, to an auction of promises, to a fancy-dress dog show. The main thing to remember is that when it comes to fundraising there are no rules. The more you can innovate and the more determined you are, the more successful you will be. Make sure as many people as possible get to hear of what you are doing, and don't be afraid to step outside the box and try things that haven't been done before.

Here are a few top tips for successful fundraising:

- Give yourself a realistic amount of time to achieve your goal.
- Choose a charity that means something to you. If people see you have a personal relationship with the cause, they are far more likely to donate.
- Be creative in your approach to fundraising: think of ways to make people part with their money and get something out of it at the same time.
- Make friends with your local press and get them to publicise your cause or any events you are putting on. Publicity is one of the best ways of raising money.
- Be bold. Don't be afraid to stand out and make a fool of yourself!
- Make people laugh – humour is key to getting people to support you.
- Write a punchy letter describing what you are raising money for and why, and send it to as many people as you can think of. Family, friends, local businesses... The more people you write to, the more money you will raise. We must have written over 500 letters.
- Find out which celebrities are associated with your charity, and write to them via their agents. See whether they will endorse what you are doing in any way – even a simple quote can help. Press in particular will prick up their ears if you have celebrity endorsement.

- Find out whether there are any charitable trusts in your area and when they meet. There are hundreds of these in the UK, and they normally meet twice a year to decide where to distribute their funds.

Good luck!

a bit about mind

**For better
mental health**

Mental illness affects people from every ethnic background and walk of life – one in four people experience mental distress at some time in their lives, and a third of all GP visits relate to mental health. Depression and anxiety, two of the most common forms of mental distress, can severely affect people's everyday lives and careers and place a strain on close relationships.

Mind has been speaking out for better mental health for 60 years and is now the largest mental health charity in England and Wales. We work in partnership with over 200 local Mind associations to directly improve the lives of people with experience of mental distress. Our vision is of a society that promotes and protects good mental health for all and that treats people with experience of mental distress fairly, positively and with respect.

Mind is an independent organisation supported by your donations. Mind campaigns to influence government policy and legislation, works closely with the media and is the first source of unbiased, independent mental health information via publications, website (www.mind.org.uk) and phone service 'Mind*info*Line: 0845 766 0163'.

At present, we find ourselves at a crossroads in mental healthcare. The progress of the past few years has been threatened by resource cuts in the NHS and new policies around welfare reform, and the revised mental health legislation may lead to further neglect, discrimination and decline in services.

Despite this, the opportunities for real change remain significant. Interest in mental health is shifting from the old negative stereotypes towards the effect of mental distress on real people's lives. The fight for mental health to be seen as a part of everyday life is ongoing.

We are grateful to Jo and Ants, not only for raising money for Mind but also for raising the profile of mental health. There is still an appalling degree of stigma and ignorance and, although media attention is growing, it is often ill-informed. Recently, a number of high-profile personalities have talked openly about their experiences with mental distress. Jo, a survivor of mental distress, has had the courage to speak out about her experiences and help combat stigma by raising public awareness.

Nick Easterbrook
Publications officer, Mind
January 2007

If you would like to donate to Mind please go to www.justgiving.com/tuktotheroad or www.mind.org.uk

Mind is registered charity number 219830.

useful sources

On the web

www.adventureshow.co.uk
The Adventure Travel Show, held annually at Olympia in mid-January, is a great place to meet people, be inspired and gather information about all sorts of adventure travel, whether it's trekking in Iran or riding across Mongolia.

www.alessie.com
Providers of Green Card insurance, which will cover your vehicle for the whole of Europe, including Ukraine. The company is based in the Netherlands and is wonderfully efficient.

www.americanexpress.com/uk
Offers competitive, comprehensive travel insurance and also sells travellers' cheques.

www.cellhire.co.uk
Provider of mobile solutions such as satellite modems, satellite telephones and mobile phones. Communication is an essential consideration when planning a trip such as this. Cellhire can consult and provide you with a package to suit all needs.

www.control-risks.com
Provides security and medical back-up for expeditions, businesses and individuals.

www.dragoman.com
Specialists in overland trips throughout the world. Not only are they amazingly good value and masses of fun, but also their huge orange trucks are a little bit more robust than a tuk tuk.

www.embassyworld.com
Index of embassies and consulates around the world.

www.expat.ru
Online community of expats living in Russia. An excellent source of information on everything to do with Russia, from getting visas to the best places to eat in Moscow.

www.fco.gov.uk
A great source of travel advice, information and up-to-date reports on political and medical situations around the world. Worth reading and rereading before you enter each country.

www.gear-zone.co.uk
Suppliers of the best brands of outdoor equipment, including The North Face, Berghaus, Karrimor, Craghoppers, Vango and Terra Nova, to mention just a few.

www.go-overland.com
A good resource for anyone contemplating an overland trip.

www.gt-rider.com
Essential information for bikers (and Ting Tong) on the roads, weather, laws and much more in Thailand and Laos.

www.horizonsunlimited.com
Anything you ever wanted to know about circumnavigating the globe

by bike (or tuk tuk). This was our number one site for research purposes, providing information about routes, equipment, useful contacts and border crossings.

www.intrepid-expeditions.co.uk
Purveyors of the finest survival courses and ration boxes. A must for anyone with a penchant for skinning rabbits and building hasty shelters.

www.khaosanroad.com
An essential website for visitors to Bangkok and Thailand – tattooing, eating, sleeping, partying...

www.kkp.kz
Insurance company based in Almaty. They insured Ting Tong for us while we were in Kazakhstan. In most other countries, we simply bought insurance at the border.

www.mooncup.co.uk
A Mooncup is an environmentally friendly option to use when you have your period – throw away those tampons and towels forever.

www.nomadtravel.co.uk
Nomad have been kitting out travellers with clothing, equipment, books, maps, medical supplies and vaccinations for 13 years. They provided us with a fantastic medical kit and lots of gear.

www.prepare2go.com
Runs rallies and raids around the world, and offers advice and hands-on support to government agencies, commercial interests and independent travellers.

www.rgs.org/eac
The Royal Geographical Society's expedition advisory centre – a fantastic resource to help you plan your trip.

www.stanfords.co.uk
One-stop shop for all maps and travel books.

www.stantours.com
Run by David Berghoff in Almaty, Kazakhstan, this specialist tour operator organises accommodation, trekking, riding and anything else you fancy doing in Central Asia.

www.statravel.co.uk
STA travel offers a range of travel services, including cheap flights, insurance and accommodation.

www.travcour.co.uk
If you've got ten different visas to apply for and neither the time nor the inclination to do it yourself, then Travcour will do it all for you. A highly efficient service that is well worth the extra cost.

www.travelfish.org
An online travel guide to Cambodia, Laos, Thailand and Vietnam. Well organised, nicely designed and chock-full of good information.

www.tuk-tukimportsuk.co.uk
A UK-based company that imports traditional Thai-made tuk tuks that are road-legal throughout the UK and Europe. These tuk tuks come from the same factory as Ting Tong.

www.ultrasealuk.biz
Miraculous puncture prevention, essential for anyone contemplating any overland adventure, be it on two, three or four wheels.

www.wildernessmedicaltraining.co.uk
Specialists in teaching advanced medical skills for use in remote, foreign environments. We attended one of their excellent courses at the Royal Geographical Society.

www.yourtuktuk.com
The fantastic Expertise tuk tuk factory in Thailand where our three-wheeled mean machine was born.

China Sea International Travel Service (CSITS)
They don't have a website. Contact Lifeng Liu, tel: +86 10 6717 2699; fax: +86 10 6710 2324. The CSITS arranged our permits, licences, guides and itinerary for travelling through China. Expensive but mandatory.

Books

Boorman, Charley and McGregor, Ewan. *The Long Way Round*, Time Warner Books, 2004.
Central Asia. Lonely Planet Publications, 2004.
Central Asian Phrasebook. Lonely Planet Publications, 2004.
Central Europe. Lonely Planet Publications, 2005.
China. Rough Guides. 2005.
Collins Pocket Russian–English Dictionary
Hare, John. *The Lost Camels of Tartary: A Quest into Forbidden China*, Time Warner Books, 2000.
Hopkirk, Peter. *Foreign Devils on the Silk Road*, John Murray, 1984.
Laos. Lonely Planet Publications, 2005.
Poland. Lonely Planet Publications, 2005.
Russia and Belarus. Lonely Planet Publications, 2005.
Sclar, Deanna. *Auto Repair For Dummies*, John Wiley & Sons, 1999.
Scott, Chris. *Adventure Motorcycling Handbook*, Trailblazer Guides, 2005.
Stanhope, Nick. *Blood, Sweat and Charity: The Ultimate Charity Challenge Handbook*. Eye Books, 2005.
Streatfield-James, Dominic and Wilson, Paul. *The Silk Roads: A Route and Planning Guide*. Trailblazer Guides, 2003.
Thailand. Rough Guides, 2005.
Thai Phrasebook. DK Eyewitness Travel Guides, 2003.
Ukraine. Lonely Planet Publications, 2005.

Finally, we used a wide selection of maps, which we purchased both from Stanfords in the UK and when we were on the road.

εquipmεnt list

Clothing

We each took: underwear ×5, socks ×2, swimwear, trousers ×4, T-shirts ×4, hooded top, hat, respectable skirt, sarong, shawl, sunglasses, prescription glasses ×2, trainers, flip-flops, Nomad tropical poncho.

Health and hygiene

Soap, toothpaste, toothbrush ×2, dental floss, razor, shampoo, Mooncup, sanitary protection, condoms, cotton-buds, wet-wipes, tissues, hairbrush, travel towel ×3, multi-use travel wash, moisturiser, hand sanitiser, Nomad Bathroom Cabinet, tweezers, nail scissors, insect repellent with DEET, multivitamins, echinacea, Lemsip, antimalarial pills, high-protection sunscreen, Optrex, prescription medication, Nomad medical kit.

Luggage

Large rucksack ×2, small rucksack ×2, bum-bag ×2, waterproof rucksack cover ×2, money belt, wallet, compression sack ×2, stuff sack ×3.

Sleeping

Nomad tropical quilt ×2, travel pillow ×2, eye-mask ×2, earplugs ×5, three-man tent, roll-mat ×2, Boovy and Wirral.

Cooking

Thermos flask, knife, fork, spoon, Trangia cooker, methylated spirits, Trangia fuel bottle, Sigg water bottles ×2, chemical water purification tablets, Katadyn Mini Water Filter, 2-litre water bladder ×2.

Miscellaneous essentials

Leatherman, sewing kit, Gaffa tape, worldwide adaptor ×2, Paracord, universal bathplug, matches, lighter, watch, compass, notebook and pens, guidebooks, reading books, backgammon board, maps, phrasebooks, Swedish FireSteel, playing cards, head-torch, small Maglite torch, chain, padlock ×4, tarpaulin, rope, bungee ×5, badminton racket ×2, shuttlecock ×5, cable lock, nylon map case, Silva solar panel.

Technical equipment

Fuji Z1 digital camera, Canon still camera, camera films, Sony PD170 DV camera, Sony mini DV tapes ×50, Portabrace camera case, DV batteries ×8, battery charger, tie-clip mike, mini-tripod, Rycote softie, DV camera rain cover, headphones, XLR cable, Garmin Etrex Yellow GPS, AA batteries, iPod and charger, laptop and case, Skype webcam, Skype headphones, Inmarsat BGAN and charger, USB key, Bluetooth-enabled mobile phone and charger, SIM4travel.

Documents

Passport ×2, UK driving licence ×2, international driving permit ×2, travel insurance ×2, visas, $500 in $1 notes, air tickets ×2, American Express travellers' cheques, credit cards, passport photo ×8, third-party vehicle insurance, photocopies of all documents.

Ting Tong's spares and accessories

Ultraseal, two-tonne jack, tyre-pressure monitor, digital tyre inflator, spare front tyre, spare rear tyre, bulbs, accelerator cable ×2, brake cable, clutch cable, front shock, radiator, oil filter ×5, fuel filter ×3, air filter ×2, front disc brake, front brake pads ×5, rear drum brakes, oil, coolant, wing-mirror ×2, rear-view mirror ×2, spark plug ×9, rain cover, toolkit with screwdrivers, wrenches, WD40, etc.

acknowledgements

This trip would never have happened had it not been for the massive amount of support we got from people at every stage. We are eternally indebted to each and every one of them. First and foremost we would like to thank Bob: without him this dream would never have become a reality. Thank you from the bottom of our hearts. Thanks also to the rest of our families – Pip, Nick, Dod, Fi Fi and Zed – for putting up with us, supporting us and listening to us until they never want to hear the word 'tuk tuk' again.

A very special mention goes to Anuwat and Dow, who not only built us the queen of tuk tuks but also treated us like sisters and looked out for us all the way. They were always there when we needed them and never short of Coke, cigarettes and laughter. Thanks also to all Anuwat's mechanics who dedicated so much time to building Ting Tong.

Next in line are our sponsors. Of the multitudes of individuals and companies that we wrote to asking for money, equipment, flights, websites, books, these are the kind people who came up trumps: Brian, our wonderful website guru at www.indrum.com; Hannah at Skype, PID, Brighton Square; Joanna, Grace and Christine at Thelma & Louise; Activair; Liftshare; Imperial Hotels; Stuart at Travelfish; Mike and Vanda at Toniks languages; Ultraseal; Paul and Jason at Nomad; Cellhire; Silva; Whitby & co; Matt at Sqare peg; Toby; Alice McLaughlin; Ben Johnson and PDC. For more information about all our sponsors, please visit our website www.tuktotheroad.co.uk.

We'd also like to thank the following, in no particular order: Cath Hibberd, Aidan Warner, Paul Farmer and the rest of the team at Mind for their belief and support throughout; David and Gwendolyn Fall; Jack – the best guide in China; Lifeng at the CSITS; Shane Winser at the RGS; Dan, Bobby and Pete at ITV Anglia; Sam and Bea Rutherford; Mike and Gemma Steen; Catherine Inglehearn and Yulia Kaufman at the British embassy in Almaty; Peter Wickenden and Linda Duffield at the British embassy in Prague; Evgenia Salagdinova and the Kazakh Feminist League; Daniel and Susi; Scott Wallace; Richard Batson at the EDP; Trisha Goddard; Chaz – editor extraordinaire; Hugh Sinclair; Simon W-S; Neil Cranston; Julian and Bob at GFS; Al; the Wycombe girls; Rudy, Oleg and Ivan – our boys in Yekaterinburg; Jenna, Kate and all the *Cosmo* crew; Duncan at Dragoman; Jo Winchester; Tom and Nik at www.gapyear.com; Hannah and André; Bert; Mark Edgar; Lou, Jang and the team at Visualeyez, Bangkok; Stephen Fry and Jo Cocker; Sir Elton John; Melvyn Bragg; David Manson; Heather and the Clares at The Friday Project; Mark at RDF; Maxat; the Armed Technician; Stan, Heid Honcho and all the other Tuk to the Road blogging faithfuls; Russ Malkin; Uncle Nobby and Kim from Intrepid Expeditions; the Bantam Trust; Sue and La La; Olly Hicks; Pestos; Jim, Sandi and Norman at The Stable Gallery; Sally, Lara, Kaye and Patsy for looking after the ferrets; and all those people out there who supported us and Mind and have helped us get so close to our £50 000 target.

Finally, thanks to all those strangers out there who went out of their way to help us when we were on the road: the family who gave us petrol in the steppes, the truckers who bought us lunch, the people who showed us the way, the mechanics who wouldn't take our money, the border guards who made our days, and the Tartars who gave us free veggies. Big tuk tuk love to you all.

Love,
Jo, Ants and Ting Tong xxx

index

Note: page numbers in bold refer to maps.

Index

Index

Index